Our War Paint Is
Writers' Ink

SUNY series, Native Traces
———————
Jace Weaver and Scott Richard Lyons, editors

Our War Paint Is Writers' Ink

Anishinaabe Literary Transnationalism

Adam Spry

Published by State University of New York Press, Albany

© 2018 State University of New York

All rights reserved

No part of this book may be used or reproduced in any manner whatsoever without written permission. No part of this book may be stored in a retrieval system or transmitted in any form or by any means including electronic, electrostatic, magnetic tape, mechanical, photocopying, recording, or otherwise without the prior permission in writing of the publisher.

For information, contact State University of New York Press, Albany, NY
www.sunypress.edu

Production, Ryan Morris
Marketing, Kate R. Seburyamo

Library of Congress Cataloging-in-Publication Data

Names: Spry, Adam, 1984– author.
Title: Our war paint is writers' ink : Anishinaabe literary transnationalism / Adam Spry.
Description: Albany : State University of New York Press, [2018] | Includes bibliographical references and index.
Identifiers: LCCN 2017017031 (print) | LCCN 2017031160 (ebook) | ISBN 9781438468839 (ebook) | ISBN 9781438468815 (hardcover   ) | ISBN 9781438468822 (pbk.   )
Subjects: LCSH: Ojibwa literature—History and criticism. | Ojibwa language. | Ojibwa Indians—Government relations.
Classification: LCC PM853.5 (ebook) | LCC PM853.5 .S67 2018 (print) | DDC 897/.333—dc23
LC record available at https://lccn.loc.gov/2017017031

10 9 8 7 6 5 4 3 2 1

*To my father, who taught me the meaning of nibwaakaawin,
and my mother, who taught me the meaning of sisu*

Contents

List of Illustrations	ix
Acknowledgments	xi
Miigwech	xiii
Ozhibii'ige	xvii
Introduction: Whence These Legends and Traditions?	1
1. Revolutionary in Character: Translating Anishinaabe Place and Time in the *Progress*	27
2. Englishman, Your Color Is Deceitful: Unsettling the North Woods in Janet Lewis's *The Invasion*	65
3. What Is This I Promise You?: The Translation of Anishinaabe Song in the Twentieth Century	101
4. A Tribe of Pressed Trees: Representations of the State in the Fiction of Louise Erdrich	139
Conclusion	181
Notes	187
Index	213

Illustrations

Figure 1.1　Front page of the *Progress*, December 17, 1887.　45

Figure 2.1　*Mort de Montcalm* by Moret, after original by Desfontaines.　83

Figure 3.1　Score and translation of "No. 64 'Initiation Song'" as it appears in Densmore's *Chippewa Music*.　105

Figure 3.2　Detail of Mide pictograph from "No. 64 'Initiation Song.'"　126

Figure 3.3　"Initiation Song" as reexpressed by Gerald Vizenor in *Summer in the Spring* (1993).　137

Acknowledgments

Figure 3.3: Verse originally published in *Summer in the Spring: Anishinaabe Lyric Poems and Stories*, by Gerald Vizenor. Reprinted by permission of the University of Oklahoma Press. All rights reserved.

Portions of chapters 1 and 2 appeared in a much different form in an essay titled, "'It may be revolutionary in character . . .' The Progress, A New Tribal Hermeneutics, and the Literary Reexpression of the Anishinaabe Oral Tradition in Summer in the Spring," from *Gerald Vizenor: Poetry and Poetics*, ed. Deborah Madsen. © 2012 University of New Mexico Press, 2012.

Miigwech

THE FIRST WORD OF ANISHINAABEMOWIN my father ever taught me was "miigwech"—"thank you"—because it is the most important. I have had many opportunities to use the word over the course of writing this book, but I would be remiss if I didn't take the time to say it once again in recognition of all of those who have helped to make this work possible.

This book has benefited immeasurably from the insightful comments of a huge number of people, including those affectionately known to me as "the cohort." Alastair Morrison, John Hay, Tim Donahue, Gania Barlow, Nijah Cunningham, Emily Cersonsky, Jessica Teague, Lindsay Van Tine, Deborah Aschkenes, and Oliver Batham are all amazing friends and accomplished scholars who have patiently listened to me talk about this project for more than a decade. During my time at Yale, I was lucky to workshop a section of this book with the Yale Group for the Study of Native America—an remarkable group of students and faculty led by the brilliant and tireless Ned Blackhawk. While at Florida Atlantic University (FAU), I received incredible support and encouragement from my colleagues Eric Berlatsky, Sika Dagbovie-Mullins, Taylor Hagood, Warren Kelly, Elena Machado, Mark Scroggins, and most especially Adam Bradford. Many students, both graduate and undergraduate, helped me to refine the ideas in this work. Special thanks to the graduate students in my "Transnational Native American Literature" seminar at FAU for stimulating conversation and brilliant insight into the work of early Anishinaabe writers.

Finally, I must thank my mentors, both formal and informal, for all of their advice and guidance. Karl Kroeber was the first to take me under his wing at Columbia, and although our time together was all too brief, he remains an important influence on me to this day. Rachel Adams gave me incredibly generous feedback and help in shaping the comparative approach of this project. John Gamber has been a kind, supportive, and tenacious advocate and friend, and I benefited greatly from his capacious knowledge of Native literature. Bruce Robbins helped guide my thinking on a number of important issues regarding transnationalism, the state, and structure. At the beginning of my studies, Frances Negrón-Muntaner gave me important advice on how to be a politically engaged scholar. After great effort on his part, Michael Golston finally made me understand the critical importance of poetry to this project, and for that I will be forever in his debt. Last, but certainly not least, is Scott Richard Lyons, who has not only been a model of scholarship for me, but perhaps one of the most generous and committed mentors a young scholar could hope for—miigwech. Every page of this work bears the traces of their influence.

Several organizations generously supported this project throughout its long development. Thanks to both the Council of Independent Colleges and the anonymous donors who underwrote the American Graduate Fellowship, which supported me during the early part of my graduate studies, as well as gave me a grant to study Anishinaabemowin. The Department of Ethnicity, Race, and Migration at Yale University was my home away from home during the last year of graduate school, where I produced the first draft of this work as a dissertation during my time as the Henry Roe Cloud Dissertation Writing Fellow. I also benefited immensely from the time to write provided by a McKnight Junior Faculty Fellowship from the Florida Education Fund. Everyone at SUNY Press has been incredibly helpful and supportive in getting this book to print, especially Amanda Lanne-Camilli, whose patience and guidance kept me afloat. And I must thank *Native Traces* series editors Jace Weaver and Scott Lyons for believing in my project, even when it was little more than a disseration.

All those Anishinaabeg of White Earth who have tirelessly worked to improve their people's lives have my deepest gratitude, and must be recognized here. My thanks to Winona LaDuke for access to the amazing collection of Anishinaabe literature housed at the offices of the White Earth Land Recovery Project (and for turning a blind eye to my reading while I should've been writing grants); and to Erma Vizenor and Jill Doerfler for their efforts—still ongoing—to ensure that all the Anishinaabe at White Earth can participate in the civic life of their community. Finally, I must thank Gerald Vizenor for his brilliance, generosity, and humor—his vision of survivance has guided this work from its conception.

Of course, my family has been my greatest source of strength and inspiration. This book is as much a product of their efforts as my own.

To Kageet, for tail wags and gentleness. I am forever in debt to my brother-in-arms, Dru Söderlund, for coming up with the portmanteau "Finnishinaabe." Gunalchéesh ho ho to Laurie and Rob Hoyt and ax káani, Ken Neish Hoyt, for being a constant source of wisdom—and for remembering my name. My sisters, Hannah and Emily, and nieces, Marley and Mia, have shown me what true courage and fortitude is, as only Anishinaabekweg could. To my parents, Michael and Melinda Spry, who instilled in me a respect for others (both human and other-than-human), pride in my complicated heritage, and a lifelong love of books—this is for you. And to my partner, Katie Shaax Hoyt: thank you, Kiddo, for your endless patience, compassion, and love. Chi-miigwech.

Ozhibii'ige

The word [Ojibwe] is very loaded and bears a host of meanings and interpretations and theories. I've heard that Ojibwe refers to the puckering of the seams traditional moccasins, or makazinan. Or that the Ojibwe roasted their enemies "until they puckered up." Gruesome. I've heard that Anishinaabe means "from whence is lowered the male of the species," but I don't like that one very much. And then there is the more mystical Spontaneous Beings. The meaning that I like best of course is Ojibwe from the verb Ozhibii'ige, which is "to write."

—Louise Erdrich

In 1842, the Anishinaabe historian William Warren was allowed to examine a plate of native copper, which had been carefully guarded by his great uncle, an ogimaa[1] named Tug-waug-aun-ay, for many years. In his *History of the Ojibway Nation*, Warren recounts that the plate was covered with "rudely marked indentations and hieroglyphics," which depicted important events from Anishinaabe history. Warren estimated that members of Tug-waug-aun-ay's family had been recording their memories on the copper plate for at least three hundred years—as testified to by "eight deep indentations, denoting the number of his ancestors who had passed." Next to the indentation marking the third generation, Warren notes, there was carved "the rude figure of a man with a hat on his head," which depicted the historic moment "when the white race made his first appearance" among the Anishinaabeg.[2] According to his reckoning, this written record proved the Anishinaabeg had known about European settlers as early as the first decade of the seventeenth century—"fifty-six years before," Warren drily notes, Europeans "first discovered the Ojibways."[3]

For their part, the first Euro-American account of the Anishinaabeg comes from 1640, in a letter included in the *Jesuit Relations* bearing the heading, "Of the Hope We Have for the Conversion of Many Savages." Despite its auspicious title, the report is little more than a list of Indian tribes whose existence a priest named Father Superior Paul le Jeune had learned of from Native informants. Buried among descriptions of the "Amikouai, or the nation of the Beaver" and that of the "Ouinipigou . . . the 'Nation of Stinkards,' Father le Jeune briefly mentions the Baouichtigouian: "that is to say . . . the nation of the people of the Sault, for, in fact, there is a Rapid, which rushes at this point into the fresh-water sea."[4]

Baawitig, the place of the rapids, had long been an important fishing grounds and summer meeting camp for the Anishinaabeg. According to their oral histories, Baawitig was one of the first permanent homes for the Anishinaabeg after completing a long migration from the Atlantic coast centuries earlier. Located at the confluence of Lakes Superior and Huron, the Baawitig offered the Anishinaabeg easy access to the multiple river tributaries and vast hunting territories adjoining the lakes. During the short northern summers, Anishinaabeg bands from across the region would gather for celebrations and religious observances. Not long after le Jeune sent his optimistic missive to Paris, Baawitig was first visited by Jesuit missionaries—whose eagerly waved crucifixes earned them the derisive nickname wemitigoozhi, or "stick shakers."

These holy men were soon followed by those with decidedly more secular interests. The Anishinaabeg established close economic relationships (and oftentimes kin relationships) with the French *voyageurs* and *coereur des bois*, with whom they traded food and pelts—mostly beaver—for cookware, fabric, steel tools, and other European-made goods. As these newcomers increasingly came to rely on the Anishinaabe villages at Baawitig, they gave the rapids the name they still bear today: Sault Ste. Marie—affectionately referred to as the "Soo." From their central location at the Baawitig, the Anishinaabeg spread their influence through trade, alliance, and war across much of continent, creating a vast homeland stretching from the shores of Lake Erie to the prairies of Saskatchewan. By the end of the eighteenth century, the Anishinaabeg had established themselves as a major economic and political power, with unquestioned sovereignty over the heart of North America. As the region underwent successive waves of French, British, and American colonization over the next three centuries, Euro-Americans would come to know the people they variously called Sauteurs, Saulteaux, Bungi, Outchibouec, Otchiptway, Ojibbeway, Ojibwe, Chippewa, or simply Indians.

In the early nineteenth century, the Anishinaabeg had their first formal interactions with the United States, which claimed a large portion of the Anishinaabegs' territory under the auspices of the 1783 Treaty of Paris. While initial relations were cool (a few Anishinaabe bands joined Tecumseh and the British against the Americans in the War of 1812), the Anishinaabeg soon established a treaty-based alliance with the United States, just as they had with the British and French before. This process was aided by a woman named Obabaamwewe-giizhigokwe, or Jane Johnston (1800–42), the daughter of an aristocratic Irish fur trader and an Anishinaabe ogimaakwe known for her abilities as a storyteller. Mixing her mother's love for the legends of her people with her father's love of literature, Jane produced romanticized translations of Anishinaabe stories as well as lyric poems recounting the heroic deeds of her ancestors—the first poetry ever published by a Native person. Through her writings, Jane opened a pathway for understanding between the Anishinaabeg and the Americans who had come among them, introducing them to the idea of Anishinaabe "culture." By a mixture of canny diplomacy and chance, the Anishinaabeg avoided the sort of conflict that marked so much of the era, allowing them to remain on their homelands in relative peace.

The situation would change considerably during the mid-nineteenth century, as the United States developed interest in Anishinaabe land as a rich source of copper, iron, and timber. During the last five decades of the nineteenth century, settlement increased dramatically, transforming the rough and remote old Northwest into the bucolic Midwest. The Anishinaabeg resisted this invasion not through battle, but through rhetoric. During this time Anishinaabe writers like George Copway (1818–69), Andrew Blackbird (1817–1908), and William Whipple Warren (1825–53) wrote impassioned critiques of American settlement and argued persuasively for the idea of a modern Anishinaabe nation. Through the diplomatic efforts of Anishinaabe leaders and their allies, the Anishinaabeg were largely able to avoid removal from their homelands—the fate of so many of their contemporaries at the time. Despite this success, by the end of the nineteenth century, the once vast territories of the Anishinaabeg were reduced to small holdings scattered throughout the Great Lakes region.

The Anishinaabeg continue to exist today on dozens of reserves and reservations spread across Ontario, Manitoba, Saskatchewan, Montana, North Dakota, Minnesota, Wisconsin, and Michigan—as well as large urban communities in Toronto, Chicago, Winnipeg, Milwaukee, Madison, and Minneapolis. According to Gerald Vizenor, the Anishinaabeg can boast of "more published writers than any other tribe on this continent."[5]

Indeed, the last century has seen the publication of poetry, drama, and novels by Heid E. Erdrich, Lise McCloud, Gordon Henry Jr., David Treuer, Gerald Vizenor, Winona LaDuke, Kimberly Blaeser, Denise K. Lajimodiere, Drew Hayden Taylor, Jim Northrup, along with many, many others. Some, such as Louise Erdrich, have even become household names, garnering widespread critical praise and international audiences.

At the same time, the Anishinaabeg have also been the subject of many works of literature by American writers. Henry Wadsworth Longfellow's *Song of Hiawatha*—based, in part, on the writings of Jane Johnston Schoolcraft—shaped the public's perception of the Anishinaabeg (and Indians) for generations. Ernest Hemingway's ascent to the heights of literary fame began with a story about a desperate Anishinaabe lumberjack. T. S. Eliot and Yvor Winters debated the aesthetic merits of Anishinaabe song in some of the most august literary publications of their day. Contemporary readers are gripped by the adventures of the Chippewa detective Cork O'Connor in William Kent Krueger's best selling paperback mysteries.

From the time of Tay-waug-aun-ay's copper plate and le Jeune's letter to the best sellers of Erdrich and Kreuger today, Anishinaabeg and Euro-Americans have used the act of writing to imagine one another—sometimes as bitter enemies, sometimes as cautious allies, sometimes even as kin. Taken as a whole, the resulting texts comprise a shared archive of a tendentious relationship that stretches back centuries. This book is an attempt to enter into that archive, to recover from it texts which may shed new and unexpected insights into a sometimes vexed relationship between two nations contentiously occupying the same land. Such a transnational perspective, I believe, is an important way of drawing attention to interesting texts that seem to have fallen through the cracks—works of drama, fiction, and poetry that challenge our understanding of the role literary writing plays in the ongoing dynamic of settler-colonialism and indigenous resistance. In doing so, I hope to illustrate a method of reading across the boundaries of settler-states and indigenous nations—one that may offer new ways of understanding both Native American and American literatures.

Introduction

Whence These Legends and Traditions?

> The Ojibwa have received a vicarious distinction, unique among aboriginal American tribal groups. They have achieved an enduring fame, not through wars or conquests . . . but through the projection of an artistic image of them that has become an integral part of American literary tradition.
>
> —Alfred Irving Hallowell

> The Ojibwe language has given English the words "moccasin," "toboggan," "wigwam," "moose," "totem," and "muskeg." We've even met on the middle ground. We provided "musk" from "mashkiig," or swamp, English provided "rat" and together we built a word for a swamp dwelling rodent that looks an awful lot like a rat—muskrat. If that's not a fine example of cultural exchange I don't know what is.
>
> —David Treuer

ON A SUMMER DAY IN 1900 a large crowd assembled on the shore of Lake Huron, just a few miles downriver from the rapids at Baawitig. They sat in rapt attention of a man standing near the water as he prepared to address them. He cut a striking figure, dressed in a decorated buckskin tunic, fringed leggings, and the large war bonnet of a western chief—its many eagle feathers draping nearly to the ground. Speaking in loud and steady Anishinaabemowin, the man told the crowd that he was about to travel back to his home, located somewhere in the far distant west. As those gathered around him shouted their farewells, he launched a small birch bark canoe into the open waters of Lake Huron. Standing, in the traditional fashion, on the frail cedar ribs of the canoe, with his eyes fixed on the horizon, the man uttered a single word: "Ningaabii'an." As if by magic, the canoe began to move across the water, gradually picking up speed on a steady westward course. As the canoe and its noble passenger receded into the distance, the audience left behind on the shore burst into waves of rapturous applause.

The hidden mechanical winch pulling the canoe was just one part of the elaborate staging put together for *Hiawatha, or Nanabozho*, which also included choreographed stage combat, a full-sized re-creation of an Anishinaabe village, and a gutsy high dive into Lake Huron in the play's climactic third act. First performed near the village of Desbarats, Ontario, in 1900, *Hiawatha, or Nanabozho* was an adaptation of Longfellow's epic poem, *The Song of Hiawatha*, performed by an all-Anishinaabeg cast from the Garden River community. The play was comprised of thirteen short scenes depicting several of the more memorable episodes from Longfellow's poem, including Hiawatha's miraculous birth, his wooing of the Dakota maid Minnehaha, and his eventual defeat of the evil trickster Pau-Puk-Keewis. The dialogue was performed exclusively in Anishinaabemowin language, with an English-speaking narrator reciting corresponding passages from Longfellow's poem through a bullhorn. A true spectacle of singing, dancing, and romance, the highlight of the play was its carefully timed finale, in which the actor playing Hiawatha departed for "the portals of the sunset" on his pulley-driven canoe into the light of the real setting sun.

Hiawatha, or Nanabozho was the brainchild of two very different men. The first, George Kabaosa, was a member of the Anishinaabe community located on the Canadian side of the Sault, at the Garden River reserve. Educated in a missionary school in Michigan, Kabaosa was part of a new class of political elite among Anishinaabeg, who blended their knowledge of Anishinaabe tradition with a savviness for the workings of the Euro-American culture. At the time of the play's first performance, Kabaosa was in the employ of Louis Olivier Armstrong, an adman from Montreal hired by the Canadian Pacific Railway (CPR) to help colonize the Canadian interior. Having achieved a degree of success in enticing Anglo-Canadians to settle in Manitoba in the aftermath of the Riel Rebellions, Armstrong now had the unenviable task of making the remote forests of northern Ontario seem like a good place to take a vacation. Part of the large-scale effort to restructure the economy of the Great Lakes region after the collapse of the timber industry, Armstrong hoped to market Desbarats as a sportsman's paradise, rife with opportunities to hunt, fish, and—of course—meet real Indians.

As a means of drawing urban tourists to an otherwise unremarkable stretch of Lake Huron coastline, staging *Hiawatha* at Desbarats was, as we would say today, good branding. At the time, *Hiawatha* was one of the most widely read works of poetry in North America, and for many a beloved childhood classic. Seeing *Hiawatha* performed by Indians in rural Ontario presented an opportunity for the fans of the poem to feel like they were not just witnessing their favorite book, but embedded in its romantic setting. In actuality, Longfellow's poem was set more than a hundred miles to the west (on the American side), at the pictured rocks of Lake Superior, but for geographically challenged *Hiawatha* fans, any stretch of the Great Lakes' shoreline could reasonably stand in for the poem's iconic "shores of Gitche Gumee." Staging the play at Desbarats ensured that fans of the poem took CPR trains—the only rail line to service the village.

By 1901, *Hiawatha, or Nanabozho* was being performed twice a day, drawing in crowds as large as five hundred.[1] Part of this success, no doubt, was due to the fact that it was one of the few things tourists could actually *do* once they got to Desbarats. Besides fishing, the sparsely populated region had little to offer by way of entertainment—especially for those used to creature comforts of large eastern cities. Armstrong and Kabaosa took advantage of this captive audience, supplementing the play with woodcraft demonstrations, staged canoe races, and Anishinaabe vendors who sold pieces of beadwork and makakoon—handmade birch bark baskets—filled with fresh berries. In 1904, *Hiawatha, or Nanabozho*, along with its original Native cast, made an off-season tour of Chicago, Boston, and New York. The next year, the play was performed in Belgium, the Netherlands, and Britain—spending five months in residence at Earl's Court in London.[2] The play would be taken up and performed by Anishinaabe communities across the region, with productions taking place as far away as the White Earth Reservation in Minnesota. In 1905, the Odawa of Little Traverse Bay began to put on regular performances of *Hiawatha, or Nanabozho* near Petoskey, Michigan, that would continue in various forms for the next five decades. The Garden River Anishinaabeg, meanwhile, continued to produce *Hiawatha, or Nanabozho* in various forms well into the 1960s.[3]

I begin with *Hiawatha, or Nanabozho*, in part, because it represents something of a historical nexus for this book as a whole—a point of convergence from which we may trace connections between a surprising set of writers, translators, and critics. The text of *Hiawatha, or Nanabozho* reflects the contributions of several prior generations of Anishinaabe writers, including Jane Johnston Schoolcraft, John Tanner, and George Copway, on whose works Longfellow based his poem, and whose descendants would eventually sit in attendance at performances of the play. Another regular attendee was a young Ernest Hemingway, who would later launch his career as a writer with a tragic story about an Anishinaabe logging camp. Hemingway's classmate, Janet Lewis, also attended the show, several years before writing a novel about the troubling family history that lay behind *The Song of Hiawatha*. At White Earth Reservation in Minnesota, a performance of *Hiawatha, or Nanabozho* was organized by an Anishinaabe schoolteacher named Mary English, whose translations of Anishinaabe song would spark heated debate among the foremost minds of American Modernism. English's production was almost certainly taken in by Theo Beaulieu, whose own adaptation of the Nanabozho mythos would provide a spark of inspiration for a young Gerald Vizenor.

These connections show an important aspect of Anishinaabe cultural identity essential to the argument of this book: the way in which writing allows cultural material to move independently between indigenous and settler contexts, taking on new meanings and different political valences as it goes. When traced back to its sources, *Hiawatha, or Nanabozho* is revealed to be staggeringly intertextual. It is a play produced by a Canadian and an Anishinaabe, performed in Anishinaabemowin, based on an English-language poem (with a meter cribbed from a German translation of a Finnish epic) written by an American poet, which was, in turn, based on an ethnographic text that reprinted English translations of Anishinaabe stories made by the Anishinaabemowin-speaking children of a Scots-Irish aristocrat. This complicated history of production and reception (to be more fully unpacked over the coming pages) makes *Hiawatha, or Nanabozho* a particularly difficult object of analysis. Sitting on the borders of Euro-American and Anishinaabe culture, the nineteenth and twentieth centuries, and the literal border of the United States and Canada (with the memory of Anishinaabewaki's continued presence beneath it all), *Hiawatha, or Nanabozho* doesn't seem to comfortably fit into the received categories by which we tend to think about literature.

It should come as no surprise that scholarly responses to *Hiawatha, or Nanabozho* have been markedly ambivalent. The sociologist Margot Francis, for instance, argues that the Anishinaabeg used *Hiawatha, or Nanabozho* "to symbolically enter the culture of modernity, at least partially, on their own terms," by encoding Longfellow's poem with meanings that "would *only* have been available to other Ojibwe speakers in the audience."[4] On the other side of the coin, the cultural critic Alan Trachtenberg takes a particularly jaundiced view of what he calls the "Indian minstrelsy" of the play, in which the Anishinaabeg "perform[ed] their loss in someone else's version for the pleasure of white audiences."⁵ The historian Michael McNally is more measured, suggesting that, despite the compromised nature of the play itself, "what happened onstage might have been less of a concession than it might seem at first glance to a modern-day observer,"⁶ arguing that *Hiawatha, or Nanabozho* "kept alive a repertoire" of cultural knowledge "on which, decades later, the resurgence of traditional culture, and related assertions of sovereign peoplehood, could build."⁷

The range of opinions regarding *Hiawatha, or Nanabozho* speaks to the difficulty the play presents to our understandings about identity, agency, and culture. The idea that the Garden River Anishinaabeg were willing (perhaps even eager) to be associated with Longfellow's famously kitschy poem does not seem to jibe with our current understanding of the cultural politics of indigeneity, in which the power and coherence of "the people" comes from a reverence for, and the desire to protect, the sanctity of traditional culture. *Hiawatha, or Nanabozho*'s explicit commodification of Anishinaabe culture, its willingness to sacrifice dignity for the sake of spectacle, its imbrication in the economics of settlement, makes the participation of the Anishinaabeg in the play deeply uncomfortable to consider. To make sense of it, we imagine the Anishinaabeg variously as being strategic, coerced, or merely assimilated—in every case, their ability to make meaningful decisions about their own destiny severely limited by the circumstance of history.

But should it be so? Can we imagine the Anishinaabeg's participation in *Hiawatha, or Nanabozho* differently? Can we read the obvious pride of the performers as anything other than complicity? Can we not celebrate *Hiawatha, or Nanabozho* as an act of Anishinaabe persistence and survival even as we acknowledge its complications? Can we find value as a significant work of Anishinaabe literature—as one of the first dramas written by a Native?

It is worth noting that Francis, Trachtenberg, and McNally all examine *Hiawatha, or Nanabozho* in terms of performance, but largely dismiss its existence as a *text*.⁸ Part of the reason may be because the earliest printed version of *Hiawatha, or Nanabozho*'s script seems hopelessly compromised.⁹ More of a tourist brochure than a working script, the short booklet is full of paratextual elements meant for the benefit of the play's audience, rather than its performers. Scattered throughout the play's dialogue are photographs of the cast posing in full costume, as well as several of the scenic landscapes around Desbarats. The text is also regularly accompanied by small engravings depicting an assortment of unmistakably "Indian" artifacts, including a parfleche bag, a buffalo-horn headdress, and a large number of war clubs. The last page of the booklet is the most explicitly commercial, comprised of detailed instructions on how the "countless virgin lakes and rivers" of northern Ontario could be reached "by the Canadian Pacific Railway from Boston, New York, and the East generally" (32).

Yet, the most interesting aspect of *Hiawatha, or Nanabozho* is the script itself, presented in both English and Anishinaabemowin in facing-page translation. The inclusion of a complete Anishinaabemowin translation of *Hiawatha, or Nanabozho*'s script seems particularly odd, given the obvious degree to which the published version of the play seems meant for tourist consumption. For the play's average audience member, seeing written Anishinaabemowin would have had little meaning outside of lending the script an air of authenticity. The same effect, however, could have been achieved far more easily—perhaps with the inclusion of a few lines of Anishinaabemowin dialogue given for exotic flavor. Instead, the translation seems to dominate the script, taking up thirteen pages of *Hiawatha, or Nanabozho*'s thirty-two pages (the English version, for comparison, is only eleven). Moreover, the Anishinaabemowin pages are largely bare, featuring almost none of the decorative elements present in the rest of the booklet. Rather, the reader is confronted with large blocks of unbroken text, a mass of hyphenated polysyllables filling the page from the top margin to the bottom.

The commercial presentation of *Hiawatha, or Nanabozho*'s script reflects the interests of the play's ostensible librettist, L. O. Armstrong. The idea that Armstrong wrote the play is testified to by the play's title page, which reads: "*Hiawatha, or Nanabozho*, Ewh Ojibway Ahnishenahba, E nuh Kuh me ge ze win (oduhmenowin) owh Waubungay or L.O. Armstrong"[10] (An Ojibwe Indian Performance [Play] by Waubungay or L.O. Armstrong). Armstrong's claim to sole authorship is troubled, however, by the inclusion of the Anishinaabemowin translation—the only part of the script that isn't merely a reproduction of Longfellow's poem. As an Anglophone Canadian living in Montreal, the idea that Armstrong knew enough of the (notoriously difficult) Anishinaabe language to produce his own translation seems unlikely. As one contemporary reviewer acknowledged, Armstrong's involvement in the play's script was limited to "realizing the wonderful possibilities of the poem as a drama" and "ha[ving] it translated into the Ojibway language, and dramatized."[11] Indeed, it is tempting to read evidence of Armstrong's lack of participation on title page of the script itself, which bestows on him the dubious honorific "Waubungay" (Waabange), meaning "He watches," or more appropriately, "He is a spectator."

Although there is no direct evidence linking George Kabaosa to the text of *Hiawatha, or Nanabozho*, a very strong circumstantial case can be made that it was he, not Armstong, who was the translator and editor responsible for dramatizing Longfellow's poem. Kabaosa had developed an interest in Longfellow's poem as a child, after hearing it recited in missionary school and recognizing the stories it contained as those of his own people. In 1901 Alice Longfellow, who had met Kabaosa and kept a correspondence with him, wrote that he was "engaged in writing out all [the Hiawatha] legends to preserve them for posterity."[12] In July 1903, the Fox ethnologist William Jones wrote that he stayed up until two in the morning listening to Kabaosa relate "the Indian versions of the things used in the poem."[13] A 1929 obituary reports that Kabaosa "was sought after by Canadian writers because of his ability as a linguist."[14] Reviewers who saw the earliest performances of the play also note that the Anishinaabe cast (led by Kabaosa, who played Hiawatha) had final say over its content—adamantly refusing, for example, to stage any scenes depicting the death of Minnehaha.[15] Whatever his role, Kabaosa certainly expressed considerable pride in *Hiawatha, or Nanabozho*, saying of his fellow Anishinaabeg collaborators: "We don't act; we live the legends of our people."[16]

Kabaosa's emotional investment in *The Song of Hiawatha* was not without reason. Longfellow's poem was based, in part, on stories originally told by his grandfather, Shingwaukonse, and his uncle, Buhkwujjinini in the early nineteenth century. The fact that his family had played a role in the creation of what was, at the time, one of the most famous works of literature in North America must have been a source of considerable pride for Kabaosa. Although the poem took many liberties with its source material, and cast Indians in a grossly stereotypical light, Kabaosa seems to have recognized how *The Song of Hiawatha* was, in some small way, a testament to perseverance of his people's culture. By translating the poem into Anishinaabemowin, Kabaosa showed how Longfellow's poem was capable of speaking to that culture, making it visible in a way that hadn't been done before—creating a new form of Anishinaabe written expression that may not have been traditional, but was nonetheless true. But doing so would mean having to grapple with *The Song of Hiawatha*'s dark assumptions about writing's role in Native life.

Wild and Wayward Stories

Broad critical consensus has it that the ideological core of *The Song of Hiawatha* is the poem's fourteenth canto, titled "Picture-Writing." In it Hiawatha invents a system of pictographs meant to preserve "the great traditions" of his people for "the generations / That, as yet unborn, are waiting / In the great, mysterious darkness / Of the speechless days that shall be!"[17] Coming nearly two-thirds of the way through *The Song of Hiawatha*, the picture-writing canto represents a significant shift in the poem's tone, beginning with Hiawatha's sorrowful lamentation: "Lo! how all things fade and perish!"[18] The mournful tenor of the canto's opening line marks, as Joshua Bellin notes, "the poem's first step toward decline,"[19] foreshadowing the deaths of Chibiabos, Kwasind, and Minnehaha, the betrayal of Pau-Pau-Keewis, and Hiawatha's own bittersweet journey to the West.

The picture-writing canto, unlike almost every other episode in *The Song of Hiawatha*, has no apparent antecedent in the Anishinaabe oral tradition. Instead, it is likely a product of Longfellow's own imagination—one with disconcerting implications. In Hiawatha's words, writing allows the Anishinaabe to "speak when absent,"[20] ensuring that knowledge of Anishinaabe traditions can survive the disappearance of actual Anishinaabe people—prefigured in his own disappearance at the end of the poem. Having established a way of preserving his teachings for "the generations . . . as yet unborn," Hiawatha disconnects Anishinaabe culture from its communal context, allowing it to be transmitted perfectly across time and space without relying on the fallible memories of Anishinaabe people, who "May pervert it, may betray it."[21] For Bellin, Hiawatha's invention of pictograph writing is "an act of pure translation, translating literally nothing, or translating nothing into literature" that both reflects and enacts "Longfellow's effacement of his source[s]."[22]

Indeed, much of the narrative material *The Song of Hiawatha* was based on was taken from stories originally translated and edited by Jane Johnston (Obabaamwewe-giizhigokwe) and her siblings in the first decades of the nineteenth century. Educated in the literary arts by their Irish father, the Johnstons were avid writers, composing multiple poems, memoirs, and stories in Anishinaabemowin, French, and English. Importantly, they also recorded and translated dozens of Anishinaabe stories from around the Sault—many from their mother, Ozhaawashkodewekwe. It was this "fund of fictitious legendary matter"[23] that Henry Rowe Schoolcraft claimed to have discovered after being installed as the head of the Indian Agency at the Sault in 1822. Marrying Jane in 1823, Schoolcraft set out to publish the Johnstons' stories as a work of ethnography, thinking that they would reveal insights into what he called "the dark cave of the Indian mind."[24] The resulting work, *Algic Researches* (1839), reprinted forty-six stories originally collected and translated by the Johnstons, lightly edited by Schoolcraft, along with a brief consideration of the "mental characteristics" of the Anishinaabeg. It was from this text that

Longfellow drew the bulk of the narrative material that comprises the plot of *The Song of Hiawatha*.

The Johnstons, moreover, were hardly Longfellow's only Anishinaabe sources. Several years before he began work on the poem, Longfellow was introduced to a young Anishinaabe lecturer and writer named George Copway (Gaagigegaabaw) who had stopped in Boston to give a lecture on the manners and customs of his people. Longfellow would maintain a correspondence with Copway that would last through the composition and publication of *Hiawatha* and use his writings on Anishinaabe history to supplement Johnston Schoolcraft's stories.[25] After publishing the first edition of *Hiawatha*, Longfellow was also visited in Cambridge by James Tanner, the son of John Tanner (Zhaazhaawanibiisens), the former captive whose memoirs Longfellow had plumbed for details about Anishinaabe language and hunting practices. The younger Tanner helped to correct several mistakes Longfellow had made in his use of Anishinaabemowin words, so that they could be rendered accurately in subsequent editions of *The Song of Hiawatha*.[26]

Yet, by the time the reading public encountered the first lines of Longfellow's poem—"Should you ask me, whence these stories? / Whence these legends and traditions?"[27]—the existence of these Anishinaabe interlocutors had been completely obscured. Instead, *The Song of Hiawatha* claims that these "wild and wayward" stories were discovered "In the bird's-nests of the forest, / In the lodges of the beaver, / In the hoof-prints of the bison, / In the eyry of the eagle" by Nawadaha, "the sweet singer," a pseudonym for Henry Rowe Schoolcraft.[28] In a short postscript to *The Song of Hiawatha*, Schoolcraft is briefly credited with "rescuing from oblivion so much of the legendary lore of the Indians,"[29] but there is absolutely no mention of the literary contributions of Jane Johnston Schoolcraft, George Copway, or John Tanner. As Birgit Rasmussen argues, "the differences in Longfellow's intertextual relationship to his sources mirror and enable his construction of a national epic based on the simultaneous appropriation and erasure of indigenous culture."[30]

The effacement of Anishinaabe sources performed by *The Song of Hiawatha* speaks to an underlying monologism that structures the poem as a whole. According to Mikhail Bakhtin, monological texts work to obscure their relationship to previously written texts by "join[ing] and personif[ying] others' words, others' voices" into anonymizing rhetorical figures such as "'the voice of life itself,' 'the voice of nature,' 'the voice of the people,' 'the voice of God.'"[31] Presenting itself as having a relatively unmediated relationship with what we would now call "the oral tradition," Longfellow's poem could claim to speak with the cultural and historical authority of an "Indian consciousness" untouched by the corrupting influences of modernity. The ponderous trochaic tetrameter of *The Song of Hiawatha* further serves to give the poem a sense of monological cohesion, smoothing over its awkward welds and gaps with a steady, driving rhythm.

The inclusion of the picture-writing canto in *The Song of Hiawatha* is meant to legitimize Longfellow's project of speaking for (and, in many ways, as) an Anishinaabeg. Hiawatha's invention of pictographic writing posits the existence of a "pure" record of Anishinaabe culture untarnished by contact or colonialism—heavily implying that such a text is the basis for *The Song of Hiawatha*. For Alan Trachtenberg, the picture-writing canto offers "a meta-action, a reflection on the reading of the poem itself,"[32] explaining:

> The illusion of the translation, the illusion that Longfellow's verse is as transparent as pictures, is the poem's ultimate act against the native and for the nation. . . . It makes Hiawatha or "the Indian" disappear in the act of seeming to give him voice; its own metrical and figurative system disarticulates aboriginal culture from its own systems of thought and speech by subsuming the aboriginal into the Anglo-Saxon nationality of the narrative verse form. The poem thus constructs a "white man's Indian" by suggesting that we can hear the picture speech of natives only by the means of the mediating voice of the poet.[33]

According to Trachtenberg, *Hiawatha* leverages the authority of text to speak *as* the Indian, ventriloquizing an indigenous voice in order to speak back to Euro-Americans, reassuring them that their destruction of Native peoples was not just necessary, but preordained by fate itself. As Roy Harvey Pearce argues, this aspect of *The Song of Hiawatha* was critical to its success, as it offered a way to receive absolution for an act that "was still heavy on American consciences," by making Indians part of "a dim and satisfying past about which readers could have dim and satisfying feelings."[34]

Gakina Banaadad

Despite removing from *Hiawatha, or Nanabozho* a great many of the episodes depicted in Longfellow's poem, Kabaosa chose to retain the picture-writing canto in his translation, albeit in a very condensed form. In the script for *Hiawatha, or Nanabozho*, the entire scene is reduced to a single piece of dialogue—Hiawatha's lament—adding another layer of significance to an already overdetermined moment.

English Script:
Lo! how all things fade and perish!
From the memory of the old men
Fade away the great traditions (16)

Anishinaabemowin Script:
Enuh Gah ken uh ga goo-ahnooj kah
Kahya gah keen uh bah nah dud
Emah ode nan dah mowine waung
Egewh uhke-wan-ze-yang
Kahya ah-nooj-kah ah-dis-oka-win (19)

Modern Orthography:
Inaa gakina gegoo anoshka
Gaye gakina banaadad
Imaa od-inendamowiniwang
Ingiw akiwenziiyag
Gaye anoshka aadizookewin

English (Re)Translation:
Oh! Everything fades
And all is destroyed
In the thoughts
Of those old men
And sacred storytelling is fading[35]

A reader familiar with ideological implications of Longfellow's poem may find the faithfulness of this translation troubling. The speech is a tacit admission that responsibility for the inevitable decline and disappearance of tribal cultures lies at the feet of the people who abandon them to the passage of time and the frailty of memory—seeing it rendered in an indigenous language makes it all the more disturbing. Some critics may want to read this passage as evidence of Kabaosa's assimilationist mind-set, molded by the efforts of missionaries and boarding school-teachers to weaken the strength of the Anishinaabe nation. A critic of settler-colonialism may point to this moment as evidence that Kabaosa translated *Hiawatha, or Nanabozho* under duress, constrained by imperial forces beyond his control or ken. We may want to read it as evidence of mental illness, material greed, or simply a lack of respect for tradition. We may want to minimize and disregard this moment, ignoring it as many already have—reducing the existence of an Anishinaabemowin translation of *The Song of Hiawatha* to a mere historical curiosity, an embarrassing relic of an imperfect past.

But to do so, I think, would be to make a grave mistake. If we are to dismiss Kabaosa's translation as too culturally compromised, too inauthentic, too liminal to count as a work of independent Anishinaabe expression, we deny Kabaosa the same kind of agency to interpret and translate texts that we freely accept in Longfellow. More importantly, to read Kabaosa's translation as a mere stand-in for Longfellow's poem is to invest in *The Song of Hiawatha* a kind of transhistorical immanence that we do *not* invest in the Anishinaabe stories from which it was adapted. That is to say, if we allow a Eurocentric interpretation of *The Song of Hiawatha* to be the *only* possible interpretation, we deny the idea that the Anishinaabe stories embedded within it may retain significances for an Anishinaabeg reader to which a Euro-American reader may not have access. The artificial monologism carefully constructed throughout *The Song of Hiawatha* is allowed to remain intact, its definitional authority unthreatened by the heterogeneous mass of stories, histories, and languages it seeks to obscure.

If we instead read Kabaosa's translation as a text that both departs from, and reflects on, *The Song of Hiawatha*, we may see how it destabilizes the monologism of Longfellow's poem while drawing out beneficial cultural and political significances latent within it. The most immediate difference one notices between Longfellow's poem and Kabaosa's translation is, of course, linguistic. Anishinaabemowin is a polysynthetic language that uses conjugation, affixes, and compounding to express complex ideas in a single word—usually much longer than those found in English. Breaking up complex Anishinaabe words into simpler mono- or disyllabic units,[36] Kabaosa's translation makes it easy for a nonspeaker of Anishinaabemowin to read each line aloud. Doing so, the reader would not only be confronted by deep unfamiliarity of Anishinaabemowin's elongated vowels and tricky consonant clusters, but also discover that the language has no underlying metrical or rhythmic resemblance to *Hiawatha*'s iconic trochaic tetrameter. In Kabaosa's translation, the familiar lines of *Hiawatha* stretch and contort to accommodate unfamiliar Anishinaabemowin words, as the three lines of English become five lines of Anishinaabemowin. The fundamental incompatibility of Anishinaabemowin with *Hiawatha*'s meter casts a layer of opacity over the original poem's claim to translational transparency, revealing the poem's most defining characteristic as an artificial construction imposed on the Anishinaabe language, rather than some sort of racial rhythm endemic to it.

Kabaosa's translation of the picture-writing canto does much more, however, than simply challenge Longfellow's understanding of Anishinaabemowin. To borrow Alan Trachtenberg's terms, Kabaosa's translation *re*articulates the "aboriginal culture" presented in the picture-writing canto with "its own systems of thought and speech," revealing an alternative interpretation of the scene's relevancy for the Anishinaabeg of the time. The original salience of the picture-writing canto relies on an imagined future in which non-Natives could be the only possible readers of Hiawatha's texts. While such a future may have seemed imminent to Longfellow's nineteenth-century readers, the mere existence of Kabaosa's translation offers direct evidence that it never came to be. Kabaosa's translation radically reframes the temporal assumptions of Longfellow's poem, transforming *Hiawatha* from a narrative of Indian disappearance into a story about Anishinaabeg's use of writing as a tool of adaptation and survival. The continued presence of the Anishinaabeg as both readers and writers of texts forces us to reconsider the prophetic implication of the picture-writing canto, transforming it from an augur of the Anishinaabeg's inevitable decline and disappearance to the mythic origin of written Anishinaabe literature. If, as Trachentenberg argues, the picture-writing canto offers a metacommentary on *The Song of Hiawatha*'s effacement of Anishinaabe writing practices, Kabaosa's translation of the scene provides an equally compelling metacommentary on their persistence.

Moreover, Hiawatha's anxiety over the potential disappearance of Anishinaabe storytelling practices expressed in the picture-writing canto takes on a different kind of urgency in the historical context of Kabaosa's translation. While the action of Longfellow's poem is self-contained in the prepolitical time of the epic form,[37] the facing translations of *Hiawatha, or Nanabozho* act as a constant reminder of the play's colonial context. The overlapping of English and Anishinaabemowin on the page reflects the overlapping (and conflicting) political claims of Euro-American settlers and the Anishinaabeg themselves—including a claim to language. As Margot Francis points out, "The significance of Ojibwe as the language of performance is particularly important when one realizes that the local idiom was discouraged by the Canadian state and usually forbidden in the local residential school."[38] The compulsory use of English was just part of a systematic assault on indigenous cultural traditions being carried out at the time by the U.S. and Canadian governments, which also forbade certain forms of singing, dancing, and religious practice. In such a context, the desire to preserve "aadizookewin" ("sacred storytelling") before "gakina gegoo anoshka / gaye gakina banaadad" ("everything fades / and all is destroyed") takes on a distinctly political edge.

In Longfellow's poem the invention of pictographic writing is meant to create the possibility of cultural continuity between the Anishinaabeg and Euro-American settlers, but in *Hiawatha, or Nanabozho* this causality is flipped on its head, as colonization becomes a motivating precondition for the Anishinaabeg's adoption of graphematic writing. Presenting Hiawatha's invention of pictographic writing in graphemetic Anishinaabemowin, Kabaosa's translation imagines a continuity between the two practices, offering a potential way to keep aadizookewin alive in a time of duress. At the same time, the translation calls attention to the fact that this mode of preservation depends on a set of technologies (alphabetic script, the printing press, etc.) adopted from nonindigenous sources. Unlike *The Song of Hiawatha*, however, the political significance of writing is never truly resolved in Kabaosa's translation, but remains weighted with ambivalence—acting as both an expression of traditional Anishinaabe cultural practices *and* as evidence of their disruption by Euro-Americans.

Crucially, we must recognize that this alternative meaning only makes sense embedded *within* the context of *The Song of Hiawatha*, not despite it. Kabaosa's translation makes no attempt to tell the true story of Nanabozho, neither does it depart from the meaning of Longfellow's original language. Kabaosa's translation does not append overtly critical language into Longfellow's poem, or attempt to present a more "authentic" understanding of traditional Anishinaabe culture. Instead, the anticolonial implications of Kabaosa's translation lie in the way it uses *writing* to reveal and activate the ambiguities already present in the pastiche-like nature of Longfellow's poem, showing how its monological claims to define Indian identity as primitive, illiterate, and vanished are contradicted by the very conditions of its production. Kabaosa's translation asks us to read Longfellow's poem as a single utterance in an ongoing conversation between Anishinaabe and Euro-American *writers* that encompasses the work of Jane Johnston Schoolcraft, Henry Rowe Schoolcraft, George Copway, John Tanner, and many others—a conversation that had been already going on for centuries. By translating *The Song of Hiawatha* into Anishinaabemowin, Kabaosa made his own contribution to the conversation, one that challenged Longfellow's vision of the future as a time without Indians while reclaiming the stories that belonged to his family and people.

Like the Anishinaabeg themselves, *Hiawatha, or Nanabozho* bears the marks of Euro-American contact in its graphemetic script, its dramatic form, and the deeply compromised nature of Longfellow's original poem, but at the same time it insists that it is "iw Anishinaabe . . . inakamigiziwin" (5),—literally, an Anishinaabe *act*. Instead of a record of decline or assimilation, *Hiawatha, or Nanabozho* should be read as an expression of agency that finds power in crossing the boundaries that separate Anishinaabe and Euro-American, authentic and appropriative, past and present. Rather than passively assert identity, *Hiawatha, or Nanabozho* lays claim to nonindigenous ideas, technologies, and languages, subjecting them to a process of translation (what we might call indigenization) that fundamentally alters their meaning, and makes them into something the Anishinaabeg can use to their own ends. This expression of agency is, to my mind, what makes *Hiawatha, or Nanabozho* a significant text, as it replicates, in miniature, a larger dynamic that has largely defined literary writing both by and about the Anishinaabeg.

Translation, Transmotion, and Transnationalism

While the history of U.S.-Anishinaabe relations has been relatively free of armed violence, it is littered with literary confrontations of the kind seen between Longfellow's *Song of Hiawatha* and Kabaosa's *Hiawatha, or Nanabozho*. Focusing on such moments, this book presents literature as a representational battlefield on which the Anishinaabeg and Euro-Americans have met to contest the future of their respective nations. Where most (but not all) texts by Euro-Americans examined in this work use the conventions of literary writing to set imaginative limits on Anishinaabe identity, those written by Anishinaabeg (and their allies) are all engaged in the project of troubling the boundaries—appropriating and tweaking literary forms, questioning narrative convention, and refusing categorization. *Our War Paint* argues that Anishinaabe literature works to support the project of Anishinaabe sovereignty and nationhood not by asserting its cultural separatism, but by resituating monological narratives of Indianness as part of an ongoing discourse comprised of multiple—even conflicting—understandings of Anishinaabe nationhood. Reading across the contested boundaries of indigenous nation and settler state, I argue, allows us to reassess the ways literary writing gives definition to otherwise vague ideas about identity, authenticity, and temporality within a political context where such abstractions are expected to carry the force of law.

According to the political theorist Kevin Bruyneel, the history of U.S. settler-colonialism since the nineteenth century has been defined by attempts to "create and perpetuate monological identities" for Native people, which are meant to "deny the multiplicity and contingency of [their] political identity, agency, and autonomy."[39] As Bruyneel argues, U.S. colonial policy during this period has sought "to narrowly bound indigenous political status in space and time" in order to "limit the ability of indigenous people to define their own identity and develop economically and politically on their own terms."[40] By establishing and policing the boundaries between what is "Indian" and "non-Indian," the United States maintains the exclusive right to define "the people, the power, the space, and the time of legitimate sovereignty."[41] According to Bruyneel, the most important of these boundaries are temporal ones, which create a division between "an 'advancing people' and a 'static' people, placing the latter out of time . . . where they are unable to be modern, autonomous agents."[42]

In simpler terms, U.S. colonial policy depends on the ability to define modernity as coterminous with Euro-American culture, and that for indigenous peoples to participate in either is for them to implicitly accede to Euro-American political dominance. Indigenous communities, therefore, can only experience social, political, or cultural change at the cost of their political rights as indigenous peoples. The result is a political situation in which non-Natives retain complete authority to define the limits of Native political subjectivity according to their own needs and desires. Although the temporal boundaries that separate Indians from modernity are ultimately codified through legislation, according to Bruyneel, they originate in "economic, cultural, and political narratives that place limitations on the capacity of certain peoples to express meaningful agency and autonomy, especially in the modern context."[43]

Given the significance of narrative in this process, it should come as no surprise that literature has been a particularly privileged site for examining settler-colonial ideology. Starting with the inestimable work of Roy Harvey Pearce in the 1950s, there has been a long tradition of examining the role of literature in defining the boundaries separating the "savage" Indian from the "civilized" American. In works such as James Fenimore Cooper's *The Last of the Mohicans*, Disney's *Pocahontas*, and many, many others, Euro-Americans have created an image of the Indian that is, in Pearce's words, "bound inextricably in a primitive past, a primitive society, and a primitive environment."[44] More recent works such as Joshua Bellin's *Demon of the Continent* (2001), James Cox's *Muting White Noise* (2006), and Mark Rifkin's *Settler Common Sense*

(2014) have done much to investigate and elaborate Pearce's idea of the "savage" as an ideological construction, showing how literary representations of Indianness have served to legitimize artificial boundaries set on indigenous people by the American state. By examining such narratives, we can gain incredible insight into what Raymond Williams describes as the "structures of feeling"[45] that underlie and give rise to specific colonial policies.

Of equal importance has been the scholarly work that shows, in Craig Womack's words, how "Indian people exercis[ing] the right to present images of themselves and to discuss those images" constitutes a "part of sovereignty."[46] Works such as Louis Owen's *Other Destinies* (1992), Robert Warrior's *Tribal Secrets* (1995), Jace Weaver's *That the People Might Live* (1997), Daniel Heath Justice's *Our Fire Survives the Storm* (2006), Womack, Weaver, and Warrior's *American Indian Literary Nationalism* (2006), among many others, have shown how Native literature works to transgress the temporal boundaries meant to contain it by offering an alternative narrative of continuity and survival in the face of colonization. According to Jace Weaver, critical attention should be focused on Native literature that presents itself as "separate and distinct from other national literatures," and "sees itself as attempting to serve the interests of indigenes and their communities, in particular the support of Native nations and their own separate sovereignties."[47]

These critical approaches, while important and sound, also have an inadvertent tendency to reproduce existing assumptions that limit our understanding of the texts with which they engage. Nationalist criticism, as Scott Richard Lyons has ably argued, has a tendency to overlook the historical development, within indigenous communities, of the idea of nationhood as a specific kind of social organization with broad economic and ideological implications for tribal peoples.[48] Meanwhile, work that examines the settler-colonial assumptions of Euro-American literature has a tendency to produce symptomatic readings that serve to reaffirm Euro-American literature's complicity in structures of power, but do little to show how that power expresses itself differently in relation to particular tribal nations.

More importantly, in treating the literary output of indigenous peoples and Euro-Americans separately, these two lines of criticism run the risk of reifying many of the same temporal and cultural boundaries Bruyneel identifies as intrinsic to U.S. colonial power. By emphasizing the ways in which Native literature displays its "cultural separatism" or "intellectual sovereignty," nationalist criticism inadvertently participates in the highly suspect politics of recognition, in which indigenous political rights are tied to the continuity of specific historical practices. Settler-colonialist criticism, for its part, has a tendency to reify U.S. colonial authority even as it critiques—setting severe limits on Native peoples' ability to act as meaningful agents in the face of the supposedly totalizing force of U.S. imperialism. Both approaches, I would argue, have a tendency to present the idea of the nation—both settler or indigenous—as a transhistorically stable concept, far more immutable (in terms of politics) and far more impermeable (in terms of cultural influence) than the observation of history would seem to suggest. Both approaches, importantly, also have a tendency to privilege texts that reaffirm the ideological and political assumptions of their critical approach and tend to overlook those, like *Hiawatha*, or *Nanabozho*, that trouble the boundaries between indigenous and settler in potentially productive ways.

It is the ability to trouble such boundaries, according to Kevin Bruyneel, that forms that basis of indigenous sovereignty. As he argues, "U.S.-indigenous politics, at its core, is a battle between an American effort to solidify inherently contingent boundaries and an indigenous effort to work on and across these boundaries, drawing on and exposing their contingency to gain the fullest possible expression of political identity, agency, and autonomy."[49] Where the United States asserts its power by setting limits and defining terms, "the expression of political power by indigenous tribes and citizens is more often than not a supplementary strategy,"[50] in which indigenous peoples work to destabilize the United States' "monological narratives" of Indianness. Rejecting the rhetoric of "assimilation or secession, inside or outside, modern and traditional"[51] as false binaries explicitly meant to put limits on their agency, indigenous peoples have consistently articulated their own understanding of sovereignty "that resides neither simply inside nor outside the American political system but exists on their very boundaries, exposing both the practices and the contingencies of American colonial rule."[52] By "demanding rights and resources from the liberal democratic settler-state" while simultaneously questioning "the imposition of colonial rule on their lives," Bruyneel argues that indigenous peoples "work across American spatial and temporal boundaries" in a way that draws attention to their fundamental instability—calling into question the legitimacy of the United States' settler-colonial authority.[53]

In simplest terms, *Our War Paint* argues that U.S. colonial rule over the Anishinaabeg has been upheld through the perpetuation of monological narratives of Indianness, articulated and disseminated through literary writing. Such narratives serve to lend an appearance of solidity to what are, in reality, arbitrary distinctions between past and present, genuine and inauthentic, presence and absence. Anishinaabe writers, in turn, have resisted U.S. colonial rule not by offering their own monological counternarratives, but by translating, critiquing, and co-opting dominant narratives of Indianness, imbuing them with divergent and supplementary meanings that challenge the definitional authority of the colonial narrative altogether. The resulting works of poetry, prose, and drama work to tease out the ambivalences and ambiguities of the colonial situation, redefining important terms in ways that best suit the expedient political demands of Anishinaabe communities, and exposing the fundamental instability of U.S. colonial authority. In response, Euro-American writers articulate new monological narratives that, in turn, co-opt elements of the Anishinaabe response, recasting their pragmatic and expedient formulations of Anishinaabe identity as the new definition of Indianness to which Anishinaabe writers must respond. The result is a network of texts linked to one another by allusion, reference, and theme—with the addition of each new text complicating and inflecting how we understand every other text.

Critical to this argument is Mikhail Bakhtin's formulation of the "dialogic" as a process by which literary texts produce, and are produced by, social processes. According to Bakhtin, the discursive nature of language means that literary works should not be understood as autonomous expressions with stable meanings, but as assemblages of previously articulated meanings that take on recognizable shapes (an idea we implicitly recognize in discussions of genre and literary influence). As new texts are produced and old texts are forgotten, the meaning of a particular literary expression can change, as it is read in the context of a new set of significations. As Bakhtin argues,

> There is neither a first nor a last word and there are no limits to the dialogic context (it extends into the boundless past and the boundless future). Even *past* meanings, that is, those born in the dialogue of past centuries, can never be stable (finalized, ended once and for all)—they will always change (be renewed) in the process of subsequent, future development of the dialogue.[54]

Thinking about Anishinaabe and Euro-American writers as engaged in a dialogical process of exchange and negotiation allows us to think about literature's relationship to indigenous/settler politics differently. Instead of reading a text like *Hiawatha* solely through the colonialist politics and patronizing cultural assumptions of its Euro-American author, we can see how it can become indigenized through an act of Anishinaabe interpretive agency.

Of course, such an approach is not without drawbacks—especially for those who wish to understand indigenous literature as principally engaged in the work of cultural expression. My approach reads Anishinaabe literary production in fairly instrumental terms as an act of resistance to U.S. colonialism, reflective of the pressing need to respond to its constant existential threat. This political context determines the way Anishinaabe authors present cultural information, sometimes causing them to distort and misrepresent cultural tradition for political purposes. That is to say, I do not see Anishinaabe literature as primarily a project of expressing cultural identity, but rather the attempt to *use* culture in expedient ways.[55] For Anishinaabe writers, giving readers an authentic account of their culture is often less important than getting them to support efforts to dismantle the colonial policies and economic structures that put Anishinaabe culture in jeopardy. As such, works of Native literature must continually define themselves relationally to dominant narratives of Indianness if they are to be made at all intelligible to a non-Native readership—those who, for better or worse, hold a disproportionate amount of power over their lives.[56]

This inherent dialogism should not be seen as a relinquishing of cultural or political authority to non-Natives, but the assertion of it. By speaking directly to non-Indians, books by Native writers are doing the important work of disrupting the colonial narratives of Indianness for a population most likely to embrace such narratives as truth. What was once a colonial monologue becomes a transnational dialogue in which once stable understandings of identity, temporality, and governance become open to reinterpretation and negotiation, allowing for Natives to shift, if only in small ways, dominant structures of feeling regarding Indianness. I should say here that this is decidedly not an argument about canon-formation—I am neither trying to suggest that we read a text like *The Song of Hiawatha* "as" Anishinaabe literature, nor the *Hiawatha*, or *Nanabozho* "as" American literature. I *am* saying that however we choose to classify these works, they are related to one another in ways that are worth thinking about. Regardless of their origin, every text discussed in this book articulates an understanding of the relationship of the Anishinaabeg and the United States—an understanding subject to reinterpretation and renegotiation as these texts circulate between Anishinaabe and U.S. national contexts.

While already seeming like a dated concept to most scholars of American Studies, transnationalism is an approach that is still treated with a certain degree of skepticism by those who wish to promote Native sovereignty. As the Dakota scholar Philip Deloria pointed out in an address to the American Studies Association in 2003, "the decentering of 'nation' comes at a particularly inauspicious time for Indian people, who have invested a great deal of political and intellectual energy building a careful argument in courts, Congress, and regulatory agencies that treaty rights and sovereignty rest upon an acknowledgement of themselves as *nations*."[57] However, a growing number of scholars in the field of American Indian Studies have begun to embrace transnationalism as a meaningful way to describe the intellectual and cultural exchanges that occur between different Native polities, as well as those that occur between indigenous communities and settler societies. Joseph Bauerkemper and Heidi Kiiwetinepinesiik Stark argue that "Because it cannot help but bring distinctions between nations to the fore, transnational discourse can be fruitfully co-opted as an avenue for rhetorical assertions of indigenous nationhood."[58]

My own use of the term is meant to articulate a similar understanding: that for a transnational relationship to exist between the United States and the Anishinaabeg, both must be in maintenance of some form of nationhood. Indeed, the Anishinaabeg have long understood themselves as having strong ties to the United States as economic partners and political equals. As the historian of Anishinaabe political leadership Rebecca Kugel argues,

> The Ojibwe had commenced their political relationship with the Americans on terms that reflected the relative weakness of the United States and, despite American growth, the Ojibwe never acknowledged any change in the basic conceptualization of that alliance. They were acutely aware of shifting power differentials between themselves and the Americans, but this recognition did not alter their insistence that they had created a reciprocal political relationship between equal partners.[59]

Of course, in the power-laden realm of *realpolitik*, the relationship between the Anishinaabeg and the United States has been, and continues to be, vastly disproportionate. But so too are many, if not all, of the relationships studied under the rubric of transnationalism. While the political and cultural relationship between the United States and a Latin American nation such as El Salvador may be similarly unbalanced, we do not seem to question the legitimacy of Salvadoran nationhood—even as we point to massive American interventions into the political, cultural, and economic lives of Salvadorans. Indeed, it could be argued that the study of transnationalism appeared, in part, as an effort to address the persistence of national identities at a time of the nation-state's diminishing sovereignty. So, too, would I examine the history of U.S.-Anishinaabeg relations from a position that insists that no matter the degree to which the United States has intervened to marginalize and disrupt Anishinaabe sovereignty, its nationhood has remained a conceptual, legal, and cultural reality.

The second reason I choose to embrace the term "transnationalism" in my study has to do with the fact that any formulation of Anishinaabe nationhood must be, by its very nature, always-already transnational. Not only do the Anishinaabeg occupy territory on both sides of the Canadian-U.S. border, they exist as dozens of individual, autonomous national polities.[60] Despite the legal separation that exists between a place like the Turtle Mountain Reservation in North Dakota and the Hiawatha Reserve in Ontario, there is a recognition not just of shared language, culture, and history, but of participation in a larger Anishinaabe community. Rachel Adams argues such relations are a form of "indigenous transnationalism," a term she uses to describe "the divisive, centrifugal forces of modernity that have dispersed North American Indians, but also . . . the drive to form coalitions across the boundaries of tribal nations and nation-states." Adams understands such coalitions as not just an expedient response to colonization, but as "the resumption of alliances and networks of filiation that were severed by the conquest and its aftermath."[61] Indeed, kinship ties form an important conduit through which an overarching sense of Anishinaabe nationhood is maintained, as internal migration between Anishinaabe communities has been (and continues to be) a fundamental aspect of Anishinaabe life.[62]

Last, I use the term "transnational" (perhaps idiosyncratically) to refer to the process by which a sense of Anishinaabe nationhood is created and maintained. Rather than understand Anishinaabe nationhood as a transhistorically stable object, I see it instead as a process—one that changes who the Anishinaabeg are—politically, economically, and culturally, both from within and without. My use of the term is meant to be a reminder that, as David Scott argues, "modernity was not a choice" for marginalized peoples in the New World, "but was itself one of the fundamental *conditions* of choice."[63] Nationhood has been a powerful rhetoric by which indigenous peoples have gained recognition, asserted self-determination, and made legal claims in a colonial context, but it is not an indigenous form of social organization. Here, I am following Scott Richard Lyons's argument that indigenous nations have not existed from time immemorial, but are "a modern invention born at the moment of the treaty."[64] Like Lyons, I see the project of indigenous nationalism as a conscious decision to embrace modernity, sometimes (but not always) at the cost of what might be called the "traditional." This is akin to what Eric Cheyfitz describes as the "colonial dynamic of translation," the process by which "Indian communities are subject to, even as they resist, cultural, social, economic, and political translation" by colonial powers.[65] Such strategic transformations are what I mean to evoke, in part, in my use of the term "transnationalism."

In thinking through this definition of *transnationalism*, I am indebted to Gerald Vizenor's concept of transmotion, defined as "that sense of Native motion and an active presence," which Vizenor argues constitutes "*sui generis* sovereignty."[66] Here, Vizenor refers to a form of sovereignty that does not refer to absolute political authority over a bounded territory, but rather "the substantive rights of motion in native communities."[67] Importantly, the motion that Vizenor describes here is not just the movement through space (although this is a vitally important part of his idea) but movement through time—the ability of a community to adapt to changing circumstances but still assert its existence as a community. As such, Vizenor sees his definition of sovereignty-as-motion as having "a natural and historical presence in the notions of and theories of transnational survivance."[68] My use of "transnational," therefore, is meant to recognize the degree to which what we call Anishinaabe nationhood can be understood as an expression of such transmotion: not an end in itself, but the process of continually asserting Anishinaabe political and cultural presence within the structures of modernity and the ever-changing context of U.S. colonial policy.

I have structured *Our War Paint* around the shifting landscape of federal Indian law in the post-treaty-making era—a period roughly covering from 1886 to the present day. Each chapter of *Our War Paint* focuses on the literary responses to (or prefigurations of) four major shifts in federal Indian policy: the Dawes General Allotment Act of 1886, the Indian Reorganization Act of 1934, the termination efforts of the 1950s, and the emergence of tribal self-determination as official policy since 1973. By employing comparative readings of both Anishinaabe and non-Anishinaabe writers, I offer a more holistic figuration of the overarching structures of feeling that determined U.S.-Anishinaabe relations at these momentous points in their shared history.

Chapter 1 examines the English translations of Anishinaabe aadizookaanag (legendary stories) that appeared in the *Progress*, a little-known newspaper published on the White Earth Reservation between 1886 and

1889. In it, I show how the newspaper's Anishinaabe editor, Theo Beaulieu (1850–1923), used these translations as an imaginative supplement to editorials that called for the transformation of White Earth into a modern, semi-autonomous nation. By translating the aadizookaanag into a form that resembled the conventions of modern fiction, I argue that Beaulieu makes an implicit case for the ability of the Anishinaabe to adapt to modern forms of social organization and governance without Euro-American interference—a task that became critically important with the contemporaneous passage of allotment legislation. Through a comparison of Beaulieu's politically motivated translations of the aadizookaanag with *Hiawatha*, I argue that the genre into which oral material is translated creates a supplementary political significance not present in the original that must be accounted for.

Chapter 2 compares the early Nick Adams fiction of Ernest Hemingway (1899–1961) with Janet Lewis's (1899–1998) little-known historical novel, *The Invasion* (1932), in order to unpack the complicated politics of settlement and recognition during the early twentieth century. Classmates and neighbors, Hemingway and Lewis both wrote about their formative experiences with the Anishinaabe people of upper Michigan. But where Hemingway's fiction eventually erases the Anishinaabe from the Michigan landscape, Lewis's novel asserts their continued presence, even as they were denied legal recognition from the U.S. government. Through substantive archival research, I uncover the remarkable history of Lewis's collaboration with a family of Anishinaabe activists who provided her with the historical narratives on which *The Invasion* is based. Showing how *The Invasion* uses its content and form to make an explicit demand for the recognition of indigenous sovereignty, I argue it be read as an important example of Anishinaabe nationalism—despite Lewis's non-Anishinaabe identity.

Chapter 3 traces the politicized publication history of Frances Densmore's (1867–1957) translations of Anishinaabe nagamonan (songs). Initially recorded as a project of salvage ethnography, these translations drew the interest of multiple generations of non-Native poets who published their own reworked versions of the songs, often inflecting them with their own misguided assumptions about Anishinaabe culture. Through a detailed reading of Jerome Rothenberg's midcentury versions of the songs, I argue that many such reinterpretations rely on the same misguided sense of cultural authenticity that underwrote the U.S. government's contemporaneous efforts to terminate tribal nations. I then go on to show how Anishinaabe author Gerald Vizenor (b. 1934) subjects Densmore's translations to a radically different kind of poetics in various editions of *Summer in the Spring* (1965, 1970, 1981, and 1993). I argue that Vizenor's reexpressions act as a critique of the temporal logic of termination by embracing a formal logic of instability and fragmentation, recasting the songs as the ephemera of colonization rather than as artifacts of an authentic tribal culture.

Chapter 4 returns to the relationship between genre and nationhood, this time by examining the fiction of Louise Erdrich (b. 1954) as the paradigmatic fiction of the self-determination era. Asserting that critics have overlooked the representational significance of state institutions in her fiction, I show how Erdrich's much-discussed "magical realism" is the manifestation of a reformist politics. Through close readings of *The Plague of Doves* (2008) and *The Painted Drum* (2005) I show how Erdrich works to rehabilitate reservation bureaucracies by showing them to be extensions of the Anishinaabe communal identity. Like Theo Beaulieu a century earlier, Erdrich uses generic translation to legitimize the existence of the modern Anishinaabe nation-state by recasting the plots of well-known dibaajimowinan (didactic stories) into a realist mode. This allows Erdrich to show state institutions as capable of helping Anishinaabe attain the philosophical ideal of mino-bimaadiziwin (the good way of life). By making the case for the state-form of Anishinaabe nationhood as ethically consistent with traditional tribal values, I argue that Erdrich's fiction reflects an indigenous internationalism emergent at the beginning of the twenty-first century.

I conclude with a brief consideration of Liz Howard's "Of Hereafter Song" (2015), a poem that rewrites Longfellow's *Song of Hiawatha* to address emerging threats to the Anishinaabe Nation in the form of ecological contamination and exploitation by transnational corporations. Ultimately, I argue that such answering threats might mean reassessing the value of indigenous nationhood as a project of political separatism, and embracing a more capacious understanding of the Anishinaabeg's place in a globalized society.

Chapter 1

Revolutionary in Character

Translating Anishinaabe Place and Time in the *Progress*

> The Progress shows all the way through that considerable war paint has been put on . . .
>
> —Paul Bodeen, editor of the *Red Lake Falls News*

> We are fearful lest friend Bodeen may have took [sic] an extensively magnified view of the war-like aspect of our exterior, and thereby caused anxiety to our neighbors across the line, so we rise to explain that our paint is of the mildest order—being simply writing fluid, and our knife and tomahawk, only the 'stick' and 'rule,' and Esterbrook and Faber's patent for our arrows and our backbone (a good one for it staid bent for nearly two years and when loosed assumed a handsome perpendicular) for the bow.
>
> —Theodore Beaulieu, editor of the *Progress*, in response

On a March day in 1886, the Indian agent went with armed guard to an unassuming clapboard shack in White Earth village. He believed the place to be the haunt of a dangerous group of subversives who were trying to foment revolt among the Indians of White Earth Reservation. The interior of the shack was small and spare, taken up almost entirely by a sizable letterpress, the deep wooden drawers of a type case, and stacks of bundled newsprint. Neatly mirrored on the galley, already sitting in the press, was the front page of a newspaper. At its head, set in large, plain type was its title: THE PROGRESS. Underneath, in smaller letters, appeared the words: "A higher Civilization: the Maintenance of Law and Order." The agent intended that the first issue of the *Progress* never leave this shack. To that end, he had the doors chained, and posted a watchman to guard the shack both day and night. With this done, he set out to find the paper's publisher, Augustus Beaulieu, in order to remove him from the reservation.

Augustus Beaulieu was the scion of the most affluent and politically influential mixed-blood family at White Earth. His father, Clement Beaulieu, used his family connections among the Anishinaabeg to rise through the ranks of the American Fur Company, becoming a major trader first at La Pointe, then at Lac du Flambeau, and finally at Crow Wing village in central Minnesota—where Augustus was born in 1852. Along with the rest of the Mississippi Band, Augustus relocated to White Earth in 1869 under the terms of a treaty his father and his uncle, Paul Beaulieu, had helped negotiate two years prior. Over his lifetime, Augustus (or Gus, as he preferred to be called) would find employment variously as a clerk, shopkeeper, interpreter, real estate agent, and uncredentialed lawyer ("Indian claims against the United States a specialty"[1]). At the time of the *Progress*'s publication, however, Gus was an acting U.S. Marshal working to curb illegal alcohol sales on several of Minnesota's Anishinaabe reservations. Despite the extensive travel demanded by his job, Gus was an active voice in Anishinaabe politics at White Earth, having largely taken over his father's role as the informal leader of the reservation's mixed-blood contingent. It was this commitment that inspired Gus to found the *Progress*.

While the *Progress* was hardly the first newspaper to be published by American Indians—the *Cherokee Phoenix* had come into existence nearly sixty years prior—it was the first independent paper to be published on an Indian reservation outside of Indian Territory.[2] Funded without the aid (or permission) of Indian agent, religious organization, or tribal government, the *Progress* would be a bold experiment that blended free enterprise and free expression unlike anything previously seen in Indian Country. Through their long history as traders, the Beaulieu family had amassed a decent amount of wealth and political influence, ensuring them a degree of autonomy unknown to most Natives at the time. Moreover, their trade connections both on and off the reservation gave their fledgling newspaper a ready-made base of advertisers—including the reservation's two hotels, the Headquarters and the Hindquarters. Gus purchased a press and accompanying typeset in St. Paul, as well as a subscription to a "patent-inside" service that provided newsprint with items of national or international interest preprinted on the inside fold. With the materials and the funding secured, the only thing the paper needed was an editor.

While Gus Beaulieu provided the capital, it was his cousin, Theodore Beaulieu, who gave the *Progress* its distinctive voice. Born in 1852 in the newly created state of Wisconsin, Theo (as he preferred to be called) came from a less prestigious branch of the Beaulieu family who had settled years earlier in the small village of Appleton, just outside of Green Bay. It was there that young Theo was apprenticed to Samuel Ryan, the editor and publisher of the *Appleton Crescent*, a small, pro-Republican weekly. After the settlement of White Earth, Theo Beaulieu, like many mixed-bloods in the region, relocated to the reservation, where he married his second cousin (Gus's sister) Julia Beaulieu. On the reservation, he found employment as the superintendent for the Indian schools at White Earth and Leech Lake, a post he held for several years until the election of Grover Cleveland in 1884. Theo, like many Republican appointees, lost his position as the newly empowered Democrats gave positions in the Indian Service to their partisan supporters. Not only a trained printer, but also naturally gifted in the rhetorical arts, the freshly unemployed Theo was a perfect candidate to run Gus's fledgling newspaper.

The first issue of the *Progress* was meant to be distributed throughout the White Earth Reservation on March 25, 1886, but by the time the agent raided its offices, Theo had only managed to strike five copies.[3] Fortunately, at least one of these copies survived, as it was entered into evidence at a subsequent congressional hearing on the matter. Despite the extreme actions of the Indian agent, there is actually very little about the first issue of the *Progress* that could be considered incendiary. The first article was a salutatory blessing written by an Episcopalian minister, the Rev. Clement Beaulieu Jr. (Gus's brother). The minister's opening words proved ironically prophetic: "With this number we make our bow to the public. The novelty of a newspaper published upon this reservation may cause many to be wary in their support and this from a fear that it may be revolutionary in character." Against this perception, the reverend offered his reassurance.

> We shall aim to advocate constantly and withhold reserve, what in our view, and in the view of the leading minds upon this reservation, is the best for the interests of its residents. And not only for their interests, but those of the tribe wherever they now are residing. The main consideration in this advocacy, will be the political interests, that is in matters relating to the general Government of the United States . . . We may be called upon at times to criticize individuals and laws, but we shall do so in a spirit of kindness and justice. Believing that the 'freedom of the press,' will be guarded as sacredly by the Government, on this Reservation as elsewhere we launch

forth our little craft, appealing to the authorities that be, at home, at the seat of government, to the community, to give us moral support . . .[4]

Despite the reverend's moderating words, the Beaulieus' little craft foundered almost immediately on the rocky temperament of White Earth's Indian agent, Timothy Sheehan. At the time Sheehan's tenure as agent at White Earth was new, but already seemed doomed to hostility and misunderstanding. An Irish immigrant and military man, Sheehan had gained distinction as an Indian fighter, having led the defense of Fort Ridgely during the Dakota Uprising two decades earlier. After mustering out, Sheehan spent eleven years as the Sheriff of Minnesota's Freeborn County, a prairie outpost of white settlers on the border with Iowa.[5] A committed Democrat, he was swept into the office of Indian agent on the same wave that had removed Theo Beaulieu from his position as school superintendent. By all accounts stern and officious, Sheehan proved almost immediately unpopular among the residents of White Earth, especially among the mixed-bloods, who were accustomed to conducting their affairs with little interference.

For Sheehan, the publication of the *Progress* was the last straw in an ongoing conflict with the Beaulieu family that had been escalating for more than a year. The Beaulieus had taken advantage of every opportunity to challenge Sheehan's authority. Members of the Beaulieu family played cards and held dances at their homes—threatening to disrupt the moral education of the Natives at White Earth.[6] Gus Beaulieu, in the course of his business as U.S. Marshal, traveled on and off the reservation without securing signed permission to do so from Sheehan—an ostensible requirement for all Natives, regardless of occupation. Prior to taking on the editorship of the *Progress*, Theo Beaulieu publically accused Sheehan's son of committing acts of indecency against a girl at the Red Lake Indian School.[7] The Beaulieus' publication of the *Progress* gave Sheehan the excuse he needed to crack down on the family.

Claiming that the Beaulieus intended to use the *Progress* to promote sentiments that were, in his words, "revolutionary to the United States Government and a detriment to the welfare of these Indians,"[8] Sheehan seized the press.[9] In a formal writ, Sheehan declared, "Gustavus [sic] H. Beaulieu and Theodore B. H. Beaulieu, or any other person or persons, are hereby forbidden to print, publish or issue a newspaper of any kind upon White Earth Agency, until you first obtain from the Honorable Secretary of the Interior or honorable Commissioner of Indian Affairs, a license or permission for the publication of said paper," in accordance, he claimed, with the Indian Trade and Intercourse Act.[10] Seeing Gus Beaulieu as an intolerable threat to his authority, Sheehan ordered the marshal removed from the reservation and barred from ever returning. Gus, thinking himself shielded by both his office and position, ignored the order and continued to come and go as he pleased.

On the cold night of December 4, 1886, Sheehan's anger at Gus's impudence finally boiled over into a frothing rage. Gus had not only returned to White Earth Village, but was staying just across the street from Sheehan's offices at the home of his father, Clement. Going with an armed posse, Sheehan burst into the Beaulieu home, ordering Gus to leave at once. Gus, in turn, produced his pocket watch and a pistol, and told the agent he would give him two minutes to leave his father's house. Sheehan said Gus was not man enough to fire. Both Clement and Theo Beaulieu intervened, putting themselves between the two men to deescalate the situation. Sheehan ultimately left the house without achieving his aim, but Gus no longer felt safe on the reservation. The next day he went back to St. Paul, not to return to White Earth for six months. Soon after the altercation, Sheehan tried to have Clement and Theodore removed from the reservation, claiming that both men had threatened him with weapons—a fact disputed by one of the agency clerks who had accompanied Sheehan to the Beaulieu home.[11]

The legality of Sheehan's actions was far from clear. At the time, U.S. Indian policy put almost total control over reservation administration in the hands of Indian agents, like Sheehan, who often acted with little oversight or accountability. Natives, as noncitizen wards of the government, had only a questionable claim to rights under the U.S. Constitution—including the right to a free press. Furthermore, it was unclear if the mixed-blood Beaulieus could even be considered Indian under the law. Nonetheless, Gus Beaulieu sued Sheehan for the loss of his press, as well as for denying him and his cousin the right to publish under the First Amendment. The case went before Judge R. R. Nelson of the U.S. Circuit Court at St. Paul in November of 1886. Considered by many at the time to be a test case for Indians' right to sue agents of the U.S. government as individuals, the case was covered by both the local and national press.

On July 18, 1887, the front page of the *New York Times* announced the court's decision with the unequivocal headline: "A HALF BREED HAS RIGHTS." As the *Times* reported, "Judge Nelson decided that Beaulien [sic] could claim jurisdiction from the court upon the same terms as any other citizen of the United States, despite the fact of his being of Indian parentage."[12] The Judge forced Sheehan to return Beaulieu's property and compensate him two hundred and fifty dollars. After the embarrassment of the trial, a special hearing of the U.S. Senate's Committee on Indian Affairs was convened at White Earth seemingly with the sole purpose of chastising Sheehan.[13] The commissioners found his actions contributed to the further degradation of the public's already tattered perception of the Bureau of Indian Affairs—currently being wracked by accusations of graft, inefficiency, and corruption. At the committee's insistence, Gus Beaulieu was allowed to return to White Earth, where he would be free to publish the *Progress* without censorship or interference on the part of Sheehan or the U.S. government.

The legal victory the Beaulieus secured over Sheehan was one of the very first recognitions of Natives' right to free expression under the U.S. Constitution, and a crippling blow to Sheehan's reputation. In his overbearing response, Sheehan had revealed himself as exactly the kind of arbitrary and capricious despot the Beaulieus claimed him to be. Now that they had the courts on their side, the Beaulieus no longer had to mask their opinion of him with tact and subtlety. After resuming publication of the *Progress* in October of 1887, Theo Beaulieu took evident pleasure in flexing his newly recognized rights, especially in regards to his former adversary.

> In an interview with a Globe reporter lately, agent T.J. Sheehan amongst other things said: "So far as the Beaulieu's [sic] are concerned, they are accepting the situation, and will soon be good Indians if they are not already."
>
> Well now, really, that's generous! But we think if that was changed vice verse a little muchee in this wise, viz: "that so far as Timmothy [sic] Jerrimiah [sic] Sheehan was concerned he was accepting the situation and was getting to be somewhat of a good Irishman, especially since he received such seasonable hints-lessons at the hands of the Circuit Court and the Hon. U.S. Investigating Committee," there would be more truth and less poetry in the assertion.
>
> We have strong hopes (with a little judicial intervention occasionally) to civilize, and make a good democratic Irishman out of "Tim" yet, that is if he remains in White Earth long enough to undergo the necessary transmogrification.[14]

Far from the cautious and measured tone of the paper's initial issue, the remaining run of the *Progress* would be defined by articles such as this—bold, provocative, and deeply funny. At a time when most critique of U.S. Indian policy was couched in the careful language of honor and respectability, Beaulieu's defiant fusillades against "the Freaks In the Employ of the Indian Service"[15] offered a stark reflection of his people's harsh treatment at the hands of the government. To both his Euro-American and Native readers, such sentiments must have seemed revolutionary indeed. In the end, Sheehan's fear of the *Progress* proved to be a self-fulfilling prophecy.

The significance of the *Progress* to Anishinaabe writing goes far beyond the legal struggles of its editor and publisher. Over the two short years of the *Progress*'s print run, its editor would try to express an entirely new kind of Anishinaabe identity. Over the course of many editorials, features, and reports, Theo Beaulieu worked to change his readers' perceptions about who the Anishinaabeg were and who they could become, articulating a radical plan to remake White Earth into the center of a modern, self-governing nation-state. Printed alongside these editorials, Beaulieu would also publish the traditional stories of the Anishinaabeg, including many of their most culturally significant legends. More than a cultural curiosity, these stories would work to overcome Euro-American prejudices of Anishinaabe inferiority while simultaneously working to convey a sense a shared heritage capable of uniting a heterogeneous tribal community into a modern nation. For Beaulieu, such a task was of the utmost importance as a rapidly changing political climate threatened to put the very existence of White Earth into question.

Beaulieu's Vision

The confrontation between the Bealieus and Sheehan would prove to be a minor skirmish compared with the battle to come. The historical moment at which the *Progress* came into existence was one of massive upheaval in the relationship between the United States and indigenous people. With the open hostilities between the plains tribes and the United States nearing a détente, the imperial impulse of the United States began to be directed outward. Support for the agency system, which had been the primary form of colonial control in Indian country for decades, was beginning to crumble under sustained accusations of cronyism, fraud and abuse. Across the United States, Indian reservations were being threatened by illegal settlements of non-Natives emboldened by the racist promise of manifest destiny and the lure of free land. The Anishinaabeg of White Earth followed the news closely as their erstwhile rivals, the Lakota, found their expansive South Dakota reservation being chipped away by squatters and congressional fiat.[16] Concern mounted that they would be next.

White Earth, due to its large size and distinctive geographic mix of open, arable prairie and vast stands of pine, was exceptionally desirable to potential farmers and timber interests. Moreover, much of the 900-square-mile reservation was unsettled. White Earth was originally intended to be the only Anishinaabe reservation in the state, with enough space to resettle the various bands spread from Grand Portage to Mille Lacs. Organized and sustained political resistance to removal, however, had allowed many of these bands to stay on their traditional lands, with only a sporadic few agreeing to resettle on the reservation. The largest of these groups, the Mississippi Band, had agreed to relocate only after the murder of their charismatic ogimaa Baagone-giizhig (Hole-in-the-Day) who had threatened to go to war to avoid removal. Suspicion that Clement Beaulieu had orchestrated the assassination in order to consolidate his own power—or possibly to avoid a repeat of the disastrous Dakota uprising Hole-in-the-Day had helped to foment a few years prior—worked to fragment the Mississippi Band politically, limiting their ability to resist the encroachment of white settlers. But as long as the land remained in communal trust, access to White Earth was effectively cut off.

The passage of the Dawes General Allotment Act during the paper's hiatus had changed the situation dramatically. Ostensibly meant to usher Natives into modernity by breaking up communal land into private allotments, Dawes Act also contained a provision that would allow non-Indians to buy "surplus land" after the reservations were broken up. While such a scheme had been previously attempted in a piecemeal fashion on several reservations (including those of the Anishinaabeg of Michigan—see chapter 2), the passage of the Dawes Act signaled Congress's embrace of allotment as its official policy in regard to Indian Country as a whole. The effort to enact the new legislation in Minnesota was spearheaded by Knute Nelson, a U.S. congressperson representing northern Minnesota's fifth district, who formed a commission to treat with the various bands representing the Anishinaabeg of Minnesota. In preparation for his negotiations, Nelson reintroduced legislation that once again called for the consolidation of the Minnesota Anishinaabeg at White Earth, where each of the bands would be resettled and given allotments. Nelson's bill proposed that the land of the former reservations (as well as any of White Earth's "surplus") would then be sold to white settlers, and the proceeds used to form a trust that would fund the "civilization" of the Anishinaabeg.[17]

The editorial stance of the *Progress* to Nelson's plan was equivocal and strained. At various points, Beaulieu expressed his cautious optimism for the proposal to bring better education and more agricultural technology to White Earth, but remained somewhat skeptical of the system of land allotment proposed by the Dawes Act. The idea of allotment was not new to the Anishinaabeg of White Earth. Under the terms of the original 1867 treaty, each Indian who resided on White Earth was entitled to claim as much as 160 acres of land as private property. Yet taking up such allotments was never mandatory under the treaty, and few Anishinaabeg had actually bothered to do so. Moreover, the provisions of the 1867 treaty (unlike Nelson's bill) made such allotments inalienable, save to other members of the band. The scheme proposed by Nelson was very different. Not only did the Nelson bill make allotment mandatory, but it also capped land grants to a maximum of 80 acres and created a hierarchical system that gave more land to legally married couples (i.e., Christianized heterosexuals) and less to the "unmarried" and children. The Nelson bill was especially onerous to married women, who were barred from claiming allotments altogether—ostensibly as a means of protecting them from exploitation. In an essay written for the *Progress*, Gus Beaulieu puts Nelson's proposal into stark relief by reframing the revisions to existent allotment policy as forfeitures.

> Therefore the proposed treaty requires every person belonging to that band . . . to relinquish without remuneration a certain amount of land as follows: each person under 18 years of age, 120 acres; each person over 18 years of age, 80 acres; and every married woman not the head of a family, 160 acre[s] . . .

Imagining the effects of Nelson's proposal on a hypothetical Anishinaabe family of a husband, wife, and three children, Gus calculated the potential loss at "520 acres of land or equivalent to a cash value of $2,600 if worth the nominal price of $5.00 per acre."[18]

Another concern the Beaulieus expressed over Nelson's bill was the ambiguity with which it treated the taxation of Indian lands. As it currently stood, the Anishinaabeg were not required to pay local taxes, even if they had taken up allotments under the treaty of 1867. However, if the land was allotted under the provisions of the Nelson Act, it was unclear if it could be taxed and if so, by whom. The fear was that state and county authorities could use tax forfeiture as a means of taking Anishinaabeg land and property—as was currently taking place on the Turtle Mountain reservation in North Dakota, just a few hundred miles to the northwest of White Earth. Several years prior, the Anishinaabeg at Turtle Mountain had agreed to an allotment scheme similar to that proposed by Nelson for White Earth. Ever since, the mixed-bloods residing on the reservation had received conflicting information about their tax status. In an April 1889 issue of the *Progress*, Theo Beaulieu reprinted a letter he had received from two such mixed-bloods, Alexandre Jeanotte and Louis Lenoir, who claimed to be facing a constant barrage of legal challenges. They write:

> Last fall a special agent came to Turtle Mountain and informed the half-breeds that they were under no obligation to pay taxes. And the civil authorities promised the special agent would not again bother the half-breeds until such affairs were consistently arranged. Hardly had the agent gone when the county authorities again renewed their endeavors and by threats attempted to collect taxes and succeeded in seizing some twelve horses belonging to one Napoleon Renville . . .

The two men also claimed that their farming implements had been siezed by the local Indian agent as forfeiture. "These are but a few instances," Jeanette and Lenoir report, "of the injustices and indignities we have been subjected to since taking our land in severalty."[19]

The plight of the mixed-bloods at Turtle Mountain could not help, it seems, but remind Beaulieu of a similar conflict being played out among their kinsmen to the north. Alongside the letter from Jeanette and Lenoir, Beaulieu published an article reporting a new wave of unrest among the Métis being fomented by Gabriel Dumont, the former lieutenant of Louis Riel. Two years prior, a political crisis over land rights had erupted on the plains of the North-West Territory, leading to the second armed rebellion by the Métis in as many decades. Although Beaulieu was somewhat cautious to throw his support behind a man who had previously led his people into a failed rebellion, he nonetheless believed in the Métis's cause. "There is no doubt but the half-breeds of the Northwest have grievances," Beaulieu writes:

> Why Canada, in pursuance of the English policy of treating with the Indians, has suffered the grievance to exist, is past comprehension. But, setting aside all the fine distinctions which imperial and colonial policies have set up, the fact remains that the treatment of the Northwest half-breeds is one which is against sound moral sense. Louis Riel and Gabriel Dumont doubtless made a mistake in the extremes

to which they carried the rebellion. The rebellion in itself may be looked upon, both by governments and individual sympathizers, as a rash act.

"Yet, one cannot help but seeing that underneath," Beaulieu writes, "all through, outcomes were inconsiderate, and that the causes were just."[20]

The roots of the conflict lay in the 1860s, when Canada began an aggressive push to acquire and settle more of the continent's territory before the United States could. In doing so, the Canadian government ran roughshod over the claims of the region's indigenous inhabitants, including the Métis. An ethnic group largely comprised of the French-speaking descendants of *voyageurs* and Native women, the Métis had strong ties to both local indigenous groups and francophone Canada. The Métis had been settled on the Red River (near present-day Winnipeg) for a generation, supporting themselves through a mix of trade, subsistence hunting, and farming. When Canada sought to acquire the title to the land on which the Red River settlement was built, it chose to ignore the preexisting claims of its Métis occupants, and treated instead with the nominal owner of the land, the Hudson's Bay Company.

The Métis were initially supportive of incorporation into the Canadian state, but were concerned that their land claims would not be recognized as legitimate. In order to get ahead of any Canadian attempt to simply annex the territory, the Métis organized their own provisional government. Under the leadership of Louis Riel, a young Métis educated at the elite Collège de Montréal, the provisional government worked with both First Nations and Anglo-Canadians to organize the new territory of Manitoba, hoping that doing so would give them more bargaining power with Canada. In his negotiations with federal authorities, Riel made Manitoba's entry in the confederacy conditional on the promise of equal citizenship for Francophones and strong protections for indigenous land claims. Such demands, however, did not jibe with Ottawa's vision of a white, Anglophone Canada, and hostilities soon erupted. Under Riel's leadership, the Métis twice offered armed resistance to Canadian expansion, first at Manitoba's Red River settlement in 1869, and again sixteen years later in the North West Territories. The conflict ended at the Battle of Batoche on the Saskatchewan River, where Riel, Dumont, and a small band of Métis made their last stand against five thousand Canadian soldiers. Captured during the battle, Riel was tried for treason and publicly hanged in November of 1885.

For the Anishinaabeg at White Earth, the Métis political crisis was not some distant affair. Decades of trade with the Red River had created deep ties between the Minnesota Anishinaabeg and the Canadian

Métis, who shared the same languages, history, and ancestry. Indeed, many Métis had even sought refuge from Canadian persecution with the Anishinaabeg in the United States—including Riel, who fled to Minnesota after his defeat at the Red River settlement. Theo Beaulieu took a particular interest in Dumont's renewed efforts to organize the Métis, likely because he saw something of his own politics reflected in their demands for equal rights and secure land title. The Métis were driven to armed rebellion, Beaulieu suggests, not because they did not wish to incorporate into the body politic of Canada, but because the Canadian government had refused to treat with them as their intellectual and moral equals. Beaulieu argues that it was the Canadians' insistent belief in "race distinction" that led to their "always presenting a front exciting the animosity of the red man and his half-brother," and ultimately forcing the Métis's hand. "Similar conditions," Beaulieu ominously warns his readers, "have existed on this side of the boundary line, and exist today!"[21]

On December 17, 1887, Theo Beaulieu reprinted, in its entirety, an editorial from the *Duluth Herald* under the headline "Prejudicial Vagaries!" Spurred by the murder of a local white trader near the Red Lake Reservation, an anonymous editorialist had taken up his pen to criticize the "Boston Indianidiocy" for their support of continued government negotiations with the Anishinaabeg, acidly remarking, "to those who know these Indians, the habits, manners and customs, this gush is simply sickening." Against the sentimentalism of the urbane and effete friends of the Indian, the editorialist offers his own wisdom, borne (apparently) of his own experiences.

> Indians have a profound contempt for all whitemen. They fear them it is true, but an Injun is an Injun clear through, and when he gets a chance, he will never fail to do a white man up. The Indians upon the Red Lake reservation are a very bad lot. So are the Pillagers, and the Bois Forte bands, at Net Lake. . . . Red Lake is a reliable redskin "Alsatia." It was there that the notorious Riel took refuge after the first Red River rebellion. When an Indian commits an outrage upon the Rainy River settlers or lumbermen he crosses the river and snaps his fingers in derision at the law.

The editorial concludes, "There are thousands of acres of splendid timber lands and farming lands within the boundaries of this reservation that are now simply used as a resort for murderers, loafers, whiskey pirates, and fur thieves."[22]

In rebuttal, Theo Beaulieu accused the editorialist of sustaining his own "prejudicial sentimentality," arguing that his exaggerated depiction of Anishinaabeg as marauders and thieves was "befitting only the cheap vaporing of the writers of 'dime novels.'" For Beaulieu, the *Duluth Herald* editorial was but the latest barrage in an ongoing war of propaganda fought between the Anishinaabeg and a mass of Euro-American political and economic interests arrayed against them. The *Duluth Herald*'s portrayal of the Indians at Red Lake, Beaulieu wryly notes, served only to obscure a more nefarious intent.

> . . . when such gush is boiled down, one cannot fail to discern midst the dregs, the conclusive motor of this 'wishy-washy' hella-belloo of 'murderers, loafers, pirates, thieves, etc.[']*,* is simply used to guard the frantic efforts of the ghouls and vultures of outright robbery and fraud. . . . The thousands of acres of land, the millions of feet of pine timber, etc.,—there's the rub, that's the eyesore of the hordes of vampires who are endeavoring by fair or foul means to get the "lion's share" of this "Redskin Alsatia."[23]

At the time, the only experience with Natives most American voters would have had came through the sporadic accounts of the bloodshed and violence of the Indian Wars. It was not hard for those with an interest in reservation land to prey on Euro-Americans' worst fears of Indian savagery and barbarism in order to sway public opinion against further negotiations with the Anishinaabeg at Red Lake—despite the fact that they, like most Anishinaabeg, had a remarkably peaceful record of cohabitation with their white neighbors. In order to win over his Euro-American neighbors, Theo Beaulieu would have to challenge such perceptions, showing them to be based on little more than bigotry.

The most biting critique of Euro-American racism to be printed in the *Progress* came in a sweeping and eloquent essay published on June 23, 1888. Titled simply "Race Prejudice" and printed under the name "Wah-Boose" (Wabooz, or "Rabbit," likely a pseudonym for one or both Beaulieus), the essay is a forceful indictment of those who think of Indians as "incapable of advancement to that plane which, in this century, and in this country, is deemed a necessary requirement, by those who desire to occupy a recognized position in social life." Wah-Boose states that "in most instances, comparison has been made . . . from the conditions of the average red man and the educated white," despite the fact that "there are thousands upon thousands in the slums of American and European cities whose conditions, intellectually and morally, are far below those of the average Indian." Wah-Boose continues, contending: "intellect, being a common heritage, cannot be one thing in one race and another thing in another. It differs not in kind, however it may in degree, and we hold that opportunities being equal the white, red, and black man will not, on the average, exhibit difference in degree." Following the idea that intelligence is a product of historical circumstance rather than racial difference, Wah-Boose goes on, stating, "he who draws comparison between the Caucasion [sic] of *to-day* and the Indian of to-day, commits a serious blunder," accusing those who do so of a "lack of literary acumen, or with absolute deficiency."

Instead, Beaulieu urges his Euro-American readers to "turn to the pages of history and review the early condition of your own ancestry." Illustrating his point, Wah-Boose quotes an evocative passage taken from Hippolyte Taine's popular *History of English Literature*, in which the ancestors of modern Anglo-Saxons are described as barbarous savages.

> Huge white bodies, cold blooded, with fierce blue eyes, reddish flaxen hair, ravenous stomachs filled with meat and cheese, heated by strong drink; of a cold temperament, slow to love, homestayers, prone to brutal drunkenness, pirates at first; of all kinds of hunting, the man-hunt the most profitable and most noble. They dashed to sea in their two sailed barks, landed anywhere, killed everything, and having sacrificed in honor of their gods the tithe of their prisoners, and leaving behind them the red light of their burnings went further on to begin again.

Building off of Taine's description, Wah-Boose continues, "How many centuries he lived as a savage and a heathan [sic] we do not know, but we do know that his civilization and enlightenment are of comparative[ly] recent date, and more than that, were not indigenous, but importations, having dawn and zenith in what is now termed the 'effete East.' To the proud Caucasion [sic] we may say 'et tu brute.'" Driving the comparison even further, Wah-Boose concludes with a radical prophecy: "Macauley says that history has a tendency to repeat itself; in his mind's eye he saw the New Zeelander gazing from the bridge upon the ruins of London! Pursue the analogy, and might not the future red man gaze upon the ruins of New York and Brooklyn from their great suspension bridge?"[24]

Curiously, this fantastical image of the future may have been inspired by Taine's *History*. A combination of sociological theory and literary analysis, *The History of English Literature* (1864) was, as Wah-Boose describes it, "remarkably successful"—popular enough to reach places as far afield as White Earth. This was due, in part, to both the liveliness of Taine's prose as well as the grand scope of his history. Tracing English literature from the earliest work of the Anglo-Saxons through the Renaissance and into the present day of the Victorians, Taine produced a holistic account of British cultural development at the height of their global hegemony. Drawing on Darwin's recent efforts to describe the evolution of animal species, Taine's work attempted to determine a scientific approach to the study the evolution of artistic production among different national traditions. What unifies the works of Caedmon, Chaucer, Shakespeare, and Scott into a single tradition, Taine argues, is not simply a shared language or nation-state but the combined effects what he calls "race" and "milieu" over the course of a millennia-long history. One of Taine's primary conclusions was that the "natural bent" of the ancient Anglo-Saxon race remained a defining feature of English literature, despite the massive linguistic and cultural disruption brought about by the invasion of the Normans in 1066, in large part because it was better suited to the geography and environment of the British Isles.[25]

In reading Taine's description of the Anglo-Saxon response to the Norman Conquest, it isn't difficult to see how the *History* would have found an interested audience in a nineteenth-century Anishinaabe.

> Oppressed, enclosed in the unyielding meshes of Norman organization, [the Anglo-Saxons] were not destroyed although they were conquered, they were on their own soil, each with his friends and in his tithings; they formed a body; . . . They endure, protest, struggle, resist together and unanimously; strive today, to-morrow, daily, not to be slain or plundered, to restore their old laws, to obtain or extort guarantees; and they gradually acquire patience, judgment, all the faculties and inclinations by which liberties are maintained and states are founded. (314)

Grappling with foreign settlers who shared neither their language nor culture, stripped of the title to their ancestral lands, and offered little political enfranchisement, if any at all, Taine's Anglo-Saxons bore more than a passing resemblance to the White Earth Anishinaabeg. Moreover, Taine's work implicitly suggests that, given the right circumstances, indigenous peoples are not just capable of adapting to colonization, but of outlasting it. According to Taine, however, the Anglo-Saxons were slowly able to regain political supremacy in England by offering a united resistance to Norman policies at the local level.

> The towns laid waste by the Conquest are gradually re-peopled. They obtain or exact charters; the townsmen buy themselves out of the arbitrary taxes that were imposed on them; they get possession of the land on which their houses are built; they unite themselves under mayors and aldermen. Each town now, within the meshes of the great feudal net, is a power. . . . Thenceforth the conquered race, both in country and town, has risen to political life. If they are taxed, it is with their consent; they pay nothing they do not agree to. (89–90)

While never intended to do so, Taine's *History* may have offered the White Earth Anishinaabeg a template for reasserting their indigenous political power—one that would allow them to avoid the fate of their Métis kin. Indeed, Taine's description of Anglo-Saxon political resurgence bears a remarkable similarity to Beaulieus' vision for the future political organization of the Minnesota Anishinaabeg. In an editorial titled "What Do We Want?" Theo Beaulieu makes the argument that the future of the Anishinaabeg depended on their ability to organize themselves at the local level.

> Some of the things we are promised under the Dawes bill, is titles to our lands taken in severalty, and then we are to become citizens—sui generis—and be endowed with all the rights citizens of the United States have. As citizens we must have *rights in the courts*, but shall we be obliged to the courts outside the reservation? Rather let us have *a county by ourselves* comprising the whole of White Earth reservation, with a judge and juries of our own . . .[26]

In other editorials for the *Progress*, Beaulieu called on the other Anishinaabeg bands spread across the rest of the state to voluntarily leave their current reservations and consolidate at White Earth, where they would organize as a single tribal body. Doing so would not only give the Anishinaabeg a better position from which to negotiate the implementation of allotment at White Earth, but also increase the population density of the reservation—meaning there would be little or no "surplus land" for Euro-Americans to buy.

Beaulieu's vision depended, however, on the government instituting allotment policy in a manner that honored prior agreements with the Minnesota Anishinaabeg. Printed on the same page as his plan to organize White Earth as its own county, Beaulieu also ran a portion of the 1867 treaty that created White Earth, under the headline "It Still Lives." The reprinted section concerned language that protected allotments at White Earth from taxation and alienation in perpetuity: ". . . the land so held by *any* Indian shall be exempt from taxation and sale for debt, and shall not be alienated except with the approval of the Secretary of the Interior, and in no case to any person not a member of the Chippewa tribe." Beaulieu believed, perhaps naively, that the language of the Dawes Act (which ostensibly deferred to preexisting treaty provisions) would be interpreted in favor of the Anishinaabeg's right to hold land privately without risk of sale or forfeiture, arguing, "There is moral ground . . . for this inalienation and therefore [it is] the right thing for the Government to impose."[27] By gaining U.S. citizenship through allotment, the Anishinaabeg at White Earth would gain the capability to organize their own governmental institutions at the county level, while the wording of the original 1867 treaty meant that the Anishinaabeg of White Earth could keep the land base of the reservation intact. As it happened, Nelson's proposed legislation would do both. With a certain degree of reluctance, the Beaulieus threw their support behind Nelson's bill.

By embracing consolidation and allotment, the Beaulieus' plan would have entailed an enormous amount of risk, but offered the potential for something greater than their present conditions. Returning to the old ways was no longer an option. Beaulieu likely understood that a return to traditional modes of living was all but impossible in the context of advancing colonization—the technological, material, and legal advantages of modernity had already allowed Euro-Americans to deplete the resources on which traditional Anishinaabe life depended. The continued existence of the Anishinaabeg depended on their ability to embrace modernity—renegotiating their system of government, modes of production, and relationship with the land itself. For Beaulieu, such changes didn't represent assimilation, but the chance for his people to survive the tide of colonization as a unified Anishinaabe nation.

During a brief historical moment in the late 1880s, such a plan looked vaguely possible—but only by convincing the drafters of the allotment plan to preserve the territorial integrity of the reservation as a homeland for the Anishinaabeg, while extending them the rights of citizenship. Doing so, however, would not just entail a great deal of legal and political maneuvering, but cultural work as well. In order to make his vision of a modern, self-governing Anishinaabeg homeland a reality, Beaulieu had to convince two different audiences of two distinct ideas. First, the various bands and factions of Anishinaabeg at White Earth and the other Minnesota reservations would have to be convinced to see themselves as a single, cohesive group. Second, Euro-Americans had to be disabused of their beliefs in Indian backwardness and savagery (such as those espoused by the editor of the *Duluth Herald*) without fully endorsing the whole-scale assimilation of Native people into Euro-American culture. In order to achieve both goals at once, Beaulieu had to present the Anishinaabeg's cultural heritage as something unique and valuable, as well as show how that culture was capable of adapting to modernity without losing its essence. Fortunately, he found a means to do so using one of the few resources the Anishinaabeg had left: their stories.

When This Country Was One Great Reservation

Theo Beaulieu published the first installment of "The Ojibwas, Their Customs and Traditions" on December 17, 1887, alongside the *Duluth Herald* editorialist's unsympathetic assessment of Anishinaabe "habits, manners, and customs." The series appeared in the *Progress* sporadically over the winter of 1887–88, always on the front page, in two or three full columns. Beaulieu printed each installment with a distinctive header and a copyright notice—something he omitted from his other articles (fig 1.1). In an introduction to the "The Ojibwas," Beaulieu described the content of the articles as "Indian stories, traditional and legendary," a distinction that would have had little meaning for a Euro-American reader, but special significance for an Anishinaabe.[28] Beaulieu's description of two different kinds of stories reflects an understanding of the generic distinction the Anishinaabeg made between two different forms of storytelling, dibaajimowin and aadizookaan.

Dibaajimowin can refer to almost any form of narrative—anecdotal, historical, or even fictional—as long as it is not primarily concerned with the activities of the manidoog—the other-than-human spirits that populate the Anishinaabe world. Although the term refers to all forms of narrative, the term "dibaajimowin" carries an etymological connotation of instruction. The root of the noun, "dibaa," is common to the class of Anishinaabemowin verbs that deal with measurement (dibaabiigin), inspection (dibaabam), and judgment (dibaakonan), which reflects this class of story's informative function. The first of the two suffixes appended

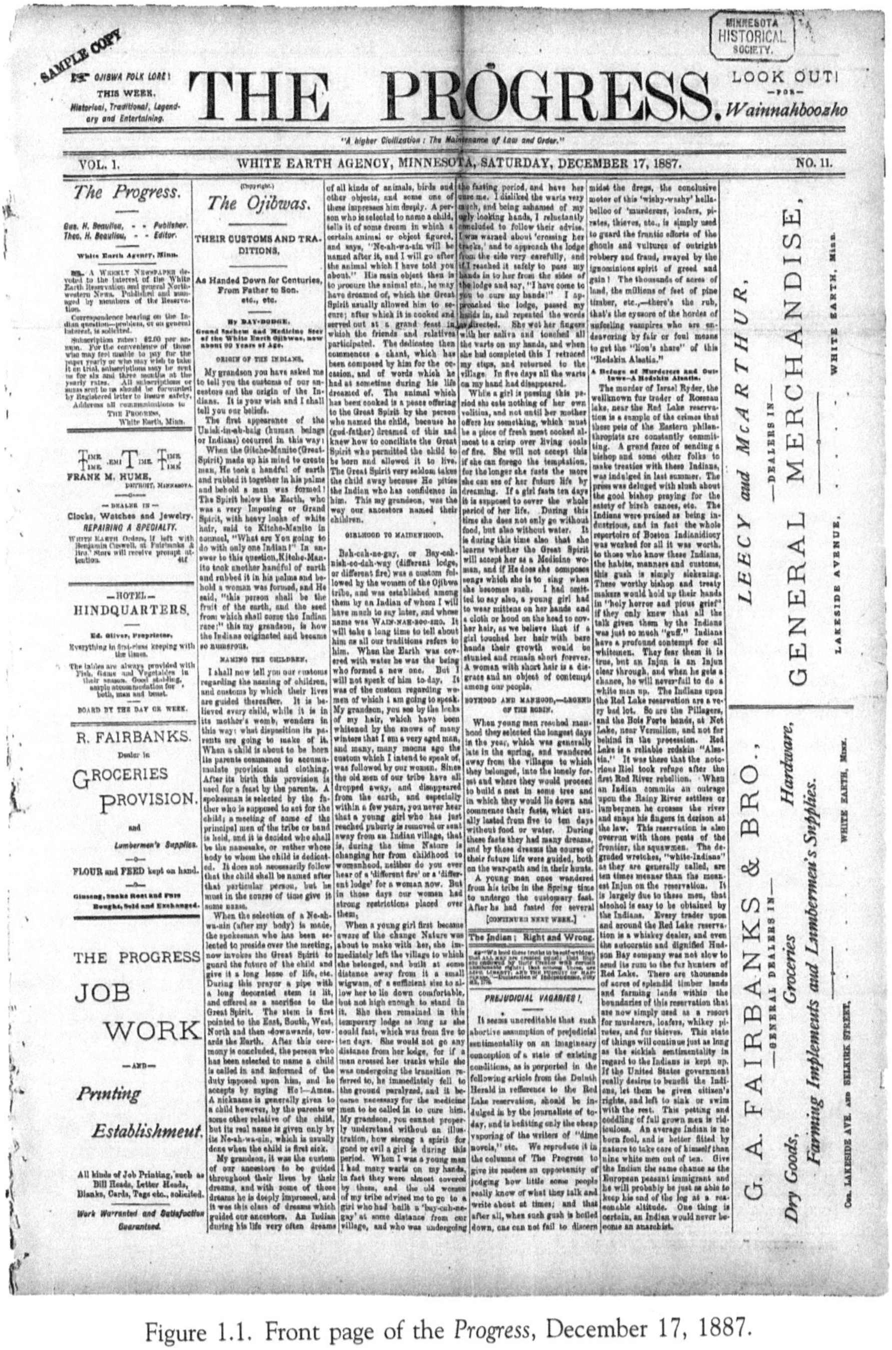

SAMPLE COPY

☞ OJIBWA FOLK LORE! THIS WEEK. Historical, Traditional, Legendary and Entertaining.

THE PROGRESS.

LOOK OUT! —FOR— Wainnahboozho

"A higher Civilization: The Maintenance of Law and Order."

VOL. 1. WHITE EARTH AGENCY, MINNESOTA, SATURDAY, DECEMBER 17, 1887. NO. 11.

The Progress.

Gus. H. Beaulieu, - - Publisher.
Theo. H. Beaulieu, - - Editor.

White Earth Agency, Minn.

☞ A WEEKLY NEWSPAPER devoted to the interest of the White Earth Reservation and general Northwestern News. Published and managed by members of the Reservation.

Correspondence bearing on the Indian question—problem, or on general interest, is solicited.

Subscription rates: $2.00 per annum. For the convenience of those who may feel unable to pay for the paper yearly or who may wish to take it on trial, subscriptions may be sent us for six and three months at the yearly rates. All subscriptions or sums sent to us should be forwarded by Registered letter to insure safety. Address all communications to THE PROGRESS, White Earth, Minn.

TIME TIME .EMI TIME TIME TIME
FRANK M. HUME,
DETROIT, MINNESOTA.
—DEALER IN—
Clocks, Watches and Jewelry.
REPAIRING A SPECIALTY.
WHITE EARTH Orders, if left with Benjamin Caswell, at Fairbanks & Bro.' Store will receive prompt attention. 4tf

—HOTEL—
HINDQUARTERS,
Ed. Oliver, Proprietor.
Everything in first-class keeping with the times.
The tables are always provided with Fish, Game and Vegetables in their season. Good stabling, ample accommodation for both, man and beast.
BOARD BY THE DAY OR WEEK.

R. FAIRBANKS.
Dealer in
GROCERIES
PROVISION.
and
Lumbermen's Supplies.
FLOUR and FEED kept on hand.
Ginseng, Snake Root and Furs Bought, Sold and Exchanged.

THE PROGRESS
JOB
WORK
—AND—
Printing
Establishment.
All kinds of Job Printing, such as Bill Heads, Letter Heads, Blanks, Cards, Tags etc., solicited.
Work Warranted and Satisfaction Guaranteed.

(Copyright.)

The Ojibwas.

THEIR CUSTOMS AND TRADITIONS,

As Handed Down for Centuries, From Father to Son. etc., etc.

By DAY-DODGE,
Grand Sachem and Medicine Seer of the White Earth Ojibwas, now about 90 Years of Age.

ORIGIN OF THE INDIANS.

My grandson you have asked me to tell you the customs of our ancestors and the origin of the Indians. It is your wish and I shall tell you our beliefs.

The first appearance of the Unish-in-ah-baig (human beings or Indians) occurred in this way:

When the Gitche-Manito (Great-Spirit) made up his mind to create man, He took a handful of earth and rubbed it together in his palms and behold a man was formed! The Spirit below the Earth, who was a very Imposing or Grand Spirit, with heavy looks of white hair, said to Kitche-Manito in counsel, "What are You going to do with only one Indian?" In answer to this question, Kitche-Manito took another handful of earth and rubbed it in his palms and behold a woman was formed, and He said, "this person shall be the fruit of the earth, and the seed from which shall come the Indian race;" this my grandson, is how the Indians originated and became so numerous.

NAMING THE CHILDREN.

I shall now tell you our customs regarding the naming of children, and customs by which their lives are guided thereafter. It is believed every child, while it is in its mother's womb, wonders in this way: what disposition its parents are going to make of it. When a child is about to be born its parents commence to accumulate provision and clothing. After its birth this provision is used for a feast by the parents. A spokesman is selected by the father who is supposed to act for the child; a meeting of some of the principal men of the tribe or band is held, and it is decided who shall be the namesake, or rather whose body to whom the child is dedicated. It does not necessarily follow that the child shall be named after that particular person, but he must in the course of time give it some name.

When the selection of a Ne-ah-wa-ain (after my body) is made, the spokesman who has been selected to preside over the meeting, now invokes the Great Spirit to guard the future of the child and give it a long lease of life, etc. During this prayer a pipe with a long decorated stem is lit, and offered as a sacrifice to the Great Spirit. The stem is first pointed to the East, South, West, North and then downwards, towards the Earth. After this ceremony is concluded, the person who has been selected to name a child is called in and informed of the duty imposed upon him, and he accepts by saying Ho!—Amen. A nickname is generally given to a child however, by the parents or some other relative of the child, but its real name is given only by its Ne-ah-wa-ain, which is usually done when the child is first sick.

My grandson, it was the custom of our ancestors to be guided throughout their lives by their dreams, and with some of those dreams he is deeply impressed, and it was this class of dreams which guided our ancestors. An Indian during his life very often dreams of all kinds of animals, birds and other objects, and some one of these impresses him deeply. A person who is selected to name a child, tells it of some dream in which a certain animal or object figured, and says, "Ne-ah-wa-ain will be named after it, and I will go after the animal which I have told you about." His main object then is to procure the animal etc., he may have dreamed of, which the Great Spirit usually allowed him to secure; after which it is cooked and served out at a grand feast in which the friends and relatives participated. The dedicatee then commences a chant, which has been composed by him for the occasion, and of words which he had at sometime during his life dreamed of. The animal which has been cooked is a peace offering to the Great Spirit by the person who named the child, because he (god-father) dreamed of this and knew how to conciliate the Great Spirit who permitted the child to be born and allowed it to live. The Great Spirit very seldom takes the child away because He pities the Indian who has confidence in him. This my grandson, was the way our ancestors named their children.

GIRLHOOD TO MAIDENHOOD.

Bah-cah-ne-gay, or Bay-cah-nish-co-dah-way (different lodge, or different fire) was a custom followed by the women of the Ojibwa tribe, and was established among them by an Indian of whom I will have much to say later, and whose name was WAIN-NAH-BOO-SHO. It will take a long time to tell about him as all our traditions refers to him. When the Earth was covered with water he was the being who formed a new one. But I will not speak of him to-day. It was of the custom regarding women of which I am going to speak. My grandson, you see by the looks of my hair, which have been whitened by the snows of many winters that I am a very aged man, and many, many moons ago the custom which I intend to speak of, was followed by our women. Since the old men of our tribe have all dropped away, and disappeared from the earth, and especially within a few years, you never hear that a young girl who has just reached puberty is removed or sent away from an Indian village, that is, during the time Nature is changing her from childhood to womanhood, neither do you ever hear of a 'different fire' or a 'different lodge' for a woman now. But in those days our women had strong restrictions placed over them.

When a young girl first became aware of the change Nature was about to make with her, she immediately left the village to which she belonged, and built at some distance away from it a small wigwam, of a sufficient size to allow her to lie down comfortable, but not high enough to stand in it. She then remained in this temporary lodge as long as she could fast, which was from five to ten days. She would not go any distance from her lodge, for if a man crossed her tracks while she was undergoing the transition referred to, he immediately fell to the ground paralyzed, and it became necessary for the medicine men to be called in to cure him. My grandson, you cannot properly understand without an illustration, how strong a spirit for good or evil a girl is during this period. When I was a young man I had many warts on my hands, in fact they were almost covered by them, and the old women of my tribe advised me to go to a girl who had built a 'bay-cah-ne-gay' at some distance from our village, and who was undergoing the fasting period, and have her cure me. I disliked the warts very much, and being ashamed of my ugly looking hands, I reluctantly concluded to follow their advise. I was warned about 'crossing her tracks,' and to approach the lodge from the side very carefully, and if I reached it safely to pass my hands in to her from the sides of the lodge and say, "I have come to you to cure my hands!" I approached the lodge, passed my hands in, and repeated the words as directed. She wet her fingers with her saliva and touched all the warts on my hands, and when she had completed this I retraced my steps, and returned to the village. In five days all the warts on my hand had disappeared.

While a girl is passing this period she eats nothing of her own volition, and not until her mother offers her something, which must be a piece of fresh meat cooked almost to a crisp over living coals of fire. She will not accept this if she can forego the temptation, for the longer she fasts the more she can see of her future life by dreaming. If a girl fasts ten days it is supposed to cover the whole period of her life. During this time she does not only go without food, but also without water. It is during this time also that she learns whether the Great Spirit will accept her as a Medicine woman, and if He does she composes songs which she is to sing when she becomes such. I had omitted to say also, a young girl had to wear mittens on her hands and a cloth or hood on the head to cover her hair, as we believe that if a girl touched her hair with bare hands their growth would be stunted and remain short forever. A woman with short hair is a disgrace and an object of contempt among our people.

BOYHOOD AND MANHOOD,—LEGEND OF THE ROBIN.

When young men reached manhood they selected the longest days in the year, which was generally late in the spring, and wandered away from the villages to which they belonged, into the lonely forest and where they would proceed to build a nest in some tree and in which they would lie down and commence their fasts, which usually lasted from five to ten days without food or water. During these fasts they had many dreams, and by those dreams the course of their future life were guided, both on the war-path and in their hunts.

A young man once wandered from his tribe in the Spring time to undergo the customary fast. After he had fasted for several

[CONTINUED NEXT WEEK.]

The Indian: Right and Wrong.

☞"We hold these truths to be self-evident, that ALL MEN are created equal; that they are endowed by their Creator with certain unalienable rights; that among these, are LIFE, LIBERTY, AND THE PURSUIT OF HAPPINESS."—Declaration of Independence, July 4th, 1776.

PREJUDICIAL VAGARIES!

It seems uncreditable that such abortive assumption of prejudicial sentimentality on an imaginary conception of a state of existing conditions, as is porported in the following article from the Duluth Herald in refference to the Red Lake reservation, should be indulged in by the journalists of to-day, and is befitting only the cheap vaporing of the writers of "dime novels," etc. We reproduce it in the columns of The Progress to give its readers an opportunity of judging how little some people really know of what they talk and write about at times; and that after all, when such gush is boiled down, one can not fail to discern midst the dregs, the conclusive motor of this 'wishy-washy' hellabelloo of 'murderers, loafers, pirates, thieves, etc., is simply used to guard the frantic efforts of the ghouls and vultures of outright robbery and fraud, swayed by the ignominious spirit of greed and gain! The thousands of acres of land, the millions of feet of pine timber, etc.,—there's the rub, that's the eyesore of the hordes of unfeeling vampires who are endeavoring by fair or foul means to get the "lion's share" of this "Redskin Alsatia."

A Refuge of Murderers and Outlaws—A Redskin Alsatia.

The murder of Israel Ryder, the wellknown fur trader of Rosseau lake, near the Red Lake reservation is a sample of the crimes that these pets of the Eastern philanthropists are constantly committing. A grand farce of sending a bishop and some other folks to make treaties with these Indians, was indulged in last summer. The press was deluged with slush about the good bishop praying for the safety of birch canoes, etc. The Indians were praised as being industrious, and in fact the whole repertoire of Boston Indianidiocy was worked for all it was worth. to those who know these Indians, the habits, manners and customs, this gush is simply sickening. These worthy bishop and treaty makers would hold up their hands in "holy horror and pious grief" if they only knew that all the talk given them by the Indians was just so much "guff." Indians have a profound contempt for all whitemen. They fear them it is true, but an Injun is an Injun clear through, and when he gets a chance, he will never-fail to do a white man up. The Indians upon the Red Lake reservation are a very bad lot. So are the Pillagers, and the Bois Forte bands, at Net Lake, near Vermilion, and not far behind in the procession. Red Lake is a reliable redskin "Alsatia." It was there that the notorious Riel took refuge after the first Red River rebellion. When an Indian commits an outrage upon the Rainy River settlers or lumbermen he crosses the river and snaps his fingers in derison at the law. This reservation is also overrun with those pests of the frontier, the squawmen. The degraded wretches, "white-Indians" as they are generally called, are ten times meaner than the meanest Injun on the reservation. It is largely due to these men, that alcohol is easy to be obtained by the Indians. Every trader upon and around the Red Lake reservation is a whiskey dealer, and even the autocratic and dignified Hudson Bay company was not slow to send its rum to the fur hunters of Red Lake. There are thousands of acres of splendid timber lands and farming lands within the boundaries of this reservation that are now simply used as a resort for murderers, loafers, whikey pirates, and fur thieves. This state of things will continue just as long as the sickish sentimentality in regard to the Indians is kept up. If the United States government really desires to benefit the Indians, let them be given citizen's rights, and left to sink or swim with the rest. This petting and coddling of full grown men is ridiculous. An average Indian is no born fool, and is better fitted by nature to take care of himself than nine white men out of ten. Give the Indian the same chance as the European peasant immigrant and he will probably be just as able to keep his end of the log at a reasonable altitude. One thing is certain, an Indian would never become an anarchist.

LEECY and McARTHUR,
—DEALERS IN—
GENERAL MERCHANDISE,
LAKESIDE AVENUE, WHITE EARTH, Minn.

G. A. FAIRBANKS & BRO.,
—GENERAL DEALERS IN—
Dry Goods, Groceries Hardware,
Farming Implements and Lumbermen's Supplies.
Cor. LAKESIDE AVE. and SELKIRK STREET, WHITE EARTH, Minn.

Figure 1.1. Front page of the *Progress*, December 17, 1887.

to the root, -mo, is a verb meaning "he or she speaks the language of," while the second, -win, is a nominalizer. In combination, dibaajimowin can be translated, roughly, as something that speaks the language of judgment, or, better yet, instruction. Indeed, dibaajimowinan are often explicitly educational, imparting a lesson about which the listener must come to some kind of understanding or judgment.[29] Because their themes are predominantly secular, the act of telling a dibaajimowinan, (unlike aadizookaanag) is not limited by seasonal or ritual injunction.

The first seven installments of "Customs and Traditions" were accounts of historical Anishinaabe practices translated from dibaajimowinan given by two "centenarians of the reservation," Day-Dodge and Say-coss-e-gay. Interspersed with illustrative anecdotes taken from Anishinaabe history, these first installments are concerned with specific traditions associated with birth, puberty, and marriage, along with accounts of the special powers of the Jiisakiiwininiwag and Mide practitioners. Conveyed largely in first person from the perspective of either Day-Dodge or Say-coss-e-gay, Beaulieu's translations are simple and direct—a stark contrast to the editor's usually florid prose—indicating, perhaps, Beaulieu's desire to hew closely to the exact words of the elders.

The remaining installments of "Customs and Traditions" were Beaulieu's translations of aadizookaanag, "legendary" stories concerning the manidoog. Beaulieu's translations of the aadizookaanag were almost entirely unlike the translations of the dibaajimowinan. Instead of a set of discrete anecdotes, these last four installments were comprised of a single narrative—that of the trickster and shapeshifter Wenabozho. Occupying a central role in Anishinaabe oral tradition as the interface between humans and the manidoog, Wenabozho was sometimes presented as a hero, sometimes as a teacher, but most often as a self-obsessed buffoon. Stories about Wenabozho's exploits (particularly those relating to his humiliating failures) were a popular way for the historical Anishinaabeg to pass the long winter months—the only time when such stories were allowed to be told.

Although it too is a form of narrative, the spiritual significance of the aadizookaanag makes them an entirely different class of story than the dibaajimowinan, with special rules governing when and how they can be told. Traditionally, stories about Wenabozho could only be told during the winter months, ostensibly as a means of protecting the teller. Tradition holds that Wenabozho, equal parts proud and spiteful, will take the form of an insect or plant in order to eavesdrop on unsuspecting storytellers who speak of him. If the story being told is unflattering or embarrassing (as many are), the teller risks incurring the trickster's capricious wrath. Since most plants and animals are dormant during the winter, however, Wenabozho has fewer opportunities to disguise himself, so the likelihood of offending mischievous manidoo diminishes.[30]

This sense of literally summoning or drawing the attention of the manidoog is reflected in the very word "aadizookaan." In Anishinaabemowin, nouns are divided into two genders: animate and inanimate. The identification of nouns as animate and inanimate generally matches a Euro-American conception of animacy, however objects or concepts that have power (a nebulous, but critical concept in traditional Anishinaabe philosophy) are often given animate nouns, even if they are inanimate in a scientific sense. Aadizookaan (unlike dibaajimowin) is an animate noun. Such stories are considered to be, at least in a grammatical sense, alive. This is because the word "aadizookaan" refers not only to a class of stories, but is also the characters that appear in them. Distinction is not made between the two. Indeed, "aadizookaan" is a nominalized form of verb "aadizooke," usually glossed as "he or she tells a sacred story," but literally translated as "he or she produces the spirits." To tell an aadizookaan is, in a sense, to summon (or, perhaps simply draw attention to) the presence of the manidoog.

Though never articulated in such explicit terms, Theo Beaulieu clearly intuited the connection of the trickster aadizookaanag to the contemporary political struggles of the Anishinaabeg. In his advertisement for the stories, Beaulieu explicitly connects federal Indian policy with the aadizookaanag. Writing that they would tell of the time "when this country was one great reservation and [there were] no Indian agents but Win-ne-boo-zho, no 'U.S.I.D.' but the vast prairies and forests whose portions swarmed with game of all kind,"[31] the Wenabozho stories were often printed adjacent to Beaulieu's editorials about the failure of the Bureau of Indian Affairs to protect the land and interests of Native peoples.[32] Such a juxtaposition implies that Beaulieu thought the stories were related, in some way, to the Anishinaabeg's ongoing struggle to preserve their land base.

On an immediate level, the aadizookaanag would have offered a sense of the Anishinaabeg as the possessors of a shared cultural heritage at a time when inter- and intraband factionalism threatened to tear the entire community apart. Whether they were mixed-blood or traditional, Mississippi or Pillager Band, the Wenabozho stories would have been instantly familiar to everyone at White Earth. Presented for public consumption, Beaulieu's stories presented a deeply heterogeneous community as culturally unified, if only in its shared fondness for trickster stories. As Elizabeth McNiel argues, such cultural work was critically important at that moment: "Beaulieu's late nineteenth-century Anishinaabe readers were dealing with their own harsh fates, their worst fears repeatedly having been realized. . . . [T]he trickster story would have served to remind them of their cultural resources."[33]

At the same time, those cultural resources were being radically reshaped. Beaulieu's stories, far from resembling the aadizookaanag most Anishinaabeg would have been familiar with, show a great deal of editorial intervention in terms of both form and narrative structure. Just how much formal intervention Beaulieu made to the aadizookaanag becomes clear when one compares a more traditional account of Wenabozho's birth to the one that appeared in the *Progress*. First, a literal translation follows of an oral performance of the aadizookaan relating Wenabozho's birth, given to an ethnographer in the mid-twentieth century:

> One day Naanabozho's mother went out with her mother to get wood. After a while, the mother missed her daughter. There was a very high wind. She looked for her daughter, but she could not find her. Later when the grandmother was chopping wood, she found a little blood on one of the pieces. She brought the piece of wood into the wigwam. She knew the blood was her daughter's. The next morning there was a little baby. That was the beginning of Naanabozho's life, and he lived with his grandmother.[34]

Theo Beaulieu writes,

> One day, feeling better than usual, [Wenabozho's mother] went outside and lay down beneath the shade of the balsam tree. . . . Suddenly there was a rustle, and a great gust of wind from the north swept by and taking the young girl in his embrace disappeared from the earth. The girl's mother, who had been enjoying a nap, was awakened by the commotion, looked about the wigwam for her daughter, and, being satisfied she was not within, hurried outside searching and calling for her beloved child, but the sweet tones of the nightingale were the only sounds that answered her call. At last, worn and with grief and weeping, she returned to her now lonely wigwam, and while passing the tree under which her daughter had so lately reclined, she overheard a wee little voice say: No-ko-mis (grandmother) do not cry. I am your grandchild,

and have been left here to comfort and take care of you. My name is Way-nah-bozho and I shall do many things for the comfort of you and my people . . .[35]

Although the plot of these stories is similar in superficial terms, when examined at the level of form, Beaulieu's reexpressions of this aadizookaan features massive differences in language, characterization, and temporality. To take just one example, in the oral version of the story above, the emotional state of the characters remains opaque. As James Ruppert points out, the lack of emotional description with regard to characters is a hallmark of oral narrative traditions, which "develop identity in an essentially apyschological manner."[36] Beaulieu, alternatively, rarely missed an opportunity to describe the "grief," "enjoyment," or "loneliness" of his characters, giving them a degree of interiority unknown in the Anishinaabe oral tradition.

As Alan Velie argues, the net effect of Beaulieu's formal interventions moved the aadizookaanag "perceptibly in the direction of . . . modern fiction."[37] However, Velie offers no analysis of Beaulieu's reasons for translating the aadizookaanag into a novelistic form, commenting only on how his translations depart from traditional (and, one suspects, for Velie more "authentic") ways of telling the tales. Elizabeth McNiel rejects Velie's subtle condemnation of the stories' inauthenticity, but argues that Beaulieu's intervention was meant to only present the Wenabozho stories in a way that "best suit[ed] the intended audience" of "educated Anishinaabe."[38] McNiel's assertion, seems to fall flat when considering even educated Anishinaabeg would have likely found Beaulieu's translations quite different from more familiar oral versions—not to mention the fact that Beaulieu's "intended audience" explicitly included non-Anishinaabeg. Moreover, Beaulieu's careful translation of the Day-Dodge and Say-coss-e-gay's dibaajimowinan shows his willingness to reproduce the Anishinaabe oral tradition with a limited degree of editorial intervention. The question therefore remains: why did Beaulieu change the form of the aadizookaanag to make it more novelistic?

We may discover a potential clue by returning, briefly, to Hippolyte Taine's discussion of Anglo-Saxon political resurgence, in his *History of English Literature*. Taine pays particularly close attention to the emergence of Robin Hood as an important figure in Anglo-Saxon storytelling traditions during the first centuries of Norman rule. Describing Robin Hood as a "national hero," Taine argues that passing along the famous outlaw's legend was a way of encoding and disseminating Anglo-Saxon politics.

They remembered how in the ballads Robin Hood ordered his folk to 'spare the yeoman, labourers, even knights, if they are good fellows,' but never to pardon abbots or bishops. The prelates grievously oppressed the people with their laws, tribunals, and tithers; and suddenly, amid the pleasant banter and the monotonous babble of the Norman versifiers, we hear resound the indignant voice of a Saxon, a man of the people and a victim. (100)

Outcompeting the folktales of Reynaud imported by the Normans, ballads commemorating Robin's fight for equality and recompense in the face of unjust laws, Taine argues, kept Anglo-Saxon political identity alive for centuries after the Norman invasion. The ballad form in which such stories were disseminated, however, was not indigenous to the British isles, where alliterative verse had been the dominant poetic form of the Anglo-Saxons for centuries. The rhymed ballad was a French import—a prestige mode of the Norman court, no less. By embracing the ballad, the Anglo-Saxons raised their traditions to a cultural plane equal to that of their colonizers. If the composers of the Robin Hood ballads meant to challenge Norman power, as Taine suggests, they did so in the language of the powerful.

Beaulieu, similarly, seems to have understood the need for his stories to speak to power. As Beaulieu explained in his introduction to the Wenabozho stories, the changes he makes to the aadizookaanag are primarily for the benefit of his Euro-American readers, so that they might conform (somewhat) to their predominating literary tastes and expectations.

> . . . there is much of the legend, whilst being of amusing interest to the Indian ear, loses its sweetest charms when given an English version; there are, other portions also that would be considered proper and modest when related in the native tongue, that would sound extemely [sic] harsh, course, vulger [sic] when translated into English. And to attempt to clothe the stories of the legend with acceptable fiction and romance we must needs sacrifice much of their originality, and when we do this their traditional charms and value, alike vanish. Thus our readers will see the difficulties naturally arising in the translation and publication of the legend. If we fail to interest and entertain you it will not be from a lack of effort on our part to do so.[39]

While appearing to be little more than a writer's false modesty, Beaulieu's stated desire to "interest and entertain" his non-Native readers is not without political stakes. Facing an audience innately skeptical of Anishinaabe culture, Beaulieu's translations would need to convey the value of Anishinaabe beliefs unfamiliar to Euro-American readers in a way they would find "acceptable." As Beaulieu acknowledges, hewing to a more "authentic" version of the aadizookaanag would be disadvantageous in that regard—as any perceived "vulgarity" in the stories would only serve to confirm suspicions of Anishinaabe inferiority. At the same time, Beaulieu refuses to concede that more traditional versions of the aadizookaanag are in any way deficient, suggesting that they have intrinsic "charms and value" that Euro-Americans are simply ill-equipped to recognize. The answer, it would seem, was to take the narrative content of aadizookaanag and present it in a form of "fiction and romance" less alien to Euro-American readers. As it happened, the novel form would not only have been instantly familiar to white readers, but also has formal qualities that make it particularly well suited to reflect Beaulieu's political goals.

One of the more subtle changes Beaulieu makes to the aadizookaanag has to do with the way in which temporality is conceived of and represented in the stories. While it was common practice in the oral tradition to string several Wenabozho stories together into a single story cycle, the stories themselves were largely told paratactically, linked by extremely minimal coordination between individual stories. Beaulieu makes of Wenabozho's story a continuous narrative of his maturation and development, from his conception and birth to his ultimate confrontation with his father, the north wind. Throughout his reexpression of the aadizookaanag, Beaulieu is at pains to thematically link each story, making each one about Wenabozho's quest to find and kill the being responsible for the death of his mother. As Alan Velie argues, by taking stories that had originally been told as nontemporally specific, semiautonomous stories, and presenting them in a single narrative, Beaulieu's translations transform the "nondurational adventure time of the tribal tale into something closer to the chronotope of the modern novel."[40]

In order to understand the ways in which the novel's figuration of temporality would have helped Beaulieu's translations to reflect his politics, we must first understand the aadizookaanag's unique configuration of temporality. Velie mistakenly claims that the chronotope of the aadizookaan is that of the epic, asserting that they "take place in a time before ours . . . long past and inaccessible."[41] However, Velie's statement ignores the ways in which the aadizookaanag encodes its own unique chronotopic conventions. As the Anishinaabe author David Treuer explains, the aadizookaanag "exist outside of time," explaining: "when the story takes place is of absolutely no importance. It could have happened yesterday or three hundred years ago."[42] An aadizookaan is never definitively set in a particular historical moment (save those that describe the creation of the planet, or the formation of geographical features, which must have occurred at some point prior to the present). The chronotopic alignment of the aadizookaan is not with the past, as much as it is entirely outside of time, or—perhaps more accurately—with a time parallel to our own (what Gerald Vizenor calls "mythic time"[43]) in which events always seem to be occurring always just beyond our sight.

Indeed, aadizookaanag sometimes move fluidly between past and present tense, or even blur a sense of definitive time altogether by employing the dubitative mood, as can be seen in this short aadizookaanag told by the late White Earth elder Joe Auginaush.

[1] Ahaaw akawe bangii niwii-tibaajimaa a'aw isa Wenabozho. Inashke Wenabozho iidog anooj gii-izhichige. Anooj gegoo ogii-kashkitoon. Akina gegoo ogii-kikendaan iidog.

[2] Inashke dash aabiding iidog, inamadabid imaa—imaa sa endaad iidog. Mii sa gaa-chi-inendang, "Haa ganabaj apane inga-babaamose." Mii iidog maajaad babaamosed. Maagizhaa imaa aandi eyaad iidog wa haa bakitejii'igewag. Miish iidog omaa ezhi-biindiged imaa bakitejii'igwaad. Miish imaa bezhig iidog gaa-izhi-nandomigod, "Hey Wenabozh! Giwii-pakitejii'ige na?" "Haaw isa geget." Wa, mii sa iidog odaminod bakitejii'iged.

[3] Maagizhaa mii sa iidog wiin nitam iwidi obakite'aan i'iw bikwaakwad. Wa, hay' niibawid aazhaa gaa-izhi-bakite'ang. Waa pane iidog i'iw bikwaakwad iwidi chi-waasa iwidi ogii-ani-ga-naandaan. Miish iidog imaa gii-ipitood imaa ji-gishiibatood iidog Anishinaabeg, "Haa Wenabozh! *Home run. Home run,*" inaa iidog. Haa mii sa go Wenabozho iidog, mii sa go apane gii-kiiwebatood. Haa mii sa i'iw.

[1] *All right, first of all I want to tell a little story about that Wenabozho. You see Wenabozho must have been up to something. He must have known everything too.*

[2] *One time he was sitting there—there where he lived. He was really thinking hard, "Maybe I'll walk around." Then he left*

walking around. Maybe there where he must have been they were playing baseball. Then he went in there where they were playing ball. Then one person must have invited him [to play], "Hey Wenabozho! Do you want to play baseball?" "You bet." So he must have played, playing baseball.

[3] So maybe during his turn he hits that ball way over there. He just stands there after he already hit it. But he smacked that ball way far over there. Then as he was running there, running fast, the Indians made a ruckus. "Haa Wenabozho! Home run. Home run," he must have been told. So Wenabozho ran home. That's it.[44]

By employing the dubitative constructions using the particle "iidog" (which appends a "must have" or "maybe" to the sentence) Auginaush's story challenges a simple present/past binary with regard to its temporal setting. The events in the story did not *definitively* happen in an absolute past, but they *must have* happened, or *maybe* happened—either way the events in the story have a contingent relationship to the present, in the sense that the storyteller is conjecturing on what happened from his present position. Such a complex and unstable temporal relationship between teller and tale can hardly be said to create epic distance between the two, but rather freely mixes past and present (or perhaps rejects both) in a way that is decidedly unlike the chronotope of either the epic or the novel.

Although this use of the dubitative is by no means the way all aadizookaanag are told—most are in simple past tense—the presence of this form at all challenges the assertion that the aadizookaan is simply "like" the epic. Moreover, as the modern subject of Auginaush's story attests, the manidoog of the aadizookaanag are considered to still be present and alive on the earth, in direct contravention to Mikhail Bakhtin's observation that the epic world is "beyond the sphere of possible contact with the developing, incomplete and therefore re-thinking and re-evaluating present."[45] In the narrative world of the aadizookaan, one never knows if Wenabozho might show up to pinch-hit in a baseball game, a claim one could hardly make about Achilles.

Making a distinction between the chronotopic conventions of the epic and the aadizookaan may seem like a minor point, but is vital to understanding why Beaulieu's reexpression of the aadizookaanag into the form of the novel, rather than the epic, carries a special ideological importance. Although the epic is a genre that is usually considered one of the most explicitly nationalist genres, it offers a special challenge to a nascent indigenous nationalist such as Beaulieu. As Bakhtin argues, the primary chronotopic effect of the epic is the creation of an "absolute epic distance," which "separates the epic world from contemporary reality."[46] In Europe, the creation and valorization of epics occurred after the nation achieved a state of coherence, so that the epic distance created between past and present could be "filled with national tradition."[47] The problem of creating an Anishinaabe epic was that, to a Euro-American reader, there was no historical distance between the Anishinaabeg and the subjects of their stories, both were stuck in a hopelessly premodern past.

Indeed, most Americans were already familiar with an epic translation of the aadizookaanag. As Beaulieu explained, "It is not only the Ojibwas who are familiar with the legend of Way-nah-bozho, but almost every school child in the United States has heard of it through Longfellow's poem of *Hiawatha*, and it was from this legend that the now famous poem originated."[48] Set "In the days that are forgotten / In the unremembered ages,"[49] Longfellow's poetic retelling of the aadizookaanag is rendered explicitly in the epic mode. As has been argued by multiple critics (see introduction), the chronotopic conventions of Longfellow's epics create an impermeable barrier between an Indian past and an American present, barring any claims to contemporaneous indigenous political existence.[50] Take, for example, the section of the poem titled "The White Man's Foot," in which Hiawatha relates two distinct visions of the future—the first, a triumphal image of Euro-American modernity.

> I beheld the westward marches
> Of the unknown, crowded nations.
> All the land was full of people,
> Restless, struggling, toiling, striving,
> Speaking many tongues, yet feeling
> But one heart-beat in their bosoms.[51]

The second vision is a warning of the bleak future facing those Indians who refuse to submit themselves to the authority of the white colonizers.

> I beheld our nation scattered,
> All forgetful of my counsels,
> Weakened, warring with each other:
> Saw the remnants of our people
> Sweeping westward, wild and woful,
> Like the cloud-rack of a tempest,
> Like the withered leaves of Autumn![52]

Having presented these two possible futures, Hiawatha abdicates his authority as leader of his people, but not before exhorting his people to submit themselves to the white missionaries, who bring European modernity with them from "the land of light and morning." Hiawatha tells his people to "Listen to their words of wisdom / Listen to the truth they tell you, / For the Master of Life has sent them."[53] Hiawatha leaves his people with the choice of either accepting the missionary's gifts (the "toiling" and "striving" of an Anglo-Protestant economy) and incorporating themselves into the coming nation, or resigning themselves to the endless westward march of exile—figured here not as a forced military relocation, but as the inevitable and natural flight of "wild and woful" Indians away from labor and assimilation.

In this epic rendition of the aadizookaanag, Hiawatha's departure literally enacts the moment at which Indian sovereignty passes into irrecoverable history. The poem imagines a past pan-Indian nation held together by Hiawatha, which then collapses in the absence of his sovereign authority, so that actually-existing tribal nations can only represent a damaged, sectarian remnant. The true past of the Indian nation, Longfellow suggests, was one that looked remarkably similar to the one that happened to be expanding its colonial reach at the moment of the poem's composition. Integrated, incorporative, and geographically expansive, the United States is presented as the logical inheritor of Hiawatha's legacy in its ability to forge one nation out of many. The coming United States, still on the prophetic horizon in the poem's epic past, represents not the dissolution of indigenous sovereignty, but the glorious return of a lost continental nation. As the poem makes clear, the tradition that fills the space between the epic past of *Hiawatha* and the present is that of America, not indigenous peoples.

Beaulieu seems to be aware of the politically problematic aspects of *Hiawatha*, as well as the need for his translations to compete with Longfellow's poem in terms of both aesthetics and legitimacy. In his introduction to the Wenabozho stories, Beaulieu explains that his translations are an attempt to present "the 'unadulterated' substance of which the legend was originally composed . . . ere its originality was corrupted by the brilliant fiction and romance of a recent civilization."[54] Offering a subtle critique of *Hiawatha* as a "corruption" of the aadizookaanag, Beaulieu presents a smart, if not entirely ingenuous, means of undercutting his readers' investment in Longfellow's beloved poem. Like his compatriot George Kabaosa, Beaulieu seems to have understood that the value Euro-Americans assigned to *Hiawatha* had more to do with its promise of an authentic encounter with the Indian than the poem's aesthetic qualities (its awkward trochaic meter having been the subject of mockery since its first publication). In suggesting that Longfellow's "brilliant fiction and romance" had somehow obscured the true meaning of the aadizookaanag, Beaulieu pitted the poem's most revered quality, its authenticity, against its least: the ponderous repetition of its meter. As an Indian, Beaulieu could claim that his translations better reflected the "unadulterated substance" on which *Hiawatha* was based, while still taking as many liberties (if not more) with the form of the aadizookaanag as Longfellow had.

At the same time, the formal changes Beaulieu makes to the aadizookaanag allows the stories to articulate a sense of simultaneity diametrically opposed to that of the temporal configuration of the epic. To see this temporal simultaneity at work, take Beaulieu's rendition of Wenabozho's encounter with a monstrous whale. Thinking the monster responsible for the death of his mother, Wenabozho intentionally allows himself to be swallowed whole, hoping to destroy the whale from the inside. There he discovers one of the whale's prior victims, a weasel who had been earlier devoured. Together, the two set out to find the whale's exposed heart, and attack it. At this point in the story, Beaulieu uses complex hypotactic sentence structures in conjunction with shifts in narrative perspective to create a sense of simultaneous action that heightens the sense of suspense.

> After the whale had reached the shore he again proceeded to swallow water for the purpose of drowning Wainaboozhoo and then trowing [sic] him up, but at this time the weasel was busy biting and lacerating their victim's heartstrings, who soon ceased all efforts and in a little while, after a few convulsive flutters, lay still and dead.
>
> On the fourth day, after Wainahboozhoos [sic] departure, Nokomis arose early in the morning . . . she started in the direction of the shore. Here she was amazed to see a monster fish apparently dead and floating near the beach, on approaching nearer she was surprised and terrified to hear the sound of voices issueing [sic], as it were, from within the big fish. However, her fears were dispelled when she heard a well-known voice calling and instructing her to come and cut Me-she-nah-may-qway [the whale] open.[55]

Compare this with the extreme parataxis of a literal translation of an aadizookaan version of the same story.

The fish began to feel sick to his stomach. He thought, "I guess I'll go to the shore and throw up Wenebojo." But Wenabojo knew what he was trying to do. He put his boat crosswise in the fish's throat, so the fish couldn't throw him up. Mišinamégwe [the whale] tried another way. He wanted to move his bowels to get rid of Wenebojo. Wenebojo could see something at the other end of the wigwam [a visual metaphor for the whale's stomach] contracting and expanding. He knew that it was the fish's rectum, but he tied it up so tight that the fish couldn't do anything. Poor Mišinamégwe died from all this. Wenebojo killed him. Wenebojo, the squirrel, and the owl were beginning to get sick inside the fish. . . . Wenebojo said, "Let this fish land near my grandmother's shore." Sure enough, Mišinamégwe landed on Wenebojo's grandmother's shore. His grandmother ran to the shore. Wenebojo called to her to hurry up quick with the knife, because the insides of the fish were so hot that it was scalding them. She came with a knife and opened the fish, and they all got out.[56]

The difference with which these two passages represent temporality is immediately apparent. The oral version of this aadizookaanag presents the characters' actions in terms of discrete events, where the Beaulieu's presents them as part of an interconnected and continuous flow. In the first passage, the whale does not simply swallow water, but *proceeds* to swallow water, allowing the action to continue in the mind of the reader even as the narrative vantage point moves back inside the whale, where the weasel is attacking the whale's heart *at the same time*. One can see how the very language of Beaulieu's version of the story works to construct a specific kind of temporality. The sentence describing the death of the whale uses three different references to time—the simple adverb *soon*, adverbial use of the prepositional phrase "in a little while," and the subordinate clause "after a few convulsive flutters"—to draw out the action, both in the imagination of the reader as well as in the real time it takes to scan the sentence. The second passage, on the other hand, does not describe the whale's death at all, save as a result of Wenabozho's actions.

The most important thing in the oral version of the aadizookaanag is conveying a sense of Wenabozho's power. We don't know whether the whale died immediately after having its anus tied shut, or several hours later, because such information is simply not as important to the logic of the story. What is important is that the whale dies because of

Wenabozho's actions. Similarly, in describing Wenabozho's miraculous return to his grandmother's house, the aadizookaanag version again neglects the passage of time and privileges Wenabozho's power. Wenabozho only has to will the whale's carcass to land near Nokomis for it to be so. Beaulieu's novelistic translations, on the other hand, make Wenabozho's power subordinate to time. Not only do the translations make the whale's appearance in front of Nokomis a product of coincidence (a concept determined by temporal simultaneity), but goes out of its way to explain the trip took four days—inviting us to imagine the disgusting details such a monotonous voyage would entail.

The connection between the modern nation and the representation of temporal simultaneity is a familiar aspect of the study of nineteenth-century literary nationalism and applies equally well here. As Benedict Anderson famously argues, both the novel and the newspaper worked to solidify the emergent form of the nation in the nineteenth century by changing the popular conception of time. Both forms create a sense of simultaneity that allows far-flung persons to relate to one another across vast distances because they can imagine each other both moving through the same "homogenous, empty time" that defines modernity—the time of clocks and calendars.[57] Anderson argues that the novel does so by showing how many characters, situated in the same society, experience the same moment of time differently. Newspapers do the same on a larger scale, inviting readers to imagine a connection with their far-flung compatriots by their shared experience of time.

What we have then, in the pages of the *Progress*, is the temporal effect of both novel and the newspaper amplifying one another to create a sense of simultaneity, the "homogenous empty time" of modernity in which the nation comes to be. The stories themselves have become more modern—less alien to a Euro-American reader and more foreign to an Anishinaabe familiar with them in an oral form. Moreover, unlike Longfellow's poem, Beaulieu's translations exist in an explicit relation to secular political time, setting his version of the stories in a time "when this country was occupied and owned exclusively by Indians."[58] Beaulieu defines the setting of his story through indigenous political claims, as it exists within the history of "this country" (the nation) and not prior to it. The thing that separates the temporal setting of his stories and the reader's present is not the mythic distance of epic, but the political ramifications of Euro-American colonization.

In pursuing this strategy of literary reinvention, Beaulieu was hardly alone. Scott Richard Lyons argues that the advent of print culture in

Indian Country was an essential precursor to Native nationhood, arguing that in the nineteenth century the "scene of writing was where indigenous ethnic groups began transforming themselves into actual nations."[59] Lyons, following Ernest Gellner, argues that nineteenth-century Indian writers, such as Beaulieu, when faced with the threat of cultural dissolution reacted "by transforming 'low' cultures into 'high' national ones."[60] Embracing the temporal conventions of the novel not only allowed Beaulieu to transform the aadizookaanag into a form Euro-Americans would associate with "high" culture, but also imbue them with a sense of modernity as expressed through their very language. In short, Beaulieu's novelistic translations convey a sense of Anishinaabe cultural identity capable of existing in modernity.

At the same time, the translations deviate from the chronotopic conventions of the novel in one critically important way. While Beaulieu's Wenabozho stories definitively take place in novelistic time, they take place in the sacred (and ambiguous) *space* of the aadizookaanag. The island of giizhis manidoo, the land without sun, the realm of the North wind manidoo, the inside of the whale's stomach, none of these spaces comfortably fit into the novel's conventions concerning setting, which tends more toward the recognizable, familiar, and secular.[61] However, they are essential to the aadizookaanag's cultural significance, all representing important spaces in the geography of the Anishinaabe cosmos (except for, perhaps, the whale's stomach). Had Beaulieu changed these settings to fit the more mimetic conventions of the novel, their cultural meaning would have been lost.[62] Instead, the translated stories retain the sense that spiritual power is ineffably tied to geography.

Embracing a modern sense of time while retaining a more traditional sense of space, Beaulieu's stories offer a profound response to the looming threat of allotment. The framers of allotment policy thought that they could change the Anishinaabeg's experience of time by changing their relationship to the land, assuming that owning land as private property would usher the Anishinaabeg into modernity. Beaulieu's stories offer a different formulation, showing the potential for traditional conceptions of the land to exist, unchanged, in modern time. Overall, Beaulieu's stories create a sense of a modern Anishinaabe presence over a landscape irrevocably tied to their cultural identity.

The idea that the natural world is more than a mere resource is made clear in one particularly evocative moment in the translated aadizookaanag, in which Wenabozho asks the trees to share with him their gifts in order to create his most prized possession.

> [Wenabozho] be-took himself to the woods where he held a council with the trees of the forest . . . it finally ended in the birch trees consenting to give some of their we-gwas (bark), which was part of their snow-white garments and lined with rich purple and gold; the majestic cedar tendered him a few fragrant splinters for the keel and ribs of his craft; the stately tamarac donated some of its wa-taub (strong durable rootlets) to lace it together, and the princely pine tree assured him that it would shed a few tears of pe-giew (gum) to cement the whole together, and make it water-proof.
>
> In time the keel was laid, the light, feathery ribs were put in place and the white and gold colored robes of the queen of the forest was gracefully set about the corset and the wa-taub was made to gently clasp and lace them together while the tears of the pine—pe-giew—smoothed the creases. Thus, the first we-gwas-o-gee-mon, birch bark canoe, was finished; and a beauty it was too, the like of which none but Wainnahboozho and his descendants have ever succeeded to build to perfection.[63]

I quote here at length to show the great care taken in representing the reciprocal relationship between the natural world and the Anishinaabeg. In this story the trees take on the form of agentive manidoog, whose connection with Wenabozho are the ties of both affiliation and affection. "Stately," "majestic," and "princely," the trees are presented as possessing not only nobility, but also power, in accordance with traditional Anishinaabe conceptions of the term (see chapter 4). Not a mere resource to be taken, the trees choose to bestow their gifts onto Wenabozho, but only after proper consideration. The resulting canoe is therefore more than a commodity, but the embodiment of a set of relationships, on which Wenabozho and the Anishinaabeg depend.

These are the same trees, it is worth remembering, that the *Duluth Herald* editorialist has in mind when referring to the "thousands of acres of splendid timber" waiting on Anishinaabe reservations to be claimed by Euro-American interests. In maintaining their distinct representation of space, Beaulieu's stories offer an affective counter to such sentiments. The novelistic form of the stories goads readers to imagine configurations of humanities' ties to the land outside that of capitalist production. By presenting elements of the natural world as characters at the intimate, human scale of the novel allows Beaulieu's stories to make more visible the Anishinaabeg's nuanced conceptions of interdependency that Euro-Americans often mistook for simple-minded superstition.

Ultimately, by reinterpreting the aadizookaanag into a more novelistic form, Beaulieu could show the legitmacy of Anishinaabeg cultural practices while simultaneously undermining Euro-Americans' prejudices. Beaulieu actively reconstitutes the tribal past in the national present by interpreting the oral tradition *in* a written literary form, as opposed to translating the oral tradition *as* a written literary form. By telling his versions of the aadizookaanag in novelistic time but in the space of the aadizookaan, Beaulieu made two different arguments to his two very different audiences. In order to address both, however, Beaulieu had to transform the aadizookaanag at the most basic levels of form and structure. By presenting the traditions and stories of the Anishinaabeg in a narrative form recognizable (but still residually foreign) to both an Anishinaabe and Euro-American readership, Beaulieu's texts operate in a mediative discourse that would upset the cultural expectations of both groups.[64] In effect, the ideological power of Beaulieu's stories comes not from their ability to perfectly convey the aadizookaanag in a novelistic form, but in how they strategically *fail* at this translation.[65]

It is precisely this aspect of the *Progress* that makes it an important document for the those interested in the history of indigenous literatures. The status of the novel, as a mode of expression for Native people, has been particularly contentious among scholars of Native American literature. Elvira Pulitano, following the late Louis Owens, argues that the novel is "a genre rising out of social conditions antithetical to whatever we might consider 'traditional' Native American oral cultures."[66] Jace Weaver, quoting his own words, argues against this position, stating,

> While there are those who would like to argue that works written in English (for example) in a form like the novel for publication are something apart from Native American literature, for me the answer is manifest: "there is something still 'Indian' about it regardless of its form or the language it speaks."[67]

Both of these positions, to my mind, risk ignoring a potentially rich approach to the study of indigenous literatures. The novel is a nonindigenous technology for the Anishinaabeg, and like all such technologies, has a particular history of adoption and accommodation. Being a specific kind of expressive technology, the novel simply does things that other genres, like the aadizookaanag, do not. This isn't to say that the novel is a less "authentic" mode of address for the Anishinaabeg (no more than using an iron kettle to parch manoomin is less authentic than using a birchbark makak), but neither would I want to argue that its adoption didn't require a certain amount of change on the part of those who embraced it. By either rejecting the novel as a non-Native imposition or embracing it unproblematically as a form of indigenous self-expression, critics risk effacing the history of the novel's adaptation in Indian Country altogether, a history which—as the example of the *Progress* shows—can offer us a fascinating insights into the evolving structures of feeling that gave rise to modern Native nationhood.

A Revolutionary Legacy

Unfortunately, Theo Beaulieu's efforts to remake White Earth into a self-governing Anishinaabe homeland proved unsuccessful. Over the period of the *Progress*'s print run, public pressure to allot Anishinaabe land only intensified. Theo Beaulieu, increasingly involved with the legal battle over the implementation of the Nelson Act at White Earth, had less and less time to devote to the *Progress*. By the spring of 1889, Beaulieu's coverage of local issues in the *Progress* all but disappeared—replaced by curious or scandalous stories hastily reprinted from popular magazines. Once Knute Nelson established an official commission to broker the terms of allotment in June of 1889, Theo Beaulieu suspended publication altogether, devoting himself instead to acting as an advocate for the White Earth Anishinaabeg in the upcoming negotiations. The last issue of the *Progress* was published on July 13, 1889, with a desultory apology: "[W]e beg our friends and patrons to please be patient with us until such time as we are again enabled to avail ourselves of your kind and generous courtesy."[68]

Such a time would never come. By the end of 1889, the Nelson Commission successfully negotiated the allotment of White Earth, sparking a quick succession of events that would ultimately lead to the majority of reservation's land base slipping out of Anishinaabe control. Once begun, the process proved to be driven by the very interests Beaulieu had hoped allotment would hold back: timber conglomerates and white settlers. Contrary to the wishes of the Beaulieus, the Nelson Act did not consolidate the Minnesota Anishinaabeg at White Earth, as it contained language that made relocation largely optional. As a result, very few bands agreed to leave their established territories. An 1891 amendment to the Nelson Act halved the size of allotments to just 80 acres. The most damning event of all, however, was the passage of the Clapp amendment, an unassuming rider appended to an unrelated spending bill in 1904. The amendment threw out the protection against alienation as guaranteed in the Nelson Act and the Treaty of 1867, allowing so-called mixed-bloods to sell their allotments to any interested party without interference—leading to a rash of fraud, abuse, and outright theft that would grip White Earth for decades.[69] By the end of the 1920s, the Anishinaabeg at White Earth had been almost totally dispossessed.

Theo Beaulieu would never again have a public platform for his work as accessible and unrestricted as the *Progress*. Nonetheless, archival evidence suggests that he continued to advocate on behalf of the rights of the White Earth Anishinaabeg for the rest of his life, by giving speeches, writing editorials, and representing their legal interests. Through this work, Beaulieu continued to impress others with his intellectual and rhetorical talents. On hearing Beaulieu give a speech on Anishinaabe history in 1914, a reporter for the *New Ulm Review* described Theo as "a man of striking appearance and convincing personality," who "left little doubt in the minds of his hearers that his is a mind the equal of that of his white brothers of more than ordinary ability."[70] A writer for the *St. Paul Globe* described Theo Beaulieu as "author, orator, diplomat, adroit politician, traveler, the product of a civilization that has no recognized place for him."[71] In recognition for his lifelong efforts, the editor of the *Progress*'s spiritual successor, the *Tomahawk*, gave Theo the fond honorific of "the Demosthenes of White Earth."[72] In 1924, Theo Beaulieu passed away at the age of seventy-two. Despite leaving behind a remarkable legacy, both the *Progress* and its fiery editor eventually lapsed into obscurity.

That would change in 1965, when a journalism student from the University of Minnesota discovered the *Progress*, by chance, after a reference librarian at the Minnesota Historical Society suggested that he, as an Anishinaabe, might find it of interest.[73] Reading through the newspaper, a young Gerald Vizenor found himself "transformed, inspired, and excited by a great and lasting source of native literary presence and survivance."[74] This chance encounter with the *Progress* had a profound influence on Vizenor, giving him "a privy trace of assurance to consider a career as a writer" at a time when such a thing seemed without precedent.[75] After a time leafing through the delicate pages, Vizenor recalls that he "looked around the reference room that afternoon for someone to convince that the *Progress* was absolutely revolutionary."[76]

Indeed, to a modern critic, it is difficult not to see echoes of the *Progress* throughout Vizenor's work. Examining Theo Beaulieu's editorials, one notices early articulations of themes that would come to be the hallmarks of Vizenor's own writing—the antiestablishment sensibility, the play of language, and the rejection of imposed discourses of Indianness. In Beaulieu's imperfect, politically motivated translations of aadizookaanag, Vizenor found what he would eventually call a "new tribal hermeneutics"[77]—a way of using material from the Anishinaabe oral tradition as a means of anticolonial resistance, by transforming traditional stories and songs into critiques of contemporary politics by translating them. The *Progress* would have critically important influence on Vizenor, not just for his own translations of nagamonan (as I discuss in depth in chapter 3), but for his entire career as one of the most influential Native American writers and thinkers of the twentieth century—the heir to an intellectual tradition of literary resistance and experimentation begun in a small shack at White Earth almost a century earlier.

Chapter 2

Englishman, Your Color Is Deceitful

Unsettling the North Woods in Janet Lewis's *The Invasion*

> The effect of the practice of speaking for others is often, though not always, erasure and a reinscription of sexual, national, and other kinds of hierarchies. . . . But this development should not be taken as an absolute de-authorization of all practices of speaking for. It is not always the case that when others unlike me speak for me I have ended up worse off.
>
> —Linda Martín Alcoff,
> "The Problem of Speaking for Others"

> Hello . . . I'm representing Marlon Brando this evening.
>
> —Sacheen Littlefeather

THE DECADES AFTER ALLOTMENT brought dramatic changes to the demography and economy of the Upper Midwest. The tidal wave of the timber industry swept through the region, leveling the old growth forests and replacing them with logging camps and dirt farms. Railroads were quickly built to move huge loads of lumber from northern sawmills to the rapidly expanding cities of Chicago, Detroit, Minneapolis, and Milwaukee. By the turn of the twentieth century, the towering white and red pines that once dominated the landscape became a rarity, along with any mature oak, basswood, or birch trees. The discovery of precious metals in Minnesota's Arrowhead and Michigan's Upper Peninsula pushed these rail lines even farther north—deep into the traditional homelands of the Anishinaabeg.[1] As with any extractive economy, the boom lasted only as long as the natural resources remained. The lumber camps and mill towns vanished along with the trees, as lumbermen sought new riches in the forests of the Rocky Mountains. The rail lines that had once carried billions of board feet of lumber now stood quiet. A vast region covering the northern portions of Michigan, Wisconsin, and Minnesota was remade and renamed: the Old North West became known as the Cutover.[2]

The Anishinaabeg of Upper Michigan felt these changes keenly. Allotment had come earlier for them than it had for the Anishinaabeg at White Earth—and under worse circumstances. A treaty signed by the Ojibwe and Odawa of Michigan in 1855 had not only imposed allotment on what remained of their land, but also stripped them of their status as Indians under federal law, effectively ending the United States' trust obligations to them. The allotment process in Michigan was marked by the same kind of fraud and abuse that would take place in Minnesota, ultimately leaving many Anishinaabeg destitute and homeless. But, unlike their kin to the west, the Anishinaabeg of Michigan—no longer considered wards of the government—had little recourse to federal aid or support in their time of critical need. Many were forced to find work in the timber industry as a matter of survival, helping to level the forests that had supported their ancestors for generations. Because of their race, Anishinaabe timbermen were often paid a fraction of the wages earned by their white colleagues while doing the most dangerous work—felling trees, and guiding huge booms of logs across lakes and down rivers to be milled. Without a permanent home, many relocated their families to ramshackle timber camps, to live as migrant laborers on land that had been theirs one generation earlier. As the timber became scarce, the Anishinaabeg were forced into an increasingly marginal existence, with many slipping into abject poverty.[3]

Meanwhile, the timber companies, finding themselves in possession of huge tracts of deforested land they no longer wanted or needed, sold their vast holdings in the cutover to land speculators, who marketed it a prime farmland to unsuspecting settlers. These eager newcomers, mostly immigrants from northern Europe, found themselves in a profoundly challenging environment. Swampy and sandy, most of the cutover was completely unsuited for agriculture. Added to this, the heavy accumulations of logging slash would regularly ignite in the summers, causing huge conflagrations so hot the topsoil burned away. But by far the most overwhelming obstacle facing these would-be farmers were the innumerable stumps punctuating their fields—each needing to be removed (often by dynamite) before plowing could even begin. Facing such overwhelming conditions, many of the new settlers simply left, allowing their farms to be reclaimed by new growth.[4]

Inevitably seized as tax forfeiture, many of these overgrown farms were eventually added back into the public domain as government managed forestland. Although primarily intended to provide a renewable supply of timber, these new state and federal forests were also open to limited recreational use by hunters, fishermen, and campers. The railroad companies, anxious to squeeze more revenue out of lines built during the heyday of the logging boom, quickly saw the potential in this arrangement and began advertising the region as a tourist destination for urban vacationers and would-be sportsmen hoping to get back to nature. Soon, the cutover was flooded with upper- and middle-class families from Chicago, Detroit, and New York seeking refuge from the oppressive heat of the summer. Vast resort hotels and tiny cabins were built to take in the annual cascade, as countless bankers, doctors, and professors abandoned their sedentary lives in order to become rugged outdoorsmen—at least as long as their vacations permitted.[5]

Out of this recreational milieu emerged two Euro-American writers—one famous, one forgotten—whose lives and work would be profoundly shaped by the region and its indigenous people. The similarities between the biographies of Janet Lewis and Ernest Hemingway are astounding. Lewis and Hemingway were both born in Chicago, less than a month apart. Lewis's father was a professor, while Hemingway's was a successful physician. Both were raised in the tony suburb of Oak Park, where they were high school classmates. Both moved to France shortly after the First World War, although Lewis's time in Paris would be far briefer than Hemingway's. Both would make important contributions to the developing stylistic revolution of literary modernism, with Lewis developing a poetics that merged imagism and ethnography, and Hemingway establishing his distinctive prose style. Importantly, both also spent their childhood summers in northern Michigan, where they would come to know Anishinaabe people, developing relationships that would arguably define their identities and careers as writers.

At the same time, the ways in which Hemingway and Lewis portrayed the Anishinaabeg in their writings differed dramatically. Just as business interests transformed the cutover into a wilderness by obscuring its industrial history, Hemingway's fiction obscures the violent history of Anishinaabe dispossession in order to present them as a noble, if primitive, people. Janet Lewis's work, in contrast, is invested in making the settler-colonial history of Michigan visible, showing how the impoverished state of her Anishinaabeg contemporaries is the direct result of Euro-American domination. By comparing the differences between Hemingway's and Lewis's work, we might begin to see how Euro-American writing is not uniformly invested in the settler-colonial project (although much of it undoubtedly is). Instead, I will argue that Lewis's work represents a potential model for "unsettled" literature, that is, literature that works to show the historical contingency of the United States and the continued legitimacy of indigenous sovereign claims. Lewis's work is able to work toward this goal only by interrogating the role Euro-American writing played in the project of indigenous dispossession, and then challenging its norms—not only at the level of theme and narrative, but even at the level of form.

Long Time Ago Good, Now Heap Shit

Ernest Hemingway's loosely autobiographical writings about life "up in Michigan" helped to shape the public's perception of the North Woods for most of the twentieth century. Hemingway spent every summer of his youth at Windemere, the fanciful name his parents gave to their simple cottage on the north shore of Walloon Lake. Situated about forty miles southeast of the Straits of Mackinac on Michigan's lower peninsula, Windemere provided a yearly refuge from the heat and congestion of Oak Park. There the Hemingway children spent their days in leisure, fishing, boating, and exploring what little remained of the old-growth forests. Occasionally their father, Clarence, would cajole them into helping him tend his forty-acre hobby farm across the lake—where, he often joked, "The best thing we raise is the flag."[6]

During his time at Windemere, Hemingway came to know several local Anishinaabeg. As a child, Hemingway regularly attended performances of George Kabaosa's *Hiawatha, or Nanabozho* at Petoskey. Clarence Hemingway was so enthused by the play that he once invited the play's star, Albert Wabunosa (Kabaosa's nephew), to visit Windemere where he taught the Hemingway children how to handle a canoe.[7] The other Anishinaabeg who lived near Hemingway were not much like the romanticized images he would've seen on stage. One of these was an "old fat Indian" named Simon Green, who owned a farm across the lake from Windemere and occasionally went hunting with Ernest and his father.[8] Others, such as Ernest's friends Rich and Prudence Bolton and Billy Tabeshaw, were Anishinaabe children who lived in dilapidated shacks at an encampment less than a mile from Windemere, to which Ernest made frequent visits. In his memoirs, Hemingway's younger brother Leicester recalled:

These Indians were the poor of the area, owning no land and seldom holding jobs for long since all the big timber had been logged out. They had regular emergencies—stabbings, broken bones, serious infections, Ernest went with Father on these calls. Not only did he admire many of the Ojibways, he learned a lot about emergency medicine under primitive conditions.[9]

Years later, Hemingway drew on these experiences with the Anishinaabeg for a short story that would ultimately become one of his best known, establishing him not only as a talented writer, but as one of the most mythologized figures in American letters.

"Indian Camp" was first published in 1924 in the *Transatlantic Review*. A year later it appeared as the opening story in Hemingway's first widely published work, a collection of short stories titled *In Our Time*. "Indian Camp" garnered Hemingway widespread praise from critics and writers alike, for its terse, vital style. The story's unflinching, almost affectless, portrayal of violence and death established the themes of self-reliance and tragic masculinity on which Hemingway would elaborate for the rest of his career. No less importantly, "Indian Camp" also established Hemingway's bona fides as a writer in touch with the primitive. At a time when many American writers were looking to urbane Europe for inspiration, "Indian Camp" announced Hemingway's bold intention to make new well-established American themes of frontier life, ritualized violence, and, of course, Indians. Indeed, the fact that Hemingway's story took place among the Anishinaabeg is likely responsible, at least in part, for the story's initial success, as Indians happened to be in vogue among America's literary elite at the time (see chapter 3).

The story opens with a very young Nick Adams on a rowboat. He has been fishing with his father and uncle, when the three are called to an encampment where a Native woman is suffering from complications during childbirth. They arrive to find the woman in dire need of an emergency caesarian. We watch through Nick's eyes as his father, a physician, operates on the unanaesthetized woman with only what he is carrying: a jackknife and fishing line. The woman's husband, badly injured in a logging accident a few days earlier, lays in the bunk above his wife, listening helplessly to her screams of pain. The operation saves the life of the mother and child, but the celebration is cut short by the realization that, during the delivery, the husband has committed suicide by slashing his throat with a razor blade. Nick, confronted by a violent death for the first time, asks his father, "Why did he kill himself, Daddy?" To which his father can only reply: "I don't know, Nick. He couldn't stand things, I guess."[10] The incongruity of the story's heightened action with its spare, quiet tone creates a sensation of ambiguity, even mystery, which has intrigued readers and critics for the better part of a century. Central to that ambiguity is the father's seemingly inexplicable suicide. Why did the man choose to kill himself at the very moment his child is born? Theories have ranged from the idea that seeing his wife cut open by a white man proved too traumatic to handle, to speculation that presence of the baby's "real" father, Nick's uncle George, drove him to it. Over the years, however, a consensus has formed around the father's suicide as a kind of initiation rite, for both the character of Nick and the reader, into a worldview in which the human experience, from its very beginnings, is defined by loss.

While most critics have been content to see such a rite strictly in metaphorical terms, others have taken the analysis even further, arguing that the events of "Indian Camp" form a literal depiction of indigenous ritual action. Latching onto the father's Indian identity, Jeffrey Meyers argues that the unexpected suicide that ends the story is "an act of elemental nobility" in which an Anishinaabe man "punishes himself for the violation of [the] taboo" of allowing a white doctor to cut into his wife.[11] As Meyers explains, "the pregnant wife is considered unclean, vulnerable, and in danger; the husband absorbs her weakness and associates her blood with his own death, practices couvade to protect his wife and child."[12] According to Meyers, not only does this provide an explanation for mystery at the heart of "Indian Camp," but also "reveals that Hemingway . . . did not simply glorify the Indians, but based his story on profound understanding . . . of their behavior, customs, and religion."[13]

Meyers's desire to seek an answer to the mystery of the man's suicide in Anishinaabe culture makes a certain sort of sense—after all we are told almost nothing about the man besides the fact that he is Indian. Yet, the main thrust of Meyers's argument falls apart under the slightest scrutiny. Even if one were to be (overly) charitable and assume that by "Indian behavior, custom, and religion" Meyers specifically means Anishinaabe cultural practice, there is no evidentiary basis for describing the man's suicide as a ritual act. Of all the historians, ethnographers, and Anishinaabe cultural experts consulted in the writing of the present book (including A. Irving Hallowell, Johann Kohl, Frances Densmore, Basil Johnston, John Tanner, Angeline Williams, and many, many others), none has discussed a tradition of couvade among the historical Anishinaabeg, or that of ritual suicide in any form (an idea that survival-minded traditional Anishinaabe would likely have found horrific). Tellingly, the only ethnographic source cited in Meyers's essay is *The Golden Bough*, James Frazer's compendious study of "primitive superstition and religion" first published 1890—a book that, as one of Frazer's contemporaries delicately put it, "ha[d] not been subjected to proper editing of its facts."[14]

Although Meyers's essay appeared in 1988 (a millennia ago in literary criticism), its primary assumption about Hemingway's deep familiarity with Anishinaabe culture continues to influence Hemingway criticism. Take, for example, a 2002 book that asserts "the most characteristic features of the Hemingway style . . . may be traced back to a 'native' source in the Ojibway stories and culture he was exposed to in his youth."[15] Or a 2009 essay that argues that "Nick Adams does not share Hemingway's reliance on the folk wisdom of the Ojibway,"[16] because his decision to throw away fish offal in "Big Two-Hearted River" is not "in accordance with tribal practice," as described, again, in Frazer's *Golden Bough*.[17] Perhaps the most fascinating example comes from a 2014 essay in which Katalin Kállay argues that the seemingly offhand description of the Anishinaabeg as "bark peelers" in "Indian Camp" is actually a subtle allusion to the birch-bark scrolls of the Midewiwin—then goes on to speculate that the man's suicide may have been a Mide-inspired ritual meant to transfer his "spirit" to his newborn son because, as Kállay asserts without evidence, "the spirit . . . has to be born through violence."[18]

This kind of speculation is, of course, exactly what Hemingway invited when he articulated his now-famous "iceberg" theory of fiction. Writing about his own fiction in *Death in the Afternoon*, Hemingway stated: "If a writer of prose knows enough about what he is writing about he may omit things that he knows and the reader, if the writer is writing truly enough, will have a feeling of those things as strongly as though the writer had stated them. The dignity of an ice-berg is due to only one-eighth of it being above water."[19] For decades, Hemingway's invocation of the iceberg-like nature of his fiction has been taken as an explicit invitation to symptomatic reading, with countless critics attempting to peer beneath the surface of the text to find its repressed hidden meanings. For Meyers, Kállay, and many others, the submerged presence looming under Hemingway's fiction is that of the Anishinaabe—not as a people, but as a cultural sensibility that Hemingway somehow possessed, but purposefully chose to obscure in his writing.

Taking a closer look at Kállay's argument neatly illustrates the problem with this position. While it certainly is possible that Hemingway was aware of the existence of Mide scrolls, a later Nick Adams story provides a much more likely explanation for the sobriquet.

> [Y]ou went into the woods on the wide clay and shale road . . . broadened for them to skid out the hemlock bark the Indians cut. The hemlock bark was piled in long rows of stacks, roofed over with more bark, like houses, and the peeled logs lay huge and yellow where the trees had been felled. They left the logs in the woods to rot, they did not even clear away or burn the tops. It was only the bark they wanted for the tannery in Boyne city . . .[20]

While Kállay acknowledges this industrial work as a possible source for the term, she describes this interpretation as "stress[ing] insignificance and maybe poverty," whereas "a closer look at the use of birch bark in Native American (mainly Ojibwa) traditions" reveals "a surprising richness of culture."[21] Kállay's argument relies on the assumption that the early-twentieth-century Anishinaabeg with whom Hemingway interacted lived in a way that was little different from their precontact forbears. While it is easy to get this sense from Hemingway's stories, the reality of the situation was far more complicated for the Anishinaabeg of Upper Michigan.

To take Hemingway's depictions of Anishinaabe "insignificance" and "poverty" at face value is to acknowledge a history that readers like Kállay may find too unsettling to contemplate. Prior to 1872, most of the land on the western side of Michigan's lower peninsula between Walloon Lake and the Straits of Mackinac was reservation land occupied by the Little Traverse Band of Odawa. The land comprising the reservation had been set aside by the Treaty of 1855, after a hard-fought battle by the Odawa and Ojibwe to resist removal under the Treaty of 1836. While originally intended to provide a land base for future Odawa allotments, Federal authorities were slow to carry out the necessary surveying work. Without clear title, the reservation was withheld from the market, effectively cutting off non-Native access. The lack of government action or settlement pressure allowed the Odawa to continue to treat large portions of the reservation as communal property for decades. Because the Treaty of 1855 had granted blanket U.S. citizenship, the Odawa found themselves with a unique opportunity to reassert political control over this Anishinaabe territory. Under the careful guidance of leaders such as Petosegay and Andrew Blackbird, the Little Traverse Odawa organized the reservation as a county with a majority Anishinaabe population, capable of electing officials from their own communities (much as Theo Beaulieu would propose to do at White Earth three decades later). Under Odawa self-government, the communities at Weekwitonsing (Little Bay Place) and Mukwasibing (Bear Creek) flourished between 1855 and 1872.[22]

The situation of the Odawa villages changed drastically in June of 1872, when Congress passed *An Act for the Restoration to Market of Certain Lands in Michigan*. The act gave the Odawa six months to select allotments, after which the "surplus" land would be opened to sale to railroads and timber companies. In 1875 Congress opened the remaining reservation land to homesteading, resulting in a massive influx of non-Natives. Prior to the passage of these two acts, over 95 percent of the region's population was Anishinaabeg. By 1880 the Anishinaabeg were outnumbered by white settlers at a ratio of five to one.[23] The homesteaders quickly took control of the county government, passing resolutions that seriously limited the Odawa's ability to participate in local politics. The Odawa, however, still held much of the most valuable property in the county—including the harbor front on Little Traverse Bay. Desirous of these holdings, the new county government imposed a new rule that assessed taxes on Indian allotments at rates twice that of other kinds of property.[24] This lead to a raft of forfeitures, some of which became violent when the Anishinaabe resisted eviction.[25] Despite multiple appeals from the Odawa to federal officials to intervene, the dispossession of the village property continued unabated. By the mid-1880s, the Odawa had been all but evicted from the towns they had built. The newcomers rechristened Weekwitonsing as "Harbor Springs," transforming it into one of the most exclusive resort communities in Michigan. The village of Mukwasibing was renamed in commemoration of its Odawa founder, the ogimaa Petosegay—known to local whites as "Chief Petoskey."[26]

Reassessing "Indian Camp" from the perspective of this history, the motivations behind the Anishinaabeg man's suicide no longer seem noble, but merely tragic. Early on in the story, we are told that the man "had cut his foot very badly with an ax" three days prior, and that "the room smelled very bad" (68). Facing long-term, if not permanent, disability, such an injury renders him unfit for most kinds of manual labor—the only kind of labor available to an Anishinaabe man at the time. Despite having to suffer under such anti-Indian racism (Uncle George, for example, calls the pregnant woman a "damn squaw bitch" at one point in the story), the couple would have received little assistance from the federal government, since they had been stripped of their legal status as Indians after 1855. Their child, if it survived infancy, would likely be obliged to enter a school system that would actively discourage him from speaking his peoples' language or engaging in their traditions. Added to all of this was the indignity of being forced to live as a squatter on land that had, only a few years earlier, belonged to their people—before it was stripped away in a massive act of fraud. Facing a situation that seems to offer nothing but further abjection for himself, his wife, and newborn child, the roots of the man's suicidal despair are not nearly as obscure as critics have made them out to be.

When discussing the state of the Indians he knew, Hemingway often repeated the phrase: "Long time ago good. Now heap shit."[27] He claimed to have heard it from a Cheyenne elder on the Wind River Reservation while on a hunting trip, and quickly claimed it as his own. That Hemingway was fond of the aphorism should come as no surprise, given the degree to which it seems to mirrors the sentiments expressed about the Anishinaabeg in his fiction. The idea of the present as an ugly corruption of the past was an unfortunate reality for many of the Anishinaabeg during the early twentieth century, a reality that Hemingway portrayed with oftentimes brutal honesty. At the same time, the phrase also reveals the reason why Hemingway's work fails to provide a meaningful critique of this status quo. Lying in the elliptical space between the good of "long time ago" and the shittiness of "now" is the entire history of abusive policy, land seizure, and outright fraud that shaped the degraded conditions of Hemingway's present.

Without this sense of history, our affective response to Hemingway's fiction can have no shape or direction, forcing us to cast about to find something that would make sense of the horror we see depicted on the page. I see the desire of Kállay, Meyers, and others to find in Hemingway evidence of a still-whole precontact Anishinaabe culture is, at its root, a desire to exonerate him (and by extension, ourselves) from participation in the processes of dispossession that led to the dire circumstances we see on display in "Indian Camp." Divorced from the context of colonization, the pain of the Anishinaabeg loses its specificity, becoming instead a sense of existential unease, or a nostalgic longing for childhood. Such feelings may be powerful, but they are also essentially apolitical—demanding nothing from the reader but commiseration. Having already lost so much, the Anishinaabeg are thus subjected to another act of dispossession in Hemingway's fiction, as their suffering becomes a space for us readers—emotional tourists—to inhabit and ultimately make our own.

If this critical account of Hemingway seems at all familiar—and it should—it is because such an approach has become a dominant model in literary criticism over the past twenty years. With so much recent critical attention paid to settler-colonialism and its relation to American literature, we have built a substantive theoretical apparatus for understanding the ways in which non-Native writers have advocated for, defended, and rationalized the historical project of indigenous dispossession in the United States over the past two and a half centuries. This body of criticism has done much to show how novels, poems, and histories have buttressed settler-colonial claims to the land by constantly re-presenting narratives of Native removal and disappearance for public consumption. As Mark Rifkin argues, the ubiquity of such narratives creates a kind of "common sense" in which, "the dynamics of settler occupation operate as the phenomenological background, against which Indigenous survival registers as anomaly and is hived off from routine nonnative experience as an aberrant (and anachronistic) eruption."[28] Indeed the commonness of this common sense is readily apparent in even the most cursory examination of American literature, as representations of Natives from Herman Melville to Stephenie Meyer fall into the all-too-predictable patterns of Indian savagery and disappearance. The critic James Cox has gone as far as to suggest that adherence to these kinds of narratives is the sine qua non of Euro-American literature, stating: "In spite of the many different religious, national, and socioeconomic origins of European American novelists, as well as the influence of an author's gender on textual production and publication, their plots proceed inexorably toward the absence of Native individuals and communities from the landscape."[29]

The totalizing nature of Cox's claim makes it immediately suspect, of course, but at the same time it presents a provocative challenge: can there be a work of Euro-American writing that does *not* reproduce the displacement of indigenous peoples? Imagining a novel written by a non-Native that not only acknowledges, but questions, the structures of settler-colonialism seems difficult, indeed. Many of the generic and thematic norms that govern American literature make it nearly impossible to grapple with the anomalous presence of Natives in any way that does not end in their disappearance. Indeed, much of the historical fiction produced in the United States has arguably worked to domesticate and normalize the dispossession of Native peoples at the level of *form*. Any deviation from these norms would offer a profound challenge to readers, who would likely find the resulting work to be almost unrecognizable as literature. Yet, by examining the fiction of Hemingway's little-known contemporary, Janet Lewis, we may find an example of such a work, one with unsettling implications for how we think about Euro-American writings' role in the process of indigenous dispossession.

Stuck with History

In 1899 an Anishinaabe woman named Anna Maria Johnstone sold a small waterfront lot on Neebish island to a young professor from Oak Park. For several years, Johnstone had owned and managed a resort called O-Non-E-Gwud,[30] a small collection of cabins on the St. Mary's river a few miles downstream from Sault Ste. Marie, Michigan. As she approached her late fifties, Johnstone found the management and upkeep of O-Non-E-Gwud too taxing to maintain, and decided to sell the resort's waterfront lots and cabins as permanent vacation homes to secure her retirement. Edwin Lewis, a faculty member at Chicago's Lewis Institute, was looking for a place to rest and recreate during his long summer vacations. Having grown enamored of Neebish after a previous vacation to O-Non-E-Gwud, Edwin Lewis took Johnstone up on the offer, buying a plot on which he constructed a rustic cabin to house himself and his family—recently grown larger with the birth of his daughter, Janet.

The landscape and people of Upper Michigan would have a profound effect on Janet Lewis, much as it had on her neighbor and classmate, Ernest Hemingway. In many ways, Lewis considered the North Woods to be her true home. Like Hemingway, the land and people of Upper Michigan became a presence in her writing for the rest of her long life. Janet Lewis spent twenty summers at Neebish, often in the company of Anna Maria Johnstone, whom she affectionately referred to as "Miss Molly." According to her own account, Lewis adored the reserved, soft-spoken woman who would often look after her while the elder Lewises recreated. On many summer evenings the Lewis family would go to Molly's cabin, where they would gather around a campfire to be regaled with stories about local history from Molly and her brother, Howard Johnstone, who lived nearby. Molly seems to have been fond of the young girl as well, keeping an occasional correspondence with Janet, even after she moved to Paris in 1920.[31]

Unfortunately, Lewis's time as an expatriate was cut short by an illness that would drastically change the course of her life. After only six months in Paris, Lewis returned to Chicago in poor health. By 1922, she was confined to Sunmount, a sanitarium near Santa Fe, New Mexico, where she spent the next five years recovering from tuberculosis. Despite her illness, Lewis was able to publish her first collection of poems, *The Indians in the Woods*, in 1922. Written during her isolated time in Paris and Sunmount, many of the poems are nostalgic recollections of the Michigan Anishinaabeg, replete with mythic images of Wenabozho and Nokomis drawn from Molly's stories. Coming out at a time in which poetry about Indians was incredibly popular (see chapter 3), *The Indians in the Woods* gained Lewis no small degree of attention and acclaim.

In 1926, Lewis married the poet and critic Yvor Winters at a ceremony held at Sunmount, where he had also been a patient. Shortly thereafter, Lewis was discharged with a clean bill of health, and moved with her new husband to Palo Alto, California, where Winters was employed as a professor of English at Stanford. Although much of her time was dedicated to the care of her newly born child, Lewis continued to pursue a career as a writer, publishing more poetry and a few short stories in the popular literary magazines of the day. After learning of Molly Johnstone's death in 1928, Lewis set out to write a short biographical sketch to commemorate her friend. The project would turn out to be more complicated than she had originally envisioned, however. As Lewis would later state in an interview: "I discovered if I was going to do a story about Miss M[olly], I had to begin with the ancestors . . . and having once began with them, I was in over my head really, and found myself stuck with history."[32]

The history that Lewis found so troublesome was that which could account for a woman like Molly Johnstone. She may have been an Anishinaabe, but Molly lived in a manner largely indistinguishable from the Euro-American resorters who surrounded her. She was a successful business owner, educated, and had a refined manner. Molly's failure to conform to Euro-Americans' expectations of Indianness caused a degree of vertiginous uncertainty about her racial identity, even among those who knew her well. As Lewis recalls, a neighbor once casually remarked about the Johnstones, "They aren't Indian," only to add, after a moment of reflection, "But of course they're Indian."[33] Despite the profound anti-Indian racism of early-twentieth-century Michigan, Molly never shied away from her Anishinaabe identity. Along with her brothers, Molly was an active part of Anishinaabe cultural life at the Sault and regularly participated in the seasonal subsistence round. They kept up relations with the Anishinaabeg communities on the Canadian side at Garden River and as far away as Manitoulin. Molly and her brother Howard were both speakers of Anishinaabemowin, and maintained a repertoire of stories from the Anishinaabeg oral tradition, which they shared with the Lewises during their evening bonfires. As Lewis recalls, the Johnstones "were very proud of their inheritance."[34]

Quite an inheritance it was. For most of the nineteenth century, members of the Johnstone family had been political and cultural leaders among the Anishinaabeg of the Sault. Molly and her brothers were descendants of the eighteenth-century fur trader John Johnston, a Scots-Irish aristocrat who turned to the peltry business after his family's fortunes faded. After establishing a trading post at La Pointe Chegoimegon (in present-day Wisconsin), he married an Anishinaabe woman named Ozahguscodaywayquay, the daughter of the illustrious ogimaag Waubojiig, who became an important political leader in her own right. Relocating to the Sault shortly after their marriage, the couple became major figures in the settlement of Upper Michigan, helping to negotiate the first treaties between the Anishinaabeg and the United States, and establishing Sault Ste. Marie as the center of culture and trade in the North West. Their children included Jane Johnston, the celebrated Anishinaabe poet, as well as her brother George, who were both instrumental in the collection, interpretation, and translation of the material that would eventually become *The Song of Hiawatha* (see introduction). The Johnstons' youngest son, John Macdougall Johnstone[35] (father of Molly and Howard), served for many years as the personal interpreter for Jane's husband, Henry Rowe Schoolcraft, and helped to draft many of the early treaties between the United States and the tribes of the Upper Midwest.

In order to tell the story of Molly Johnstone, Lewis decided that she must tell the history of the entire Johnstone family—one that stretched back to the eighteenth century. Over the next four years, Lewis launched a massive historical investigation of the Johnstone family of the Sault. She enlisted the aid of Chase Osborn, the former governor of Michigan, who gave her access to a huge archive of historical, ethnographic, and journalistic texts housed in Michigan's various libraries, universities, and museums. Her father sent her records and materials from Chicago, in addition to his own writings about the Sault (years earlier, Edwin Lewis had written his own novel about the region called *White Lightning*). Importantly, Lewis also reached out to Molly's surviving brothers, William and Howard Johnstone, from whom she received the personal recollections of family history.[36]

The resulting book announces its project with its provocative title, *The Invasion*. Offering a searing account of the settler invasion of Upper Michigan from the earliest days of Euro-American contact to the present day of 1928, *The Invasion* takes the perspective of the Anishinaabeg, as their political power and social coherence both deteriorate under the pressure of a century and a half of Euro-American colonization. Unlike other historical novels of the time (such as Willa Cather's *Death Comes for the Archbishop*), *The Invasion* displays the effects of settlement not only in the past, *but also in the present day*—explicitly finding continuity between the historical dispossession of the Anishinaabeg with their contemporary situation. In its critical account of Anishinaabe–Euro-American relations over two centuries, *The Invasion* presages Patrick Wolfe's dictum that "invasion is a structure and not an event"[37] by almost fifty years.

The Invasion, I believe, should be read as a sustained critique of settler-colonialism as both a historical process and an ideology that persists into the present day. In rejecting settler-colonial ideology, *The Invasion* shows the potential for the recognition of Anishinaabe nationhood and sovereignty—even at a historical moment when the Michigan

Anishinaabeg had been without formal recognition as a nation for nearly a century. *The Invasion* accomplishes this by instantiating a sense of historical Anishinaabe sovereignty and making it comparable with that of Euro-American nations—and therefore recognizable. The book also shows how settler-colonial dispossession was not the inevitable, naturalized outcome of Euro-American–Native contact, representing it to be rather a product of a particular ideology driven by capitalist interests and buttressed by racism. *The Invasion* goes on to show how the hegemony of settler-colonial thought can be disrupted and even rejected by settlers, through the process of confronting the illegitimacy of their own settler privilege, acknowledging their complicity in the history of indigenous dispossession, and recognizing contemporary indigenous political rights.

Perhaps most importantly, *The Invasion* accomplishes this work by interrogating the role that *writing* by Euro-Americans played in the history of the Anishinaabeg's dispossession, showing it to be a powerful tool for rationalizing false assumptions about Native sovereignty, intellectual inferiority, and the trajectory of history itself. Throughout *The Invasion*, the act of writing is presented as the primary space in which Euro-American characters articulate their relationship with the Anishinaabeg for both good and ill. The novel shows how the resulting texts circulate in Euro-American society, giving solidity to otherwise fanciful notions of Indianness to the broader public—a process in which *The Invasion* (as a work of Euro-American writing) also participates. It is this metanarrative aspect of *The Invasion* that is its most interesting characteristic, as the novel simultaneously works on the levels of characterization, theme, and form to avoid replicating the same process of appropriation and misrepresentation it seeks to critique—resulting in a novel that might be best described as "unsettled."

Early reviewers reacted to *The Invasion* with mild praise and pronounced confusion. The *New York Times* described the book as "a curious combination of a genealogical compendium and descriptive writing of a cool, translucent beauty."[38] A reviewer from the American Library Association suggested *The Invasion* was "of limited appeal as a novel, but a fine example of regional history." Another reviewer from *Bookman* magazine admitted that "no rough and ready classification" existed for *The Invasion*, but ultimately commended Harcourt, who "wisely decided to issue it as a [. . .] novel."[39] A reviewer for the *Nation* praised *The Invasion* as "an exceptional achievement"—only to demure—"as a history rather than a novel."[40]

The difficulty the reviewers had in understanding the genre of *The Invasion* was due, in no small part, to the curious interplay of its style and scope. Accurately relating the events of nearly a century and a half in a linear fashion, the epic scale of *The Invasion* suggests it be read as history. Yet, its subject is decidedly more intimate, reducing events of historical importance to an indistinct background against which she presents a study of the domestic lives of multiple generations of the same family—Molly Johnstone's family. While such an intimately domestic setting would indicate the book's affinity with the novel, Lewis's style, characterization, and plotting resist any such affiliation. *The Invasion* employs dialogue only rarely and offers the barest glimpses into the minds of her characters. The characters themselves fall into the story only to drop out in a disorienting fashion. The narrative point of view shifts, sometimes wildly, between characters—oftentimes on the same page. No one who could be described as a protagonist ever really emerges from the story. Through it all, *The Invasion* maintains a tone of controlled, objective disinterest—relating skirmishes and soirées in what one reviewer describes as a "low monotone."[41] For her part, Lewis was insistent that *The Invasion* not be read as a novel or history, as she (somewhat confusingly) explained: "*The Invasion* . . . is not a novel. Harcourt called it a novel because novels are what they publish. But it is a fiction, called 'in the manner of fiction,' but in it I think I invented practically nothing."[42] Instead, Lewis claimed that *The Invasion* occupies an ambiguous third category between history and fiction, calling the book a "narrative," one based on the "personal legends of the Johnstone family."[43]

While it may seem like a meaningless distinction to make at first glance, Lewis's identification of *The Invasion* as a narrative is freighted with specific political and cultural implications. For most of the nineteenth century, highly romanticized historical "narratives" were a prestige mode for American writers, such as James Fenimore Cooper[44] and Nathaniel Hawthorne. As Doris Sommer argues, writers in the former colonies of the Americas, desirous to differentiate themselves from Europe, felt the need to create "a history that would increase the legitimacy of the emerging nation and . . . to direct that history towards a future ideal."[45] The fragmentary nature of the colonial archive, however, made orthodox forms of history writing difficult, if not impossible, to produce. Embracing "narrative" allowed nineteenth-century writers to turn this deficit into an asset, since, as Sommer argues, "narrative's acknowledgement of its own supplementary nature gives it a freer hand to construct history, not despite, but thanks to the gaps and absences."[46] By giving historical actors interiority, filling archival gaps with imagined scenarios, and giving a mere sequence of events the shape and direction of a plot, authors of historical romances took the inert stuff of history and reshaped it into something dynamic and emotionally satisfying. Writing between the aesthetic distance of the novel and the claustrophobic detail of modern historiography, nineteenth-century writers of narratives demanded that their nations be seen as the inevitable culmination of history—even as those nations continued to struggle in asserting their own political and cultural autonomy.

In the United States, the specific form of historical narratives that took root in the public imagination was that of the frontier romance, which, according to Gregg Crane, "use[d] the image of the frontier and violent conflicts between European Americans and Native Americans to stage the birth of an American identity."[47] Works like Robert Montgomery Bird's *Nick of the Woods*, William Gilmore Simms's *The Yemassee*, or Cooper's *Last of the Mohicans* took the relative chaos of the early decades of Euro-American colonization and transformed it into the linear story of progress, settlement, and civilization. This, of course, meant sanitizing a history of violence directed at the continent's indigenous peoples, presenting it as an unfortunate, but necessary aspect of the nation's founding.

Indeed, *The Invasion* shares many of its superficial generic conventions with a particular kind of historical romance identified by contemporary critics as the domestic frontier romance. The genre combined two of the most popular forms of nineteenth-century fiction, the frontier romance and the domestic novel, into narratives about brave pioneer women who bring domestic order to the chaos of the frontier. As Ezra Tawil points out, works like Lydia Maria Child's *Hobomok* and Catherine Sedgwick's *Hope Leslie* used the frontier domestic space as a site in which the idea of racialized citizenship was articulated through allegories of failed attempts to form kin relations between white women and nonwhite men—most often Natives. Such works "provided the conditions of possibility of an Anglo-Saxonist nationalism and the fateful articulation of race and nation," according to Tawil, "by telling the story of the English woman who crossed over into Indian culture and yet remained white."[48]

The Invasion, too, is interested in the production of racialized identities in the frontier, but with a twist. Instead of being white, the women of *The Invasion* are all Anishinaabeg. The domestic spaces in which the novel operates are almost exclusively those controlled by Anishinaabe women. This change forces us to reevaluate the operation of the genre in a different context. The domestic space being imagined is not an allegory for the U.S. nation, but rather the Anishinaabe nation—at least its earliest articulation as a nation. Moreover the frontier is not presented from the vantage of the imperial core expanding outward into the unknown, but from an indigenous core being continually enclosed on, for whom the frontier offers its own kind of chaos, disruption, and failure of law. Instead of crafting a story that shows how the frontier becomes familiar, *The Invasion* creates a narrative in which the familiar becomes frontier. In this way, Lewis's book is more like a dark satire of the domestic frontier romance—beginning with a scenario readers of the genre would instantly recognize, but deviating from its conventions in unsettling ways.

The book actively, even insistently, denies the narrative's generic coherence by forcing the homogeneous conventionality of the romance plot to contend with the extreme heterogeneity of history, with its unclear motivations, archival gaps, and partisan contestations. Indeed, one may even say that *The Invasion* calls on the qualities of the historical romance to show how history and romance are incommensurate, if not incompatible, with one another. Balancing the authority of historiography and the intimacy of the novel, *The Invasion* is a work that it is *formally* unsettled—never fully cohering into a work with a definitive identity, or a sense of overall unity. Instead, the book is messy, full of gaps and distances, awkward transitions and ambiguous motivations—unpleasantly forcing the reader to contend with the text rather than merely accept its authority. The book's ambiguity, I believe, is a document of Lewis's own unsettlement, a traumatic confrontation with a history that defined her existence and identity, but of which she remained unconscious—a history that, once acknowledged, stuck with her.

The Ogimaag

The Invasion opens with a short preface depicting the death of the Marquis de Montcalm at the Battle of the Plains of Abraham in 1759. The defeat of the French general outside the gates of Quebec City was a turning point in the Seven Years War, and a watershed moment in the colonial history of North America. The image of Montcalm's death has been fixed into the colonial imaginary through a series of famous visual depictions by Defontaines (see fig. 2.1), Watteau, and Chevillet. In these images, Montcalm is surrounded by his officers and aides-de-camp while his Indian allies look on insensibly from the margins of the image, seemingly unable to register the magnitude of the moment. Against this image, *The Invasion* gives a depiction of the event as she heard it from the Johnstones, with the Anishinaabe ogichidaa Ma-mongazid cradling the mortally wounded general, his "dark sorrowful face, with its war paint of vermillion and white, intent above the French face graying rapidly." For Ma-mongazid, the death of Montcalm is a serious blow to his tribe's interests, as the French had proven to be trustworthy allies. By replacing the image of a nameless, tribeless Indian at the literal margins of history with that of a historic Anishinaabe leader at the center of this precipitous moment, *The Invasion* signals its intent to depart from the

Figure 2.1. *Mort de Montcalm* by Moret, after original by Desfontaines.

settler account of history and take up the perspective of the Anishinaabeg. The scene continues.

> Presently they took the Marquis to the hospital at St. Charles, where he died. Ma-Mongazid with his warriors in thirty bark canoes returned to La Pointe Chegoimegon through the yellowing woods and increasing storms of autumn. The rule of the French was over, the Province of Michilimackinac had become the Northwest Territory. The Ojibways called the English Saugunosh, the Dropped-from-the-Clouds, and regretted the French.

The narrative strategy of the scene is subtle but powerful. As the canoes of the Anishinaabeg make the journey back to Chegoimegon—the center of Anishinaabe cultural and social life—*The Invasion* draws the reader further away from a Euro-American historical perspective. Like the autumnal storms it describes, *The Invasion* casts an unsettling pall over a well-known moment of colonial triumph—hinting at the historical renegotiations to come.

The Invasion takes pains to show the Anishinaabeg as a coherent social body with its own sovereign integrity—continuously invoking the language of nationhood to do so. The first chapter opens in 1791 at the village of Chegoimegon (now La Pointe, Wisconsin) during a summer gathering of the Mide (2). Settler-colonial narratives paint indigenous space as fundamentally empty and indigenous social life as too primitive to facilitate the kind of large-scale organization necessary to constitute a national identity. Yet in this section, *The Invasion* presents a coming together of many hundreds, if not thousands, of Anishinaabeg from across the region, their number adding considerably to the "sixty or more wigwams of the regular village" (7). Presiding over this convocation is Waub-ojeeg, the son of Ma-mongazid, the "hereditary chieftain of the Ojibway nation," whose military prowess against the Dakota has ensured that "Lake Superior and all the surrounding territory was Ojibway, and the center of Ojibway power was Chegoimegon" (2). Much of this portion of the novel relies on Lewis's imaginative re-creation of Anishinaabe life, yet where Lewis invents, she does so with an eye toward making the Anishinaabeg seem *less* exotic—downplaying elements of their cultural practices that would seem alien to a Euro-American reader and highlighting those that seem familiar. The effect is to take the frontier wilderness of the *pays d'en haut* and transform it into a recognizable, even familiar, homeland.

Through its characterization of Waub-ojeeg *The Invasion* carries out the most direct work of disrupting reader's expectations about the nature of indigenous political power. In settling a territorial dispute between two Anishinaabe hunters, Waub-ojeeg illustrates the Anishinaabeg's sophisticated understanding of territorial rights, and establishes a sense of Waub-ojeeg's sovereign authority. In the scene, Waub-ojeeg is approached by Little Thunder, who has found the traps of Cloud Approaching on his trapping territory. Little Thunder claimed the traps, along with the animals they contained, earning the ire of Cloud Approaching, who threatens Little Thunder for stealing his game. Hearing the facts of the matter, Waub-ojeeg gives his judgment.

> He deliberated the case with a pipeful of tobacco, and finally told Little Thunder he best return the pelts. The meat, which he had partly consumed, he might keep. He asked him to return the pelts because Cloud Approaching was a relative and it was not wise to quarrel within one's own family. More-

over the traps and the labor were Cloud Approaching's, and Little Thunder had been late in his hunting. He would give a message to Little Thunder to present to Cloud Approaching, warning him to stay in his own territory, and he would send one small mokkuk of sugar to the wife of Little Thunder as a gift from Waub-ojeeg. (28–29)

In fashioning this fictional depiction of Waub-ojeeg's political leadership, *The Invasion* works to bring out the qualities in his leadership that make him recognizable to a Euro-American reader as the source of sovereign authority. First, it shows Waub-ojeeg's authority as a civil leader as being primarily social and not martial. Waub-ojeeg is not a backwoods chieftain ruling by caprice (as the settler-colonial narrative would have it), but a reasoning political actor, whose primary role is to enforce, rationally and fairly, a previously agreed-on set of laws.

Second, and importantly, the scene depicts the Anishinaabeg as having a defined political sense of territory—that is, land use is managed and controlled through sovereign authority. Where popular settler accounts hold that Native people had no sense of property, *The Invasion* offers a more sophisticated (and historically accurate) depiction of Anishinaabe land tenure. As it is depicted in *The Invasion*, a band's land base was held in common, but exclusive usufructory rights to demarcated territories were claimed by individual hunters and trappers. Ogimaag like Waub-ojeeg managed the band's entire land-base, fixing boundaries between hunting territories and settling disputes between claimants when they arose.[49] In this capacity, the ogimaag expressed a sovereign authority over a band's territory, as they determined the rules governing property, along with deciding when to create exceptions to those rules.

The Invasion extends this sense of Waub-ojeeg's sovereignty beyond simple hunting rights, however, imagining the ogimaa's perspective on the political situation in the *pays d'en haut* after the Seven Years War.

> In some remote way [Waub-ojeeg] acknowledged a British jurisdiction over and above the Ojibway. He did not think of the land as being British, but of the Ojibways as being bound by treaty to the English as they were to the Ottawas, Potawatomis, Illinois, and Menominees. He expected to punish an Ojibway who transgressed against an Englishman, and he expected the English to do justice for the Ojibways upon French or English. He granted the English the right to trade in his territory; he admitted the day of the French was over. (2)

The description of Waub-ojeeg's power is unequivocal: it is *he* who grants the English the right to travel in *his* territory. *The Invasion* does nothing in this description to diminish or undermine the credibility of Waub-ojeeg's—and subsequently the Anishinaabeg's—claim to sovereign authority over their own land. The novel is unequivocal in its depiction of the Anishinaabeg's belief in the equivalence of their sovereign authority to that of the French or English, as well as their expectation that these powers respect it. In doing so, *The Invasion* primes the reader to conceptualize subsequent events (including the diminution of Anishinaabe territory and political rights) as deviations from the status quo of Anishinaabe sovereignty.

What comes next in *The Invasion* is a depiction of the very different ways in which two Euro-Americans, John Johnston and Henry Rowe Schoolcraft, related themselves to the Anishinaabe nation. The relationships each of these white men forge with Waub-ojeeg's descendants becomes an allegorical reflection of relations between the Anishinaabeg and Euro-Americans as a whole. Where John Johnston's relationship with the Anishinaabeg represents the potential for economic and social integration in the fur trade era (1750–1819), Henry Rowe Schoolcraft's exploitation of the Anishinaabeg as a way of achieving personal fame replicates the systematic dispossession of the treaty era (1820–55). By allegorizing the Anishinaabeg's experience of colonization through the portrait of these two men in a domestic setting, *The Invasion* gives its critique of settler-colonialism a high degree of affective charge, showing its effects on an intimate, interpersonal scale. *The Invasion* shows how the Anishinaabeg struggle to find a way to share a *home* with these white men, showing how the familiar domestic world of the Anishinaabeg is transformed into the frontier—a space of lawlessness and violence—when Euro-Americans fail to recognize Anishinaabe sovereignty.

Interestingly, *The Invasion* shows how this transformation is largely facilitated through acts of *writing*. Throughout the novel, both Johnston and Schoolcraft are presented as having an almost compulsive need to narrate their experiences with the Anishinaabeg—imagining them as both racial others and as kin. Yet, where Johnston uses writing to imagine the Anishinaabeg as his social and cultural equals, Schoolcraft uses writing to create an image of the Anishinaabeg as intellectual inferiors in need of colonial domination. The novel is careful to present the views of both men to be little more than a reflection of their own assumptions and biases, as they work to rationalize their continued presence among the Anishinaabeg. However contingent Johnston's and Schoolcraft's narratives might be, *The Invasion* shows how the act of writing gives them a sense of solidity—especially as the resulting texts circulate among Euro-American society. In this way, Lewis's novel becomes a meditation on the immense (and immensely dangerous) power a single Euro-American writer can have to shape the perception of the Anishinaabeg for both good and ill.

Writing Kinship

The relationship between John Johnston and Ozah-guscoday-waquay (Molly's grandparents) reflects the potential for a nonexploitative relationship between Native and white made possible by a particular social and cultural milieu that took hold in the *pays d'en haut* at the end of the eighteenth century. Richard White has famously described this period as being defined by a concept he calls the "middle ground," a process of cultural accommodation and compromise that came to define the era. As White describes it, the interactions between Algonquians (like the Anishinaabeg) and Europeans during this time were conditioned by "the inability of both sides to gain their ends through force," and which compelled both to "attempt to understand the world and the reasoning of others and to assimilate enough of that reasoning to put it to their own purposes."[50] White's formulation of the middle ground is essential to understanding the economic, political, and cultural work being done by the marriage of Johnston and Ozah-guscoday-wayquay, because sexual unions between Natives and non-Natives were the predominant site where the middle ground was instantiated. As Anishinaabe historian Brenda Child argues, "The necessities of the fur trade made permeable the borders of Anishinaabe and European society, with marriages between newcomers and indigenous women becoming the foundation upon which new cultural relations were constructed in the Great Lakes."[51] More often than not, the production of such new cultural understandings was a messy and imperfect project, based on, as White describes, "creative, and often expedient, misunderstandings" instead of genuine comprehension.[52]

Such creative misunderstandings form the basis of Johnston and Ozah-guscoday-wayquay's relationship, one that reflects the positive potential for a Euro-American settler to recognize—and submit himself to—indigenous sovereignty. Early on in their courtship, Johnston seems intent on partnering with Ozah-guscoday-wayquay *à la façon du pays*. Approaching Waub-ojeeg with a request to marry Ozah-guscoday-wayquay, Johnston receives the following response:

> Englishman, your color is deceitful. I have watched your people now for many years. You come among us and marry

our daughters, and when you are tired of them you say you are not married, and go away. I cannot let you marry my daughter and desert her. But I have watched you and your conduct has been right. I think you are better than the others. I say to you now, go back to Montreal, to your own people, and look among them for a wife. If you do not find a woman who pleases you, and if when the summer is gone you still wish my daughter, return to this place, and I will give her to you. If you take her you must keep her forever, as you would a woman of your own race. I have said. (38)

The way in which *The Invasion* presents Waub-ojeeg's rebuff loads it with political significance, highlighting the ogimaa's assertion of national difference and sovereign authority. Whereas the historical accounts of this moment use the term "white man," Waub-ojeeg's use of the word "Englishman" in *The Invasion* suggests the conflict not to be one of race, but of *law*.[53] In order to gain Waub-ojeeg's permission to marry Ozah-guscoday-wayquay, Johnston must recognize that such a union is as legitimately binding as any marriage conducted under Euro-American law, underwritten by Waub-ojeeg's sovereign authority, as emphasized in his definitive declaration of "I have said." In essence, Waub-ojeeg is demanding that if Johnston marries Ozah-guscoday-wayquay, that he understand that it will bind him, legally and culturally, to Waub-ojeeg and the Anishinaabeg.

Johnston complies to Waub-ojeeg's directive, doing so by imaginatively recasting Anishinaabe social organization and political power into a form that is recognizable to himself as legitimate: the patrilineal aristocracy of Europe. Writing to his semi-aristocratic Scots-Irish family about his impending union to Ozah-guscoday-wayquay, Johnston asserts "that this was to be an alliance between two noble houses," finishing his letter with a chivalric flourish by "prais[ing] the beauty of his lady, and her virtue" (41). Despite all of her vast cultural differences, Johnston imagines Ozah-guscoday-wayquay to be of equal rank to himself—and therefore worthy of binding his family's reputation and fortunes to her own. While it is impossible to know how the historical Johnston really understood his spouse's social position compared to his own, in *The Invasion*'s fictional account Johnston's rationalization is presented as completely ingenuous. Johnston truly believes that he is forming a new aristocracy in the *pays d'en haut*, even going so far as creating "a crest of his own devising" comprised of "a crane, totem of the home band of St. Mary's, several elk heads, and the motto *Vive ut Postea Vivas*" (64).

Johnston's adoption of the Crane doodem[54] is more than symbolic. After his marriage to Ozah-guscoday-wayquay, Johnston finds that: "the attitude of the Indians had changed toward him, and realized in himself also a changed attitude. A corner of the blanket of Waub-ojeeg had descended upon his shoulders, involving, besides greater favor of the Indians, greater responsibilities" (48). By recognizing and submitting himself to Anishinaabe political authority, Johnston is compelled to enter into the reciprocal-communalist system of Anishinaabe kinship networks, which in turn forces him to forgo the exploitation of Anishinaabe land and labor, and instead support his kin. Under the continued tutelage of Waub-ojeeg and Ozah-guscoday-wayquay, Johnston ultimately becomes a good kinsman who redirects wealth back to his doodem. By the time of his death, "Johnston's books [. . .] showed a loss of nearly forty thousand dollars in credits to individual Indians [. . .] and the chance that any of it would ever be repaid to the estate was, at that time, negligible" (149). Driven by his own sense of largesse, Johnston has forsaken the profit motive, imagining his gifts of trade goods to the Anishinaabeg as the noblesse oblige of a feudal lord instead of an expenditure of capital in the form of credit. Johnston has been integrated into Anishinaabe kinship networks in a manner that contradicts his identity as a capitalist, but not as a Euro-American.[55]

The key role of Johnston and Ozah-guscoday-wayquay's relationship in the narrative structure of *The Invasion* is to undermine the sense of settler-colonialism as an inevitable outcome of Euro-American-Native contact. Showing the possibility for mutual interdependence borne out of a respect for Native political authority, Ozah-guscodaway-quay and Johnston act as a model for what Lewis describes as "the weaving together of two races, and a possible way of coexisting."[56] It is vital to recognize, however, the degree to which this possible mode of coexistence is predicated on the mitigation of Johnston's capitalist impulses and adoption of Ozah-guscoday-wayquay's system of redistributive kinship obligations. This is an important distinction to make, as *The Invasion* takes pains to present Johnston as the rarest of exceptions in the otherwise exploitative and incredibly disruptive fur trade economy, which Lewis describes in an interview as "terrible for the Indians," explaining it as the embodiment of "the passion the European had for clearing out whatever could be taken from the continent."[57]

The Invasion presents the marriage of Ozah-guscoday-wayquay and Johnston's daughter, Jane Johnston, to Henry Rowe Schoolcraft as souring any potential for reciprocity. The educated, sophisticated Jane is the embodiment of the harmonious admixture of her mother and father's respective cultural traditions, making her the perfect ambassador for the coming age of increased Euro-American–Anishinaabe contact. *The Invasion* presents Schoolcraft, however, as a character who cannot see Indians—even his own wife—as his intellectual or cultural equals. The novel presents the marriage of these two as inherently exploitative, with Schoolcraft using Jane and her family as a social, cultural, and political resource on which he capitalizes for his own benefit. Where Schoolcraft is initially dependent on the knowledge and political power of Jane and her family for his very survival, by the end of his time in the narrative Schoolcraft has ascended to dizzying heights of fame and success, while the fortunes of the Johnstons have precipitously declined—along with those of the Anishinaabeg generally.

Through it all, *The Invasion* carefully fosters a sense that all of Schoolcraft's gains are ill gotten, achieved only through the efforts of the Anishinaabeg helping him.[58] The triumph of Schoolcraft's discovery of Lake Itasca is undercut with the biting description of his "having been led there by the hand, as it were, by an Ojibway from Leech Lake" (193). Despite producing a grammar and vocabulary of Anishinaabemowin, Schoolcraft continues to find the language "pleasanter to record and systematize than to speak," meaning that he "never, to the end of his career, dispensed with the services of an interpreter" (120). The culmination of Schoolcraft's career, *Algic Researches*, is described not as the product of his genius, but merely as a collection of "material which had, as it were, been selected for him by Jane Schoolcraft" (226). The combined effect of such passages is to confirm the sense that the entirety of Schoolcraft's success is predicated on settler-colonial expropriation—taking Indian land and knowledge and refiguring it as his own, all the while obscuring the agency and specificity of the Indians from whom he steals.

In *The Invasion* Schoolcraft acts, quite literally, as the agent responsible for the dispossession of the Anishinaabeg. Installed as the Indian agent of the Sault, Schoolcraft becomes the highest-ranking representative of the United States in the area, using his influence and kinship connections to gain access to the Anishinaabeg's material and cultural resources. Although he has the dubious distinction of being "associated, in one way or another, with and personally present at every treaty made with the Ojibways since 1820" (190), *The Invasion* does not pay much attention to Schoolcraft's work as an Indian agent. Instead, the novel focuses on his Schoolcraft's role as an ethnographer, showing how his idiosyncratic biases worked to shape the perception of the Anishinaabeg for centuries.

In one particularly evocative scene, *The Invasion* illustrates the degree to which Schoolcraft claims intellectual ownership over the Anishinaabeg.

Schoolcraft, frustrated by what he perceives to be Anishinaabemowin's "tendency to clutter up general ideas with particular meanings" (120), decides to "reform the Ojibway language from the foundations up" (122).

> He wanted a monosyllabic Ojibway. He was willing, for the sake of rhythmic variety, to retain a few dissyllables as well. He wanted pronouns which declined themselves regularly; he wanted nouns to form their plurals, their pejoratives, diminutives, and augmentatives regularly, and he wished to increase the number of words expressing abstract ideas. He was willing to retain all existing monosyllables, provided he might regulate their changes, but the polysyllables he intended to reduce. . . . He found it necessary to add to the language new sounds it had never contained, the English *f*, *l*, *r*, and *v*, and when he had done so, felt himself well on the way to achieving "a language of great brevity, terseness, regularity and poetic expressiveness." (122)

The imperious tone of the passage highlights the arrogance of Schoolcraft's attitude toward the Anishinaabeg, just as the repetition of the phrase "he wanted" reveals his underlying desire for possession. Even as he facilitates the conveyance of Anishinaabe land into American hands, Schoolcraft mines the intellectual resources of the Anishinaabeg, transforming the raw materials of their language, history, and culture into a narrative of racial inferiority that legitimates the U.S. project of dispossession. In the novel, Schoolcraft's desire to remake the Anishinaabe language is a metonymy for the United States' historical treatment of indigenous peoples as a whole. His desire to possess the language while reforming it according to his own desires reflects the contradictory drives of settler-colonial dominance—the desire for authentic indigenous cultural knowledge, while simultaneously demanding Indian assimilation to Euro-American cultural and social practices.

This metonymic significance is further reinforced in *The Invasion* in its treatment of *The Song of Hiawatha*, released at the exact moment that, "in accordance with the Treaty of 1855, the bands were dissolved and the Ojibway nation ceased to be a reality" (226). Schoolcraft's efforts to convey both Anishinaabe culture and land into the hands of whites lay the groundwork for the emergence of a fully formed settler-colonial regime. In a sustained juxtaposition, *The Invasion* lays bare the ideological similarity of *Hiawatha* and the Treaty of 1855, revealing how these two pieces of writing work in tandem to facilitate the dispossession of the

Anishinaabeg. As Lewis writes: "The nation in general, now that the West was safe for civilization, the Indian question having been solved by treaty, deportation, and other methods kinder not to mention, was delighted to contemplate the Indian as 'a human being capable of the tenderest emotions'" (226). Even as Euro-Americans embrace a mythic Indianness as their own cultural patrimony, they simultaneously deny the continued existence of the actual Anishinaabeg, who have been transformed into mere "citizens of the United States, having varying ancestry" (224).

The Indians Shut The Door

Despite the enormity of these losses, *The Invasion* maintains the potential for a renegotiation of the settler-indigenous relationship in a scene that comes near the end of the novel.[59] In it, an English immigrant farmer named John returns from a day of haying with his son only to discover a family of Anishinaabeg occupying his rustic cabin. John, opening the door, is taken aback by what he sees inside his own house, thinking, "My God . . . there was all the Indians of the country here!" The Anishinaabeg, who have already made a fire and have made a general survey of the contents of the house, silently invite John to sit on a bench "where they had cleared a place for him." Seemingly overcome by surprise, John glances "from figure to figure," and receiving no explanation, lapses into "a trancelike stillness, gazing steadily before him at nothing." Only after a long moment does one of the Anishinaabe men "very amiably" ask John, "'This your house?'" (242).

Confronted thus, *The Invasion* makes John into the paradigmatic settler at the moment of traumatic confrontation with the reassertion of indigenous title. Initially conforming to his role as settler, John employs a series of disavowals and rationalizing narratives in an attempt to counter the indigenous claim of prior occupancy being made against his house. John's first impulse is to describe his ownership of the cabin, explaining that he "built this house . . . about fifteen years ago." John tells the Anishinaabeg, "you can stay as long as you like. And if anyone says you can't, you say John Porter said you could." What at first seems to be a charitable offer, under closer scrutiny, proves to have a much more ambivalent significance. First, the Anishinaabeg's ability to stay in the cabin is predicated on acknowledging John's proper claim of ownership. Moreover John lets the Anishinaabeg know they can stay only because the cabin is unfit for habitation by whites: "We used to stay here, but a year or two ago some vagabones got in here and filled it up with bugs. So we ain't used it none since" (243). Bear's band can occupy the house, but only because it is suitable only for "vagabones"—unclean, uncivilized nomads who can only temporarily occupy territory instead of owning it. The sense that John's offer is somewhat cynical is compounded by the fact that, after receiving no acknowledgment from the Anishinaabeg for his offer, "he paused and turned his head aside with the movement of a man about to spit" (243).

Instead of spitting, John launches into an extended monologue (one of the longest stretches of dialogue in *The Invasion*), explaining his long history, recounting his experiences as a laborer and a farmer, and espousing his moral views on liquor and tobacco. The Anishinaabeg, for their part, simply listen. John's compulsive narration is presented as an explicitly solipsistic act, meant to distance himself from the reality he is confronted with: "At any time when he had more than a single disconnected remark to make his voice assumed a narrative tone, slightly softer and more resonant than his usual speech. It was like the steady unseeing gaze of his eyes, and it produced a certain impersonality, on the smooth ground of which figures moved." Conflating John's ability to speak with an inability to see, this description reflects what Mark Rifkin describes as "feelings of rupture, disorientation, backwardness" that mark "those moments when settler sensoria reach their limits [when] confronted by indigenous presence."[60] John's need to rationalize his presence in the house through narrative not only distances him from the Anishinaabeg, but also makes him unlike himself. The "impersonality" of John's narrative reduces the people and the land itself to mere abstractions, indistinct "figures" moving on "smooth ground." By continually narrating his claim to the house, John produces a willful kind of blindness, which keeps him from seeing himself as an interloper.

Having exhausted his repertoire of narrative claims to the cabin, John finally seems to relent, lapsing into silence once it becomes clear that most of the Anishinaabeg don't understand English. As he sits, his eyes—which were once "steady and unseeing"—begin to take in the landscape, along with the people on it.

> He could look far across the fields to the fringe of small bush where Young John was going, and above hung the Mountain, a blue lake. To the north a heavy bank of cloud, blue like the Mountain, somber and cold, was gathering with speed, but left the sunset unobstructed. [. . .] The Indians began to move about. Pitonoquod had hung his felt hat on a nail. The women were spreading quilts over the hay in the bunks. There

was a little talk, the pat and shuffle of feet on boards, slowly. Old John sat very still and felt tired. (244–45)

Only once he stops talking about his ownership of the land, does it cease being an abstraction—as do the Anishinaabeg. John's silence and stillness not only allow him to finally see the land for what it is, but allows for the Anishinaabeg to go about their business undisturbed, all too happy to ignore the presence of the old man. The moment subtly recalls the historical sovereignty of the Anishinaabeg at the beginning of the novel with its reference to the approaching clouds. The name of one of the Anishinaabeg, Pitonoquod (Bidaanakwad, "Cloud Approaching") is the same as that of the trespasser Waub-ojeeg sits in judgment of in the first chapter of the novel. Yet, where the earlier Cloud Approaching was chastised by Waub-ojeeg for trespassing on another Anishinaabe's trapping grounds, in this instance Pitonoquod's trespass seems like an act of justice. While John lapses into silence, Pitonoquod, in a richly symbolic act, hangs his hat, claiming the cabin as his home.

The coming clouds bear a different kind of omen for Old John, who is described via a particularly interesting simile: "He was covered with light, like a very fine sand thrown over body and feet; among the darker moving figures he loomed, somehow, like far shores on still, sunny mornings" (245). In a book that employs figurative language skillfully—and sparingly—the tortuousness of this simile cannot help but draw the reader's attention, creating a moment of hesitation. How, in fact, may far shores loom? The answer may lie in the simile's metonymic implication. The far away shores are, I think, those of Europe, made present in the person of Old John. The distinctness of John's light figure against that of the darker Anishinaabeg makes the implication even clearer. What really looms over the scene is the history of Euro-American colonization, a presence that suddenly seems disturbingly intrusive.

The scene ends with an unambiguous moment of unsettlement. As John leaves the house, the narrative perspective suddenly shifts to the point of the Anishinaabeg: "The Indians watched them go. As they entered into the small bush, where the wagon was, the first drops of rain struck sharply on the roof, and sang, like whips, on the tin of the stovepipe. The Indians shut the door" (245). Finally, in the final pages of *The Invasion*, we have a symbolic reversal (however minor) of the seemingly inexorable onslaught of settler-colonialism: the Anishinaabeg have regained a domestic space that they are free to manage, without interference from non-Natives. For this to happen, however, takes recognition on the part of the settler of the validity of indigenous claims *and* a willingness to relinquish his sense of sovereign entitlement. It is not simply enough to let the Indians continue to exist, the settler must also give up (as John eventually does) their right to define history exclusively by their own terms. *The Invasion* does not represent this as an easy, or even very desirable, outcome for the settler—John, after all, is left exposed to the elements without food—yet one cannot escape the sense that it is correct. The recognition of Indian rights, and the subsequent relinquishment of settler-colonial privileges, cannot be had without material and emotional sacrifice on the part of the settler—it must be an unsettling experience.

Old John's recognition of the Anishinaabeg's indigenous claim resonates with another recognition the Anishinaabeg of Michigan would receive a few short years after the publication of *The Invasion*. Since the early twenties, various Anishinaabe groups across northern Michigan had petitioned the federal government to recognize the usufructory rights to fish and game, but had met with only limited success. One of the earliest and most vocal of these Anishinaabe activists was William Meddaugh Johnstone—brother of Molly, and one of the most significant of Janet Lewis's collaborators in writing *The Invasion*.

As is all too often the case with Anishinaabeg of his time, information on William Johnstone's life is scarce, lived as it was on the geographic and social margins of the United States. What we know of him can only be pieced together from the archival fragments he left behind: mentions in local papers, his letters to Lewis, and (most incredibly) a collection of personal records discovered by chance in an abandoned house many decades after his death. Among Johnstone's personal memorabilia is the guest ledger from O-Non-E-Gwud, a program for Kabaosa's production of *Hiawatha, or Nanabozho* at Desbarats, and a number of clippings drawn from local and national newspapers—almost all of which concern issues impacting Native people. While some are merely items of curiosity (such as a proposal to build a giant statue of an Indian in New York Harbor to match the Statue of Liberty), many more are about Natives protesting issues of land fraud, treaty rights, and abuse at the hands of the government (of particular interest seems to have been the political fallout of the allotment process at White Earth).[61] From these scattered sources, a fascinating picture emerges of Lewis's interlocutor as a deeply intelligent, though uneducated, man with a strong commitment to his family and the Anishinaabeg people, and who dedicated much of his life to the fight to regain recognition for the Michigan Anishinaabeg.

From his letters, we know that William Johnstone had spearheaded efforts to reestablish treaty rights for the Anishinaabeg at the Sault during the first decades of the twentieth century. In 1915, he traveled to Washington, DC for the first time to meet with the Commissioner of Indian Affairs to plead the case for reinstating the treaty rights of the Anishinaabeg at the Sault. Johnstone's primary contention was that the second Treaty of 1855, which invalidated several provisions of the first treaty signed two days earlier by dissolving the Anishinaabeg as a political body, was made fraudulently. After laying out his case, he was told by a Bureau of Indian Affairs (BIA) representative that he needed affidavits from each claimant showing their connection to the six original bands at the Sault before any review would commence. Over the next three years, William Johnstone collected affidavits from the Anishinaabeg at the Sault, returning to Washington with Congressman Frank Scott to deliver them in 1918. The result was disappointing. As he would relate in a letter to Janet Lewis, "I went with [Scott] before some of the Committee on Indian Affairs and explained the case to them. They seemed satisfied and told me that the matter would be brought up before the whole Committee some time later and that there wouldn't be any need of my staying there under expense any longer so I came home." Despite their promises, Scott and the others members of the committee did nothing to address the concerns of the Anishinaabeg at the Sault. Johnstone soon realized, as he would write to Lewis, the committee's hollow promises were made "just to get rid of me."[62]

Two years after the publication of *The Invasion*, the political situation of the Michigan Anishinaabeg changed dramatically. After years of concerted efforts on the part of both Native and non-Native activists led by newly installed BIA chief John Collier, the Wheeler-Howard Act (better known as the Indian Reorganization Act, or IRA) was passed in 1934. The legislation ended the practice of allotment as well as the oversight of federal Indian agents, recognizing the legal right for Indian tribes to exist as self-governing bodies. Importantly, the IRA provided Indian tribes with the ability to buy private property and convey it into communal land held in trust—giving tribes a method by which to begin to undo the damage of centuries of dispossession. The potential for the Anishinaabeg of Michigan to benefit from the IRA initially seemed doubtful, however, having "voluntarily" terminated their political status in 1855.

In 1936 the Bureau of Indian Affairs published a memorandum that suggested that it had been misinterpreting the Treaty of 1855. The memo reframed the treaty's termination clause, which dissolved "the tribal organization of [. . .] Ottawa and Chippewa Indians," suggesting that the framers of the treaty merely intended to sever the formal affiliation of the Odawa and Ojibwe in the region, but left their right to exist as independent nations intact.[63] Soon, the BIA began meeting with representatives of the Sault and other Anishinaabe bands to discuss the possibility of reorganizing their governments and reestablishing their land bases. So began a process of reestablishing Anishinaabe reservations across Northern Michigan, starting with Bay Mills Indian Community in 1936, followed thereafter by the Sault Ste. Marie Tribe of Chippewa Indians in 1972, the Grand Traverse Band of Chippewa and Ottawa Indians in 1980, and the Little Traverse Bay Band of Odawa in 1994.[64]

It is not difficult to see in the BIA's dramatic policy reversal the same kind of renegotiation of history taking place in *The Invasion*, but this is not to say that the novel played a role in the BIA's decision. Instead, I believe that *The Invasion* is better understood as representing an emergent structure of feeling about the legitimacy of Native sovereignty that gained traction among left-leaning elites in the United States in the early twentieth century. In its recognition of a coherent Anishinaabe historical perspective, *The Invasion* prefigures a similar (if imperfect) attempt to recognize the validity of indigenous nationhood through the IRA. This family resemblance is not incidental, as the creative reinterpretation of history is, in many ways, a precondition for political change. As Lorenzo Veracini explains,

> all processes of constitutional rearrangement involving indigenous constituencies in settler nations have necessitated a significant revision of traditional historical narratives and a comprehensive reinterpretation of national and/or regional pasts. Indeed, the role of historians in contributing to institutional and judicial readjustment has in some cases been decisive, and historians and other academics involved in the production of indigenous and national histories in settler societies have in some cases made history by literally (re) writing it.[65]

While not explicitly acknowledged in Veracini's argument, indigenous peoples' access to the means of writing and publishing their own historical counternarratives has been (and continues to be) severely limited. This was especially the case for the Anishinaabeg of Upper Michigan in the first years of the twentieth century, as they faced incredible economic and social hardships in the wake of allotment. As William Johnstone's struggle to bend the ear of BIA officials testifies, the effort to regain recognition for the Michigan Anishinaabeg would demand a tremendous amount of political and cultural capital.

Given his involvement in the efforts of the Sault bands to regain legal recognition, it is tempting to see William Johnstone's collaboration with Lewis as a way of gaining access to the social and political circles that he had been shut out of. Lewis was, after all, no stranger to protests against the BIA and federal Indian policy. During her time at Sunmount, Lewis was part of a committee of artists, writers, and musicians who lent their voices in support of the Pueblos' effort to stop the passage of the Bursum Bill. The proposed legislation was largely seen as a Euro-American land grab, as it would have legitimated the deeds of non-Natives who had illegally settled on unceded Pueblo lands. Opposition to Bursum was led by John Collier, along with Mary Austin, Oliver La Farge, Mabel Dodge Luhan, Yvor Winters, and others who organized fund-raisers and protests against the bill. After waging a months' long publicity campaign that included bringing Pueblo representatives to Washington to testify against the bill, and the publication of a scathing *New York Times* editorial by D. H. Lawrence, opponents to Bursum won the day. Having failed to achieve his goal through official channels, it is certainly possible that William Johnstone thought of Lewis's book as a way of drawing attention to the cause of the Anishinaabeg at the Sault—the same way Lawrence's essay had for the Pueblos of New Mexico.

As a white, middle-class writer, Janet Lewis had access to exactly the kind of resources that would allow her to bring the history of the Michigan Anishinaabeg to light. Without Lewis's bona fides as a graduate of the University of Chicago, and expansive social network of well-connected friends, it is highly unlikely that a book as strange as *The Invasion* could have ever been published. The active participation of the Johnstone family in the production of *The Invasion* testifies to their belief that their story needed to be heard, just as Lewis's conscientious writing testifies to her respect for the trust the Johnstones placed in her to tell it. That Hemingway's troubling fiction remains popular while *The Invasion* remains largely unknown and unread speaks, to my mind, to the degree to which it is a story that is still in desperate need of being heard.

The history of *The Invasion*'s publication brings up a challenging question for the study of Native American literary nationalism. Should Lewis's novel be regarded alongside William Whipple Warren's *History of the Ojibway People*, or Louise Erdrich's *Tracks*, as an important work of Anishinaabe nationalism? I think so. Allow me to be clear: I am not suggesting that Janet Lewis should be thought of as an Anishinaabe person. Only that *The Invasion*, as a literary text, is aligned with the interests of the Anishinaabe nation in such a way that we may reasonably call it nationalist. This, of course, assumes that nationalism is not an identity but an ideology, a set of political convictions about the right of certain peoples to continue to exist as self-defining, self-governing political bodies. Indigenous nationalism, at least in the literary realm, is quite simply the effort to counter the representational strategies of settler-colonialism with an alternative discourse of Native continuity—biological, legal, cultural, and social—that instantiates the possibility for indigenous nationhood in the mind of readers (readers who are, it must be said, mostly non-Native). As such, indigenous nationalism seems to be an ideological position open to anyone who recognizes, and advocates for, the continuity of indigenous nations—whether or not they belong to those nations. Expanding our idea of who can participate in the political project of contemporary indigenous nationalism allows us to understand settler-colonialism as an ideology that—despite its strong entrenchment in settler society—non-Natives can learn to reject.

Chapter 3

What Is This I Promise You?
The Translation of Anishinaabe Song in the Twentieth Century

> I think myths are appropriated to our experience, myths from the long distant past, but we also appropriated things that happen to us in our daily lives, very immediate things. In the oral tradition these recent appropriations have a way of becoming merged with the whole of our experience. It is a process of renewal . . . I think that space age terminology, for example, will become a diction in mythology and in a hundred or two years or even two hundred generations will constitute a valid part of oral tradition. I see no reason to think otherwise.
>
> —N. Scott Momaday

> It's so strange you don't remember any of your poetry.
>
> —Nobody to William Blake
> Jim Jarmusch, *Dead Man*

TONY SOPRANO SITS IN A HOSPITAL ROOM, recovering from heart surgery. Across from him, Christopher, heir to the Soprano crime family, attempts to make small talk with the boss, but has difficulty breaking through Tony's morphine-induced haze. Unable to meet Tony's glassy stare, Chris looks across the room to a corkboard, covered in cards offering well-wishes and hopes for a speedy recovery. The camera lingers on one card in particular—a simple beige index card amid a tumult of color. On it is written, in block letters, is what appears to be a short poem with a curious attribution. "'Sometimes I go about in pity for myself,'" Chris reads aloud, "'and all the while, a great wind carries me across the sky.' O-jee-bwee saying." Chris looks back to Tony, who is now staring intently at the note, seemingly shocked into a degree of consciousness. Chris points at the note, and says: "Indians, right? Who put this up?"[1]

It's a very good question. Where could such a thing come from, and how did it wind up on premium cable? The answer is complicated.

The text hanging in Tony Soprano's hospital room is not actually a proverb, but the lyrics of an Anishinaabe nagamon, or song. The nagamon was originally performed by a man named Ga'gandac', who lived on the White Earth Reservation at the turn of the twentieth century. The song was recorded on wax cylinder by an ethnologist named Frances Densmore, who classified it as an example of ina'bûndjīgañ nagûmo'wīn (inaabandjigan nagamowin), or "dream singing."[2] As Densmore reports, such nagamonan were originally composed as a means of communicating with the manidoog. The imagery of the song is based on a dream that the song's composer (probably Ga'gandac') received from these powerful beings—in this case, the animikiig, or thunderbirds.

To understand how an Anishinaabe nagamon became part of American pop culture requires tracing a complicated path that winds its way through the entire twentieth century. Starting with Densmore's original recordings, this chapter charts the history of the nagamonan's production and reception as poetry, revealing the overlooked role Anishinaabe song played in the development of theories of translation, poetics, and Native identity over the course of the twentieth century. While certainly not the only work of indigenous ethnographic material to influence these debates, the case of the nagamonan is particularly rich, as they remained an item of curiosity and inspiration for multiple generations of writers—including some of the most significant voices in American poetry.

Essential to this history are the changing attitudes toward tribal sovereignty during the middle decades of the twentieth century. Starting with early readers' assumption that the songs represented a "primitive" form of poetry in need of Euro-American editorial intervention—an idea reflective of the assimilationist policies of the allotment era—this chapter goes on to show how succeeding generations of poets have interpreted the nagamonan using the same philosophical assumptions that informed federal Indian policy's dialectical shifts over the course of the century. The second half of the chapter focuses on the interpretive strategies of two poets, Gerald Vizenor and Jerome Rothenberg, whose work on the nagamonan reflects the tumultuous period of federal Termination policy and the subsequent efforts of Native peoples to resist it. In showing how the way we think about the translation of oral material into poetry entails larger questions about interpretation, culture, and temporality, I argue that the attempt to re-create an "authentic" sense of a song's original meaning in poetry serves to reify potentially damaging assumptions about the cultural authority of ethnographic recordings and the colonial archive in which they are held.

The Tireless Throb of the Drum

After hearing a Native drum group perform at the Columbian Exposition in Chicago, Frances Densmore found herself "scared almost to death."[3] Born to a white family in southern Minnesota five short years after the Dakota Uprising of 1862, her fear was understandable. Densmore likely grew up hearing tales of the wild savagery of Indians from older settlers who had lived through that tumultuous time. As a child, she occasionally heard the distant drumming of nearby Dakotas, a sound she found both disconcerting and fascinating. She carried these early experiences with her to Oberlin and eventually Boston, where she studied musical performance and composition. In 1893, Densmore traveled to Chicago's World's Fair, hoping to see performances of some of the world's greatest operatic and symphonic talents. Instead, she heard something that must have seemed both alien and oddly familiar—the steady beat of a pow-wow drum. "I saw Indians dancing and heard them singing," she later wrote, "that was my *start* on this subject."[4]

Returning from Chicago, Densmore threw herself into the study of tribal music with all of the single-minded persistence that would come to define her career and personality. "For the next ten years," she wrote in her memoirs, "I soaked my receptive mind in what army officers wrote about Indians, and what historians wrote about Indians, with some of the publications of the Bureau of American Ethnology, with which I was later to be connected."[5] Densmore started with Alice Fletcher's *A Study of Omaha Indian Music* (1893), a pioneering work that proposed the systemic study of indigenous song. Fletcher, an ethnological researcher at Harvard's Peabody Museum, was also a major figure in Boston's Friends of the Indian movement, having been one of the primary architects of allotment policy in the United States. Leveraging her Boston contacts, Densmore sought out the acquaintance of Fletcher's collaborator at the Peabody, John Fillmore, and eventually Fletcher herself, who encouraged Densmore to research tribal music in her home state of Minnesota. After securing financial assistance from the Smithsonian's Bureau of American Ethnology, Densmore began her research in earnest, traveling to Anishinaabe reservations throughout Minnesota and Wisconsin in order to record their songs.

One of Densmore's first outings was a 1906 trip to White Earth, where she hoped to observe musical performances at the annual celebration of the reservation's founding. There she met Mary Warren English, an educated Anishinaabe woman who would help to launch her career. A member of an influential family, English was the granddaughter of Michel Cadotte (an important figure in the American fur trade) and sister to the noted Anishinaabe historian William Whipple Warren. English was quite accomplished herself, having served for decades as both an educator and administrator at Indian schools in Wisconsin and Minnesota, and eventually named principal of the boarding school at Red Lake.[6] Already in her seventies by the time Densmore met her, English had retired to White Earth, where she remained an active part of the community (she organized, for instance, a production of Kabaosa's *Hiawatha* that played intermittently at White Earth between 1903 and 1917[7]). Over the next decade, English would aid in almost every aspect of Densmore's studies as a fixer, informant, and, most importantly, translator. Drawing on English's connections to Anishinaabeg communities throughout the Midwest, Densmore gained access to numerous informants, including several respected members of the Midewewin—allowing her to record, transcribe, and translate hundreds of nagamonan from Anishinaabe communities across Minnesota and Wisconsin.

The enormous scope of Densmore's research was enabled by her use of a relatively new technology: the wax cylinder phonograph. Unlike earlier ethnomusicologists who recorded Native songs by taking extensive notes in the field, Densmore preferred to record her subjects in a controlled environment, as she put it, "to free [the singers] from constraint or embarrassment, in order that the recorded song may be free and natural."[8] As she traveled to various reservations, Densmore often set up a makeshift recording studio in the offices of the local Indian Agent, where she would record her informant's performances. Not only did the phonograph let Densmore record many songs quickly, they also allowed her to transcribe both the melodies of Anishinaabe songs and their lyrics at an unprecedented level of detail, producing scores so accurate they even note when a particular tone was slightly out of pitch (fig. 3.1).

The phonograph also made translating the lyrics of the nagamonan much easier, as she needed only replay the recordings back to an interpreter who could provide a transcription of the original Anishinaabemowin as well as word-for-word translations. Densmore invariably chose her translators from the ranks of White Earth's mixed-blood elite, many of whom had received formal education. Although she retained the services of several interpreters (including Gus Beaulieu and Rev. Clement Beaulieu Jr.), Densmore seems to have preferred working with

Figure 3.1. Score and translation of "No. 64 'Initiation Song'" as it appears in Densmore's *Chippewa Music*.

English, who she thought "very discriminating in the choice of words in her translations." For example, Densmore explained that English "objected to the word 'pity' used by some other interpreters concerning the attitude of the spirits, saying it suggested condescension, while the Chippewa term was used only by persons who were equals."[9]

English's nuanced understanding of Anishinaabe traditions was likely critical for the translation of the songs of the Midewewin, which demanded, in Densmore's words, "special skill."[10] For most nagamonan, Densmore found, lyrics were relatively unimportant, observing, "In a succession of several renditions of a song it is not unusual to find the words occurring only once."[11] Midewewin songs were an exception, as they were consistently performed with the same lyrics every time, with little deviation between singers—even across large geographic distances. The lyrics of Mide songs, Densmore found, were intrinsic to their power and meaning, having been passed down to Midewewin practitioners over generations. The antiquity of the songs meant that many contained words "unknown in the conversational Chippewa of the present time," making their "literal translation . . . meaningless" to those without the linguistic faculty or proper ritual instruction.[12] Preserving these songs was of particular importance to Densmore, who saw them as both the most culturally significant to the Anishinaabeg, and the most in danger of being lost to history.

Densmore primarily understood her work among the Anishinaabeg as a pressing mission to ensure that "Indian music, or the knowledge of it, should 'not perish from the earth' "—a goal motivated by a complex mixture of scientific rationality and genuine appreciation of indigenous music.[13] Like many of her contemporaries, Densmore believed in stadialism: the assumption that all human culture developed in a linear fashion from barbarism to civilization, and that the world's various peoples occupied different levels of development.[14] By collecting Anishinaabe songs, especially those of the Midewewin, Densmore wanted to find a window back into the history of human cultural and psychological development, hoping to discover there the "natural laws which govern musical expression."[15] At the same time, Densmore's ethnographic writings—often precise and detached—occasionally betray a much less objective impulse, revealing a deep admiration for the artistry of Anishinaabe singers. Describing a recording session with Gage'bīnes, "a young man, a mixed-blood, who had a pleasing voice and a particularly agreeable manner," Densmore reported, "[h]e sang the plaintive songs so well that he was encouraged to keep to that style; he gave eight songs in all, five of which were love songs . . . ."[16]

The conflict between Densmore's role as a dispassionate social scientist and her evident love of a people and their culture colors both volumes of *Chippewa Music*. Published by the Smithsonian's Bureau of American Ethnology in 1910 and 1913, the books represent the culmination of Densmore's research, containing scores, transcripts, translations, and interpretive notes for more than three hundred nagamonan, along with analysis of Anishinaabe material culture, social custom, and ritual. More than a collection of ethnographic data, however, *Chippewa Music* also contains brief, but affectionate portraits of the women and men (such as Gage'bīnes) who performed for Densmore, along with surprisingly beautiful descriptions of the communal life their songs helped to maintain.

> The dancing, which began in the morning, was continued with little intermission until after midnight. The scene was lighted by a full moon, round and red above the pine trees. Hour after hour was heard the tireless throb of the drum and the shrill voices of the singers; at last they ceased and the camp fell asleep—all but the dogs, which barked until daybreak. At last they too were quiet, and one was reminded of the words of an old Chippewa war song, "When the dogs are still I will be ready to do mischief." A grey light struggled across the sky. It was the hour most dreaded in Indian warfare, the hour when so many terrible attacks were made. Yet in forgetfulness of the past and without fear of the future the little village slept.[17]

Chippewa Music, in its articulation of a new, systemic approach to the study of folk music, was a foundational text for the emerging field ethnomusicology. Building on her techniques, those who followed in Densmore's footsteps quickly surpassed her makeshift methods of recording and transcription, creating ever more detailed and accurate methods of collection, notation, and analysis. By the 1930s, Densmore had difficulties raising funds for her fieldwork, even while fellow musicologists John and Alan Lomax traveled the country making recordings on behalf of the Library of Congress. As is the case with any scientific text in an increasingly sophisticated field, *Chippewa Music* was eventually relegated to obsolescence. But even as Densmore's star faded in her own field, her work would gain lasting significance among a wholly different kind of audience.

The Chippeway in the Drawing Room

In 1917, *Poetry* magazine published a short, but glowing review of *Chippewa Music* by Carl Sandburg, who lamented that Densmore's work had not received "even such notice as it deserves in 'news value,'" a situation he blamed squarely on the Bureau of American Ethnology (BAE). "As no efforts are made by that organization to exploit and advertise a writer," Sandburg declared, "the researches and translations have slumbered in a more or less innocuous desuetude." Hoping to correct this oversight, Sandburg reprinted the English language translations of four songs and the evocative titles (such as "Song of the Game of Silence") of several more. Other than the omission of the Anishinaabemowin lyrics, the translations appeared in *Poetry* mostly as they had in *Chippewa Music*, but with added punctuation and more consistent line breaks.

> **Song for the Cure of the Sick**
> They are in close consultation
> With their heads together,
> Wenebojo and his grandmother.

The results, Sandburg joked, led to his "[s]uspicion . . . that the red man and his children committed direct plagiarism on our modern imagists and vorticists."[18]

Densmore's translations received even more exposure in 1918, when George Cronyn released *The Path on the Rainbow*. Ambitiously described as "the first authoritative volume of aboriginal American verse,"[19] the collection included more than forty of Densmore's translated nagamonan (along with several more from Henry Schoolcraft). In terms of line breaks and punctuation, Cronyn followed the form of Densmore's translations more faithfully than Sandburg had, but introduced a system of indentation not included in the originals.

> **Healing Song**
> They are in close consultation
>   with their heads together
> Wenabojo
> And his grandmother.[20]

The Path on the Rainbow proved to be quite popular, going through two printings in three months. Again, readers of Cronyn's collection drew a connection between Anishinaabe song and contemporary poetry. Mary Austin, in her introduction to the book, noted "the extraordinary likeness between much of this native product and the recent work of the Imagists, *vers librists*, and other literary fashionables," arguing that the songs were proof that modern American poets had unconsciously tapped into the indigenous spirit of the continent.[21]

Not all, however, were impressed with the nagamonan. In a review for *The Dial*, Louis Untermeyer called the translations "odd-shaped pieces of sentimentality" overburdened by an "arbitrary arrangement of words and a pretentious typography that is foreign to our native—though it may be native to Ezra Pound, 'H.D.,' and Richard Adington."[22] In a scathing review of *The Path on the Rainbow* published in 1919, T. S. Eliot offered this witheringly sarcastic scene.

> [S]uddenly, egged on by New York and Chicago *intelligentsia*, the romantic Chippeway bursts into the drawing-room, and among murmurs of approval declaims his
>
> **Maple Sugar Song.**
> Maple sugar
> is the only thing
> that satisfies me.
>
> The approval becomes acclimation. The Chippeway has the last word in subtlety, simplicity, and poeticality.

Eliot wasn't opposed to the publication of Native songs as poems, per se (although, one suspects, he may have made an exception for the "Maple Sugar Song"). Eliot wrote that modern poets should "welcome the publication of primitive poetry, because it has more significance, in relations to its own age or culture, than 'Kehama' or 'Aurora Leigh' have for theirs." To this end, however, he criticized Cronyn for his failing to provide adequate context for the translations, saying, "when the translator uses the word 'beauty,' the contemporary poet wants to know the Navajo equivalent for this word, and how near an equivalent it is." Despite these niggles, most of Eliot's criticism was focused on those who, on reading the poems, "yield to the weak credulity of crediting the savage with any gifts of mystical insight or artistic feeling that he does not possess himself."[23]

It isn't difficult to see Eliot's essay, with its bombastic rhetoric of savagery, as a reflection of its time. For more than five decades, federal policy had been directed toward eliminating the "savage" through boarding schools, allotment, and missionization. With his characteristic respect for tradition, Eliot endorses the idea that tribal cultures should survive, in a much diminished form, as a "heritage" for modern Americans—just as Ernest Seton was encouraging young children play Indian during their free time—but to see any special value in their continuing practice by actual Natives remains a bridge too far. The project of exploring tribal cultures, Eliot holds, should become the exclusive purview of the "artist," who Eliot describes as "the most competent to understand both civilized and primitive," and therefore the best prepared to see "how the savage, the barbarian and the rustic can be improved upon."[24]

"Improve" on the nagamonan, American poets certainly did, as they rushed to offer their own reworked "versions" of the songs. Alice Corbin Henderson, who built a career on such poetic interpretations, published several reworkings of the nagamonan in *Poetry*. One of these was the "Dancing Song of the Bi'jikiwuck'," originally sung by Maiñ'gans, which she rewrote thus:

> **Buffalo Dance**
>   Strike ye our land
> With curved horns!
> Now with cries
> Bending our bodies,
> Breathe fire upon us;
> Now with feet
> Trampling the earth,
> Let your hoofs
> Thunder over us!
> Strike ye our land
> With curved horns![25]

In a short interpretive essay, Henderson explains that she produced her poems by "tak[ing] the Indian key-note" from Densmore's texts "and expand[ing] it very slightly."[26] Henderson's additions were somewhat more extensive than she let on, however, as her poem nearly quintupled the length of the original translation, comprised of just seven words: "strike ye/our land / with curved horns."[27] While Henderson admits to "taking liberties with the originals," she insists that her revisions are "strictly within the spirit of them"—an assertion readers would have to take on faith, as she did not reprint the originals for comparison.[28] Henderson argued that interventions such as hers were necessary in order to consider "Indian poetry as poetry," since "the ethnologists" (read: Densmore) had "overlooked the literary significance of the Indian songs."[29]

In reality, Densmore was very much aware of the nagamonan's poetic potential. Two months after Henderson's reworkings appeared in *Poetry*, Densmore privately published a chapbook of her own interpretations, titled *Poems from Sioux and Chippewa Songs* (1917). With her characteristic rationality, Densmore presented the book as an experiment of sorts, explaining, "The inspiration of the poems was a desire to ascertain whether the rhythm of a song is expressive of its idea." To this end she attempted to rework the lyrics of the nagamonan in such a way that the resulting poems matched the rhythm of the original songs, which she compared using her wax cylinder recordings. This proved to be a challenge, however, since "the words were so few" in many Anishinaabe songs that it became necessary "to elaborate the idea in order that the words should fill the melody, adding such facts or concepts as are known to be associated with the song."[30] The resulting poems, like Henderson's, were many times longer than the original translations, but did include the original translations for comparison. In almost every other way, however, Densmore's interpretations were quite different form Henderson's imagistic reworkings, presented instead with a more classical hendecasyllabic meter reminiscent of ancient Greek poetry.

No. 12. To the Buffalo
Literal translation: "Strike ye our land with curved horns."

Strike ye now our land with your great curvéd
    horns;
In your mighty rage toss the turf in the air.
Strike ye now our land with your great curvéd
    horns;
We will hear the sound and our hearts will be
    strong;
When we go to war,
Give us of your strength in the time of our need,
King of all the plain—buffalo, buffalo.
Strike ye now our land with your great curvéd
    horns;
Lead us forth to the fight.[31]

Feeling her rhythmic translations to be a success, Densmore chose to publish the poems as part of yet another experiment: "to test the poetic quality of Indian songs by offering the verses themselves to those who in this manner may consider them apart from the music."[32] The results of this test, one must presume, proved inconclusive, as the book was not widely reviewed.

Another interpreter of Anishinaabe song (and arguably the most successful) was the poet and performer Lew Sarett, whose first two collections, Many, Many Moons (1920) and The Box of God (1922) consisted of what Sarett called "broad interpretations" of "Indian dance, song, and ritual."[33] Unlike Henderson and Densmore, Sarett claimed to base his poems not on preexisting ethnographic translations, but his own personal experiences. The son of Lithuanian and Polish immigrants, Sarett had briefly lived in Upper Michigan as a child, after his father moved the family from Chicago to look for work in the timber industry. During his five years in Michigan, Sarett claimed to have been adopted by local Anishinaabeg and given him the name Páy-shig-ah-deék (Bezhigadik), or "Lone Caribou." Despite leaving Michigan at the age of twelve, Sarett claimed to have amassed an extensive understanding of Anishinaabe language and ceremony. His poetry, he asserted, was an attempt to render this deep knowledge of Anishinaabe culture in the idiom of poetry. The results are less than convincing.

> "My frien', Ah-deek, you ask-um plenty hard question:
> Ugh! w'ere Kéetch-ie Má-ni-dó he live?
> W'ere all does Eenzhun spirits walk and talk?
> Me—I dunno! . . . Mebbe . . . mebbe overe here,
> In beaver pond, in t'rush, in gromping bullfrog;
> Mebbe over dere, he's sleeping in dose mountain. . . ."[34]

Coming soon after the success of Cronyn's Rainbow, Sarett's poetry received enthusiastic acclaim from critics, with The Box of God winning the prestigious Levinson Prize in 1921 (won the year before by Wallace Stevens, and the year after by Robert Frost). Reviewing the collection for Poetry magazine, Harriet Monroe compared it favorably to Eliot's Wasteland, saying: "If Mr. Eliot's subject is essentially a phantasmagoric fade-out of God, Mr. Sarett's is the search for God, for a larger god than men have ever entrapped in the churchly boxes they have made for him."[35] Louis Untermeyer, who had been so unsympathetic to The Path on the Rainbow, declared The Box of God to be "one of the most remarkably beautiful poems I've read in years."[36]

Perhaps more important than the critics, Sarett's poetry was also popular on the Chautauqua circuit, providing the up-and-coming poet with a steady stream of public readings in front of large audiences. Often appearing in a warbonnet, bandolier bag, and fringed leggings, Sarett presented himself as a cultural insider, who not only recited poetry, but also lectured on Anishinaabe customs, and performed various styles of tribal song and dance. When Sarett did read his poetry, he did so in an equally affected manner, chanting the words while accompanying himself on a hand drum. Sarett's use of costumes and props worked to blur the line between artistic and ritual performance for his Chautauqua audiences, who saw him as something more than a mere poet. As the *Boston Transcript* reported, Sarett was seen as a kind of racial medium: "Mr. Sarett makes one understand the Indian. We understand the Indian in relation to his thoughts, moods, his customs, his legends, his symbolism, his natural mysticism. With the poet's full equipment, he has psychologically become an Indian and thus his interpreter to the outside world."[37]

This quasi-shamanistic quality is evident in Sarett's poetry, which he claims is meant "to communicate something of the . . . spiritual significance of Indian ceremonies" to his readers.[38] To achieve this goal, Sarett contends, requires an entirely different approach to translating Anishinaabe song. Arguing that "[l]iteral translation . . . will rarely reveal the emotional and ideational content of a ceremony," because it produces only "fragmentary phrases . . . repeated over and over again, interspersed with apparently meaningless syllables and ejaculations." Sarett offers, instead, a more holistic approach.

> [I]f the fragmentary ideas be interpreted against a background of legend, or supplemented by the accompanying incidents of the dance,—its music, postures, gestures, and vocal embellishments,—if they be refracted through the prismatic glass of Indian imagination, the few words that are uttered may suggest a great colorful complex of ideas and emotions.[39]

Importantly, the goal of such translation is not to transmit an accurate sense of semantic meaning, but the affective experience of the ceremony itself. The embodied participation of the reader is apparent in the text of many of Sarett's poems, which include detailed instructions for reading the poem aloud, as in the following excerpt from "The Blue Duck," which Sarett described not as a poem, but as a "Chippewa Medicine Dance."

> Hí! Hi! Hí! Hi! Hí! Hi! Hí! Hi!
> Heé-ya! Hói-ya! Heé-ya! Hói-ya!
> Keetch-ie Má-ni-dó, Má-ni-dó,

> I place this pretty duck upon your hand;
> Upon its sunny palm and in its windy fingers.
> Hi-yeee! Blue and beautiful   *Faster, louder,*
> Is he, beautifully blue!   *with a vigorous*
> Carved from sleeping cedar   *lilting beat—*
> When the stars like silver fishes   *with abandon.*
> Were a-quiver in the rivers of the sky;[40]

The desired result of such poems is meant to be a kind of literary possession, in which "the consciousness of the genuine American Indian of today"[41] is made apprehendable through an incantatory act of reading—a theory that would take on increasing acceptance among poets in the latter part of the twentieth century.[42]

Sarett's sympathy for the Anishinaabeg seems not to have extended beyond the metaphysical, as he expressed a somewhat jaundiced view of their struggle for treaty rights. Writing in the notes to his "translations" of Anishinaabe oratory (what he called "Council Talks") appearing in *Many, Many Moons*, Sarett describes Anishinaabe protests over "certain alleged violations of the 'Treaty of 1889,' 'The Treaty of 1854' and other treaties" as representing "but one point of view." Taking an explicitly paternalist position, Sarett declares, "many of his complaints and hardships are due to misunderstanding, to government red tape, or to the Indian's own weaknesses and defects, and are therefore often unreasonable and prejudiced," but ultimately conceding that "there is in his cause a proper share of truth."[43]

Although Sarett attained immense popularity among the Chautauqua set, he had at least one very vocal detractor in Yvor Winters—critic, poet, and husband of Janet Lewis—who had little patience for those who "take the 'symbols' . . . of the living Indians and give them a 'meaning,' and usually . . . a damned sloppy one." Like his wife, Winters had spent several years in treatment for Tuberculosis at the Sunmount sanitarium in Santa Fe. It was there that he witnessed a recitation of Sarett's poem "Blue Duck" (excerpted above), performed by the Chickasaw actress Te Ata—a performance that moved him to write an open letter to Ernest Walsh's fashionable literary magazine *This Quarter*. Describing his letter as "a review of a review of a revue," Winters recounts the uproarious reaction of a Pueblo audience on hearing the performance of Sarett's poem.

> The Taos delegation wrapped their heads in their sheets and
> tried to strangle themselves, and one fell over backwards. One,
> in tears, pulled out a handkerchief, but had to give it up for

his sheet. Mothers from Tesuque and San Ildefonso tried to smother their infants, and all the little girls from the Indian school were lolling on one another's laps and shoulders from exhaustion. The old men from Tesuque, dressed up for the bow and arrow dance, almost ruined their makeup before they came on.

Winters takes the occasion of the Pueblos' laughter to launch a characteristically acerbic critique of Sarett and his so-called translation of an Anishinaabe ceremony, which he declares "obviously a fake." Lumping Sarett with Cronyn, Henderson, and others like them, Winters concludes, "this notion of interpreting the Indian is too much for me. They are in need of no assistance whatsoever, as anyone is aware who has ever read the really great translations of Frances Densmore . . ."[44]

Winters had been interested in Densmore's work since her translations first appeared in *The Path on the Rainbow*. Unlike many of his contemporaries, Winters was far less interested in the spiritual significance of the nagamonan than their aesthetics, writing that Densmore's translations were "far more beautiful than any of the versions of Japanese lyrics that have been made in recent years." Winters was particularly drawn to the formal aspects of the nagamonan when presented as texts, which he thought possessed a unique affective potency: "These poems, so minute in appearance, shrill as the voice of a gnat dying out past the ear, are among the most endlessly fascinating poems of my experience. What they accomplish is beyond analysis."[45]

In an attempt to capture some of the beauty he found in the nagamonan, Winters published his own collection of poetry inspired by Densmore's translations the same year Sarett brought out *The Box of God*. True to Winters's distaste for interpretation, the poems in *The Magpie's Shadow* (1922) are not reworked versions of Densmore's translations, but original compositions, in which Winters attempted to emulate what he perceived to be the formal and thematic qualities of the nagamonan.

May
Oh, evening in my hair![46]

At evening
Like leaves my feet passed by.[47]

The Aspen's Song
The summer holds me here.[48]

Presented without the stylized typography of *The Path on the Rainbow*, nor the interpretive notes of *The Box of God*, the poems of *Magpie's Shadow* bear a striking resemblance to many of the translated nagamonan, but only in theme and form. Winters never claims an Anishinaabe identity for the poems, or includes any references to their religion or culture. Winters may have avoided the inclusion of such material in his poems, in part, because he considered it incidental. As he would argue, a tribal song could "have meaning, religious, magical, ritualistic, or locally humorous," but such meanings were secondary to its appreciation, as they "sometimes complicate the poem profitably as a poem, sometimes unprofitably."[49] Of primary importance to Winters was the replication of the nagamonan as a particular *form* of poetry—a compact juxtaposition of natural imagery with a strong sense of individual subjectivity.

That Winters recognized a coherent genre where Sarett saw only fragmentary phrases likely had to do with the differences between the two men's understanding of indigenous epistemology. Where Sarett saw in the Native an alien consciousness in need of translation, Winters saw a perfectly rational being shaped by particular social and material conditions. Remarkably similar in tone and content to something Vine Deloria would articulate half a century later,[50] Winters's position on the communal and materialist nature of tribal religions put him at odds not only with Sarett, but with most primitivists of the day, writing:

> Any attempt to define the American Indian mind in terms of some neo-Confucian, neo-Buddhistic, or neo-Freudian "mysticism" is, I am inclined to suspect, pretty far-fetched. I am no ethnologist, but I take it that most primitive religion is rather definitely practical in its aims: it consists mainly of scientific formulae for perpetuating the race and for getting three square meals a day. The gods are not spiritual qualities, but natural forces: they are not in any sense abstractions but are things one can lay ones hands on and control. The Indian controls the rain and thunder by means of incantation to get crops: the modern scientist controls electricity by other means to construct engines which will make him felt hats in very rapid succession. Now the only essential difference between these two states of mind lies in this, that the first is serious and the second is relatively frivolous. But neither one has any ulterior significance.[51]

For Winters, viewing indigenous religion as fundamentally pedestrian did not detract from the appreciation of tribal songs, but allowed the reader to recognize how "the great art remains as art, the statement of valid conclusions."⁵²

Winters's insistence that Natives were not savages but rational beings with highly sophisticated and specialized modes of life reflects his involvement in the political reforms taking place in Indian Country during the twenties and thirties. Like his wife, Winters had been involved in the protests over the Bursum Bill (see chapter 2), working alongside American Indian Defense Association chief, John Collier. While Collier would go on to enshrine tribes' right to political self-determination in the Indian Reorganization Act, Winters would continue to support contemporary Native cultural expression, becoming a vocal promoter of the painters Awa Tsireh and Fred Kabotie, as well as close friend and protégé, the novelist Scott Momaday. In his insistence that the Anishinaabeg needed "no assistance whatsoever" from white poets, Winters helped to clear the way for a new generation of Native artists and activists who would revolutionize tribal political and cultural identity in the second half of the twentieth century.

Two Foxes Face Each Other

As the century progressed, interest in Densmore's work waned but never fully abated. Shortly after her death in 1957, William Carlos Williams honored Densmore's memory by using a short quotation from *The Study of Indian Music* as the epigraph of his Pulitzer Prize–winning poem "Pictures from Brueghel" (1962): ". . . the form of a man's rattle may be in accordance with instructions received in the dream by which he obtained his power."⁵³ In 1946, Margot Astrov reprinted Densmore's translations in *The Winged Serpent*, which billed itself as an "anthology of American Indian prose and poetry."⁵⁴ Meanwhile, Cronyn's *The Path on the Rainbow* remained in print (as it does today) under a succession of various titles, ensuring that the nagamonan would continue to be rediscovered by successive generations of readers. In a 1956 essay for *Perspectives USA*, Kenneth Rexroth declared Densmore's translations to be "of tremendous importance to the student of literary origins, to the aesthetician or critic, and especially to the practicing poet," describing them as "pure poems of sensibility resembling nothing so much as classical Japanese poetry or Mallarmé and . . . the Imagists at their best."⁵⁵

Even as Rexroth celebrated the beauty of the nagamonan, the Anishinaabeg were facing the worst political and cultural crisis since the passage of the Dawes Act. As early as 1943, the U.S. Congress had begun to investigate the feasibility of ending the trust relationship between the federal government and Indian tribes. On August 1, 1953, Congress made explicit its desire to do so with the passage of House concurrent resolution 108, which stated,

> It is the policy of congress, as rapidly as possible, to make the Indians within the territorial limits of the United States subject to the same laws and entitled to the same privileges and responsibilities as are applicable to other citizens of the United States, to end their status as wards of the United States, and to grant them all the rights and prerogatives pertaining to American citizenship.[56]

By calling for the eventual cessation of tribal self-government and the end of federal trusteeship over Native land and resources, the resolution effectively called for the abrogation of every existing Indian treaty in the United States, and for Native people to "assume their full responsibilities as American citizens."[57] Two weeks after passing HR108, Congress began divesting the federal government of trust responsibility to Native peoples by passing Public Law 280, which overturned more than a century of federal oversight by granting several state governments complete criminal and civil jurisdiction over Natives residing on reservation land. In an attempt, in part, to weaken tribal communities, Congress began paying for Natives between the ages of eighteen and thirty-five to leave their reservations and move to urban areas, where they would ostensibly receive housing and employment assistance. The effects of this policy, euphemistically called the Adult Vocational Training Program, were to deprive reservation communities of their existing population of wage earners, and to make relocatees subject to state, rather than federal, jurisdiction. By the official end of the Termination era in 1973, 109 tribal nations had been dissolved—resulting in the cessation of federal benefits and protections (including health-care, food, and housing assistance) for 13,263 Native people, and the loss of over a million of acres of tribally owned land.[58] During this period, over 100,000 Native people were relocated to urban centers, however many would eventually return to their home communities.[59]

The aggressively antitribal policies of the U.S. government during the Termination Era were, somewhat paradoxically, the catalyst for a nationwide renaissance of tribal identity. In an effort to avoid termination, Native communities across the country began reasserting their cultural particularity. Reviving their languages, reinstating various subsistence practices, and performing religious rites long hidden from public view, this cultural revitalization was meant to illustrate the degree to which tribal communities had refused to assimilate to Euro-American life. Reconnecting to their home communities, urban Indians also began to reassert their tribal (and pan-tribal) identities, partly as a means of drawing attention to their struggle for civil rights. Through the efforts of formal and informal organizations such as the National Congress for the American Indian, the National Indian Youth Council, and the American Indian Movement, by the late 1960s Indians had found a new purchase on the public imagination, emerging from the dark days of allotment and economic depression as separate peoples, culturally and politically distinct from their fellow Americans.

One of the most influential voices to emerge from this period was that of the Anishinaabe poet and writer Gerald Vizenor, whose theoretical works on Native culture and politics would help to shape multiple generations of indigenous scholarship. Born in Minneapolis in 1934, Vizenor lived apart from his family's community at White Earth for the majority of his youth. Largely raised by his paternal grandmother, Alice Beaulieu, Vizenor's early days were marked by loss—the murder of his father, the accidental death of his uncle, and abandonment by his mother. After living in a succession of foster homes, Vizenor joined the military at a young age, serving first with the National Guard, and then the U.S. Army. He spent two years stationed in Japan as part of the U.S. occupation force. There he became fascinated with haiku, a form he would eventually come to master in his own poetry. Returning to the United States, Vizenor took advantage of the GI Bill to attend the University of Minnesota, where he studied social work. By 1965, Vizenor was attending a graduate program in journalism at the University of Minnesota, as well as working at the American Indian Employment and Guidance Center in Minneapolis—a job that brought him into intimate contact with Natives who had been relocated to the city as part of the government's Termination policies.

Vizenor likely first encountered *Chippewa Music* in the course of his graduate studies, after he had already published two volumes of haiku, neither of which explicitly addressed Native themes. One can imagine the degree to which Vizenor would have been struck by the similarity between Densmore's translations and the haiku he had already published, given the nagamonan's condensed form and thematic emphasis on the natural world. Take, for example, the haiku-like nature of Densmore's translation of a song originally performed by A'jide'gijīg:

> they face each other
> two foxes
> I will sit between them[60]

Discovering Densmore's translations was likely an important moment in the development of Vizenor's career as a poet, providing, as it did, a link between his Anishinaabe identity and his own poetic practice.

In 1965, Vizenor published *Summer in the Spring*, a small chapbook comprised of fifty-two poetic "reexpressions" of Densmore's translated nagamonan, along with interpretive notes (mostly taken from Densmore), as well as a brief sketch of Anishinaabe history. Organized by the same categories (Mide songs, war songs, etc.) used in *Chippewa Music*, Vizenor's reexpressions do not stray far from Densmore's texts. In fact, many of the poems replicate the Densmore texts almost exactly, as with Vizenor's reexpression of Ga'gandac"s song (the same that would later show up in *The Sopranos*), which Densmore presented as follows:

> Sometimes
> I go about pitying
> Myself
> While I am carried by the wind
> Across the sky[61]

Vizenor's version is hardly different.

> Sometimes
> I go about pitying
> Myself,
> While I am carried
> By the wind
> Across the sky.[62]

The lack of editorial intervention on Vizenor's part seems to have based a sense of reverence for the original translations, many of which he felt to be "so concisely rendered by Densmore" that they required "no changes . . . except in word and line order."[63]

At a time when the idea of a Native poetic tradition would have seemed almost unthinkable, *Summer in the Spring* provided a foundation on which Vizenor could build a career as a Native writer—not by imitating the work of non-Natives, but by recovering the literature of his own people. Vizenor's book is, perhaps, one of the earliest manifestations of what would eventually come to be known as the Native American Renaissance, a period of intense literary production in which Native writers infused their novels and poetry with material from the oral traditions of their tribal groups. The power of such a juxtaposition was proven with the publication of *House Made of Dawn* in 1968, for which Scott Momaday (the apprentice of Yvor Winters) would receive the Pulitzer Prize. The next two decades would see a string of award-winning books from Native writers, including Momaday's *Way to Rainy Mountain* (1969), James Welch's *Riding the Earth Boy 40* (1971) and *Winter in the Blood* (1974), Leslie Marmon Silko's *Ceremony* (1977), and Louise Erdrich's *Love Medicine* (1983). These books found a wide audience among a curious public made newly aware of Native issues by the protests at Alcatraz and Wounded Knee. For the first time in decades, readers had access to an artistic Native voice largely unmediated by non-Native interpreters.

Not that such interpreters ceased to exist. Indeed, this period also saw a pronounced revival of the poetic reexpression of tribal material by non-Natives, under the auspices of a movement called "ethnopoetics." Unlike the earlier generation of interpreters, some of the practitioners of ethnopoetics were academically trained linguists who had at least some degree of competency in Native languages. Those such as Dell Hynes and Dennis Tedlock translated tribal songs and stories in the idiom of poetry because they thought it better suited than prose to represent the dynamic quality of oral performance. Others, like Gary Snyder, continued the modernist practice of "translation" in the tradition of Alice Corbin Henderson and Lew Sarett. Like their predecessors, these poets offered their interpretations of already translated tribal texts in order to reveal their original "spirit," which ethnographic translation had somehow obscured.[64]

Perhaps the most prolific (certainly one of the most well-known) practitioners of this kind of ethnopoetics is Jerome Rothenberg, who published *Shaking the Pumpkin: Traditional Poetry of the North Americas* in 1972. The book is a collection of poems Rothenberg "reworked" from preexisting translations of oral material from indigenous peoples across North America—including several from Densmore. This collection continued Rothenberg's work in *Technicians of the Sacred* (1968) of presenting "primitive or tribal" literature in what he describes as "total translation." Similar to Sarett's work half a century earlier, Rothenberg claims to "translate" oral narratives and songs from various tribal people in such a way that the "full & total experience" of the original oral performances can be represented in printed English. Using avant-garde formal techniques, including field composition and the integration of nonlinguistic elements (images, musical scores, mathematic equations, etc.) into the text, Rothenberg claims that "Everything in these song-poems is finally translatable: words, sounds, voice, melody, gesture, event, etc., in the reconstitution of a unity that would be shattered by approaching each element in isolation."[65]

In practice, many of the poems of *Shaking the Pumpkin* are fairly similar to the ethnographic texts on which they are based, albeit with a vocabulary more suited to the informal, counterculture milieu of the early seventies. Take, for instance, Rothenberg's "translation" of a Mide initiation song originally recorded by Densmore. The original reads,

> I that hasten around
> I shoot at a man and he falls
>   in a trance
> Then I feel with my hand
> To see if he is still alive[66]

which Rothenberg interprets as,

> I keep running around
> shoot at a man & he falls down
>   stoned
> try feeling with my hand
> see if he's still alive[67]

While lending the poem the frisson of the taboo by implying that this Mide ceremony was somehow pharmacologically enhanced, Rothenberg's revision adds little else to the original Densmore translation that wasn't already there—and even retains the translation's original line breaks and indentation.

Perhaps unsurprisingly, Rothenberg's work has proven to be exceptionally controversial. The most vocal criticism of Rothenberg's work came from Native poets—most notably Leslie Marmon Silko, Geary Hobson, Chrystos, and Wendy Rose, who have variously charged Rothenberg with insensitivity, appropriation, and religious fraud. The success of *Shaking the Pumpkin* led, in part, to an influx of what Hobson called "white shamans," non-Natives who presented themselves as poet-priests with disingenuous claims of possessing indigenous spiritual knowledge. To his credit, Rothenberg has always been careful to distance himself from white shamanism—claiming his work is more interested in revealing the underlying poetry of Native oral traditions than in expressing indigenous religious beliefs. In a note to *Shaking the Pumpkin*, Rothenberg goes as far as to say that no reader should expect to find in his translations a "spirit-of-a-people etc," explaining: "the best remains untold or its powers reserved for those who 'have ears to hear' etc. But the rest of us have to begin somewhere."[68]

A potentially more damning critique came from the critics William Bevis and William Clements, both of whom took Rothenberg to task for identifying himself as a "translator" of Native texts. Bevis described Rothenberg's claim of presenting the "Traditional Poetry of the North Americas," as "certainly misleading and perhaps opportunistic,"[69] pointing out that Rothenberg's translations not only deviate widely from the original sources "but translate with impunity from one genre (chant to lyric, impromptu oral statement to lyric) and even from one medium (action and painting to words) to another."[70] Clements's criticism was even more pointed, calling *Shaking the Pumpkin* "a dangerous book" that "perpetuates alarming misconceptions about the nature of Native American verbal art."[71] For Clements, the major flaw of Rothenberg's work was the fact that his "total translations" were based on preexisting texts—mostly translations made by late-nineteenth- and early-twentieth-century ethnographers. Like Bevis, Clements accused Rothenberg of not paying enough deference to the generic specificity of the original material, particularly the Densmore translations, stating,

> These texts are indeed songs; as such, their melodies are as vital as their words. The absence of any musicological indications prevents the reader from appreciating the integrity of the performance of this material as song. One can certainly make no claims of having achieved "total translation" when elements essential to depicting the nature of oral performance are ignored.[72]

As Clements concludes, the poems of *Shaking the Pumpkin* "seem to reflect what Jerome Rothenberg feels Native American oral poetry should be rather than what it actually is or was."[73]

For his part, Vizenor has also expressed skepticism about Rothenberg's project, stating, "I don't think the oral tradition can be translated," only "reimagined and reexpressed."[74] For Vizenor, the impossibility of translating the oral tradition has almost nothing to do with crossing the barriers of language, but everything to do with moving from one technology of expression to another. Stating that "Written languages and translations were contradictions in most tribal communities," Vizenor argues that

English and the written word were not neutral for the Anishinaabeg, but rather, imposed and deeply compromised modes of expression. However, when tribal cultures and languages were threatened with total annihilation in the late nineteenth and early twentieth centuries, writing their traditional stories and songs in English provided the Anishinaabeg with "chances to overcome tragic reason and the loss of tribal memories."[75]

According to Vizenor, the transformation from oral to written was chancy because "The translation from the heard to the written is a transvaluation of the heard to the seen, the listener once, the reader evermore." In other words, such translations risked permanently eliminating the most important aspect of oral literature: its infinite adaptability. As Vizenor sees it, in oral cultures there is no single definitive text against which future utterances can be judged. Nothing, in the most literal sense, is set in stone. The shape and content of cultural expression is always fluid—bound by convention to be sure, but a convention that is always being negotiated in a communal context. The specific words of a song or story may change, sometimes radically, but the overall shape of oral expression remains relatively stable. By recording an utterance from the oral tradition in writing, Vizenor believes, one immediately and irreversibly creates a standard against which future oral expressions can be judged, even if the written utterance was chosen arbitrarily from an infinite number of possible variations.

Uncomfortably, however, many of the accusations of inauthenticity that Bevis and Clements level at Rothenberg could also apply to *Summer in the Spring*'s lightly reworked versions of Densmore's already translated texts.[76] Like Rothenberg, Vizenor conflates different genres of expression, describing his lyric poems as Anishinaabe songs, and vice versa, despite the incommensurability of the two forms. *Summer in the Spring* also contains several romanticized descriptions of "The Indian" and his unique mental qualities, including this passage: "The Indian instinctively knew what the occidental settlers had forgotten. He was not afraid of fear. He disciplined himself against the excesses of human desire and possessions."[77] Although Vizenor makes no claim to transmit a Native "consciousness" to his readers, such descriptions heavily imply that such a consciousness exists. Given these similarities, one is tempted to ask the question: if we are to criticize *Shaking the Pumpkin* for its inauthenticity, must we then also consider *Summer in the Spring* an equally compromised text?

Comparing Vizenor and Rothenberg's treatment of a single poem, it certainly seems that we might. The original song, collected by Densmore as No. 64 "Initiation Song," was sung by Ki'tcimak'wa, a member of the Midewewin healing society. Densmore's translator presented it in English as follows:

> What is this
> I promise you?
> The skies shall be bright and clear for you
> This is what I promise you[78]

In the 1965 version of *Summer*, the poem appears with the title "Mide Initiation Song." The poem appears nearly exactly as it was translated in *Chippewa Music* (as does every other poem in the collection). Indeed, Vizenor explains in an interpretive note that "Most of the Ojibway words in this song were obscure,"[79] requiring him to follow the Densmore translation closely, only regularizing the line breaks and inserting the word "Spring" to reflect the season of Midewiwin initiation.

> What is this
> I promise you?
>
> The Spring skies
> Will be bright
> And clear for you.
>
> This is what
> I promise you.[80]

Rothenberg's translation also closely follows Densmore's prose rendition, albeit in far less formal language.

> know what I'll promise you?
> skies be bright & clear for you
> that's what I'll promise you[81]

At the level of the language, the differences between Vizenor and Rothenberg's poems are minor. At most, one may say that Rothenberg's use of highly informal language lends the poem a sort of "Red English" exoticism (à la Sarett), but hardly changes its overall meaning. Vizenor, for his part, goes in an opposite direction, using capitalization and formal punctuation to lend the text a certain gravitas. While their revisions may have different implications, neither departs widely from Densmore's original text. However, when one takes a step back from the language of Rothenberg's and Vizenor's poems and examines how each is situated contextually, differences between the two emerge.

Unlike Vizenor's reexpression, Rothenberg's version prominently features the pictograph Densmore originally published with the song (fig. 3.2). As Densmore explains in her notes, the pictograph illustrates both the content and the intent of the song: the line that emerges from the figure's mouth is the song itself, which travels upward to clear the sky, represented as a circle above the figure's head. According to Densmore, Mide practitioners incised such "Song Pictures" as mnemonic devices to record certain series of events or songs. The pictographs represent a kind of writing in that a Mide practitioner could, on seeing a pictograph, immediately sing the song that the pictograph represented, or conversely on hearing a song, draw its corresponding pictograph. Densmore notes that such pictographs could be used "to express complicated ideas,"[82] but is careful to differentiate the pictographs from forms of phonetic writing. A Mide follower who was not familiar with a pictograph would only be able to vaguely guess at its overall meaning, but would not be able to give an exact word-for-word translation—let alone perform the song it represented. In a note to his version of the poem, Rothenberg directly contradicts Densmore's assertion that the pictographs were used only as mnemonic devices, insisting that the Mide were indeed able to "read-out" pictographs. Citing an earlier nineteenth-century treatise on the Midewewin, Rothenberg argues that the pictures departed "from the mere representation of the songs' content to the presentation of new information not supplied by the words."[83]

Figure 3.2. Detail of Mide pictograph from "No. 64 'Initiation Song.'"

In his insistence on privileging the visual over the verbal, Rothenberg anachronistically makes Anishinaabe culture always-already graphematic, and thereby legitimizes his project of total translation. Indeed, Rothenberg's privileged placement of the pictograph to the left of the text invites the reader to see the text as an explanation of the pictograph, rather than the other way around. In essence, Rothenberg presents the pictograph as a text that can be read, rather than as symbols that can only be interpreted with the right kind of knowledge. This sort of interpretive logic imbues the pictograph with a meaning that is not contingent, negotiable, or fluid—but fixed in a way that places it outside of time.

While this may seem like philosophical hairsplitting, the relationship between such vague abstractions as culture, authenticity, and time took on real political urgency for Native peoples in the mid-twentieth-century. The Termination era marked a subtle, but profound shift in the philosophical basis of Federal Indian policy. For the first time in its history, the United States began to articulate an understanding of tribal sovereignty based on the recognition of cultural difference, rather than legal or historical precedent. Tribes that were deemed sufficiently "acculturated"—meaning, usually, those who had most thoroughly adopted Christianity, the English language, and free market capitalism—were the first to be terminated. In essence, Congress and the Bureau of Indian Affairs targeted specific tribal nations based on the degree to which they perceived these tribes to be no longer authentically Indian.

By tying the recognition of indigenous political rights to the performance of traditional cultural practices, the U.S. state created an irresolvable paradox—in order to continue to exist in modernity Indigenous communities had to behave as if modernity itself did not exist. As anthropologist and political theorist Beth Povinelli explains, such recognition is explicitly meant to erode indigenous rights because it "always already constitutes indigenous persons as failures of indigeneity."[84] Indeed, as Povenelli argues, indigenous political subjectivity is defined by such failure.

> To be indigenous . . . requires passing through, and in the passage being scarred by the geography of the state and topography of other social identities. Producing a present-tense indigenousness in which some failure is not a qualifying condition is discursively and materially impossible. These scars are what Aborigines are, what they have.[85]

The cunning of recognition, as Povinelli calls it, is twofold: by placing the burden on Indigenous peoples to constantly reassert their cultural authenticity, the settler-state can both suppress its own complicity in the violent repression of indigenous cultural practices, *and* further erode indigenous legal rights.[86] Ethnographic texts like Densmore's play a central role in the politics of recognition. By appearing to give an authoritative definition of what constitutes (or at least constituted) authentic indigenous cultural practice, ethnography provides the settler-state with a standard of authentic indigenous behavior against which contemporary Native people can be judged.

Yet, according to the Anishinaabe anthropologist Gail Guthrie Valaskakis, the idea that a text like Densmore's can act in any meaningful way as a repository for uncontaminated, authentic Indigenous culture can be nothing more than a fantasy. As Valaskakis explains, "both what anthropologists know about Indian practices and what Indians know of the traditional are equally perforated" by the legacy of colonial dispossession.[87] Indeed, at the time Densmore was making her recordings, the Anishinaabe at White Earth were experiencing some of the most radical upheavals to their traditional way of life since the first days of contact. The idea that the songs were not influenced by this colonial history is almost unimaginable. Moreover, Valaskakis argues that the inherent limitations of text keep Densmore's translations from ever capturing the critically important social context in which the songs were originally performed. As Valaskakis argues, "In Densmore's report, there can be no smell of buckskin and woodsmoke, no soul-searing sound of the drums, or piercing voice of the singers, no collective motion of the dancers."[88] In short, while the Densmore texts may act as "an enormously valuable goad to our personal and public memories," *Chippewa Music* remains "essentially a dictionary of historical songs—obscure, distant, and lifeless."[89]

Yet it is precisely what Rothenberg claims do—presenting his translation as conveying the "full & total" experience of the original performance—and, in so doing, recapitulating the recognitive logic of Termination. Because the total meaning of the song is meant to inhere within the pictograph, anyone should be able to gain access to the total experience of the song—with almost no prior knowledge of the cultural, material or linguistic context of its enunciation. Such an assumption would mean that if a modern Anishinaabe, like Valaskakis, reads the poem but cannot comprehend its meaning, it would not be due to the coercive legacy of colonial violence, but simply to a lack of interpretive will. In treating written texts as portals through which one may access the cultural and epistemological lives of historical tribal people, Rothenberg's project of total translation makes an implicit claim that indigenous peoples were not stripped of their traditions, but simply abandoned them to gather dust in the archive.

A New Tribal Hermeneutics

Had the 1965 version of *Summer in the Spring* been Vizenor's only foray into the reexpression of Anishinaabe song, he too could be accused of deferring to the authority of the colonial archive. Fortunately it was not. *Summer in the Spring* was but the first of four subsequent editions (printed in 1970, 1981, and 1993, respectively) of reexpressed nagamonan that Vizenor would publish. In each new edition, Vizenor offers increasingly different renditions of the Densmore texts, challenging the idea that single, definitive translation may ever be achieved.[90] By juxtaposing translations together, matching the poems with unrelated pictographs, and publishing the poems in the same volume as Beaulieu's translations, Vizenor embraces a strategy of supplementarity that undermines the very idea of an authentic translation. Taken as a single project, the four volumes of *Summer in the Spring* trace a transformative arc in Vizenor's poetic reexpression of the Anishinaabe oral tradition: beginning as accurate reproductions of Densmore's texts, only to eventually become subjective expressions of Vizenor's poetic sensibility. Through this transformation, Vizenor articulates a method of reexpressing Densmore's texts that lends them a kind of flexibility and adaptability that is similar to (but not exactly like) that of the oral tradition. Returning to a primary orality may be an impossibility for Vizenor, but by constantly supplementing, reinterpreting, and retranslating ethnographic texts, one may resist the temporally fixed idea of Indianness that they threaten to impose. Rather than reify the dominance of the colonial archive, Vizenor's poems seek to overwhelm it with conflicting versions—puncturing its authoritative facade with the shrapnel-like fragments of the very culture it seeks to contain.

One of the most important changes Vizenor makes to *Summer in the Spring* after 1965 is his pairing of the reexpressed nagamonan with Theo Beaulieu's translations of the aadizookaanag from the *Progress*. First published in 1970 as a companion volume to his reexpressed songs, Vizenor collected the Beaulieu stories under the title *Anishinabe Adisokan*. In 1981, Vizenor began publishing his poems and Beaulieu's stories as a single volume with the title *Summer in the Spring: Anishinaabe Lyric Poems and Stories*. The translated aadizookaanag represented more than just added content, but seem to have had a profound impact on Vizenor's sensibility as an interpreter of the Anishinaabe oral material. In his introduction to the 1992 edition of *Summer in the Spring*, Vizenor describes the Beaulieu translations as representing "a new tribal hermeneutics."[91] While Vizenor does not elaborate on the term, I believe it to mean that the Beaulieu translations offer replicable strategy for the interpretation of Anishinaabe oral material in writing—a method that privileges creativity and personal expression of contemporary Natives over fidelity to supposedly authentic forms of address. As I showed in chapter 1, Beaulieu's translations take liberties with the content and form of the traditional aadizookaan in order to make a specific kind of political claim about the modernity of the Anishinaabeg. In this sense, the act of reinterpreting oral material to make it address the needs of present-day Anishinaabeg, rather than recapture what it may have meant to a previous generation, comprises the practice of this "new tribal hermeneutics."

Understanding that there is no direct correspondence between oral and written forms, the new tribal hermeneutics embraces the supplementarity of nonindigenous literary genres in pursuit of explicitly political goals. As Vizenor argues, "Those who heard stories were hounded to the sense of the present," whereas written translations can only serve as "tributes to that sense of the present that is abandoned to the weakness of historical time."[92] The interpreter must recognize that the relationship between the form of the original material and the form into which it is reexpressed is always arbitrary and artificial. Despite the apparent affinities of aadizookaan with prose, or nagamon with lyric, they are not commensurate forms—translating one form into another always requires a degree of interpretation and intervention. Recasting oral material from an indigenous genre into a Western genre always means that the resulting text is loaded with a range of social, cultural, and political significations the original did not have.

When pursued in an active manner, however, a translator (or more properly reinterpreter) of oral material can productively draw on these supplementary meanings in order to make a political claim. For instance, when a nagamon is presented as a lyric poem, it will call on the historical and cultural associations of the lyric with a philosophy of individual subjectivity from ancient Greece to Wordsworth and beyond—despite the fact the original nagamon was produced outside of this tradition. Yet, by associating the nagamon with the lyric, an interpreter like Vizenor draws on that form as a prestige mode of cultural expression, transforming what was once "folk music" into high literature (see chapter 1), and allowing Vizenor to make the cheeky claim that "the first American imagist poets were the American Indians."[93]

The relationship between Beaulieu's formal interventions and Vizenor's may be difficult to discern at first, as their texts trace opposite trajectories in terms of form, yet both work toward the same political goal: articulating an Anishinaabe identity capable of existing in modernity. Whereas Beaulieu's reexpressions of the Wenabozho stories move toward greater coherence, structure, and causality in order to adhere better to the conventions of novelistic fiction, Vizenor's reexpressions move toward a greater indeterminacy, polysemy, and openness that reflect better the conventions of poetry—particularly that of haiku. By embracing an explicitly haiku-like form for his reexpressions, Vizenor makes an implicit argument for reading the poems of *Summer in the Spring* as the products of his subjective imagination, as well as for recognizing the degree to which the Anishinaabeg experience and engage in the transnational cultural milieu of modernity.

As noted previously, many critics compared the nagamonan with Japanese haiku when the Densmore translations first appeared—and many continue to do so. Kimberly Blaeser, for example, explains that both a translated nagamon and haiku, as forms, are "open text[s]," which she defines as "a text that works by suggestion, implication, absence, allusion, and juxtaposition, that works through intentional gaps, indeterminacy in various forms, and the practice of many kinds of restraint in language."[94] Blaeser believes that this openness is what links the nagamonan to haiku, but is quick to point out that there remains a "central question about whether the Japanese quality was inherent in the original Ojibway dream songs or merely 'crept into' Densmore's translations."[95]

In fact, the haiku-like nature of the Densmore translations seems to have stemmed from Anishinaabemowin's complex, polysynthetic structure. In Anishinaabemowin, individual words (most often verbs) can be comprised of a string of morphemes that each inflects its meaning. For example, take the variations possible with the single verb-stem "aabi" meaning "see." "Waabi" means "he or she sees," whereas "ogii-waabamaan" means "they saw those (animate)," and "gaa-kwiinawaabandamaan" means "that thing (inanimate) which I did not see." In the text of *Chippewa Music*, the translations of the lyrics follow a set format, with each "stanza" representing a single word of Anishinaabemowin. For example, the translation of a song by A'jide'gijīg reads as follows:

pe'dwewe'cîn . . . . the sound of his approaching footsteps
neta'micodûñ' . . . . who always hits the mark[96]

As we can see, translating single words (even those that are complex) means that each "line" of the translation is relatively brief. Moreover, the word-by-word translation tends to deemphasize the link between subject and verbs, making what would be a syntactically coherent statement in

Anishinaabemowin seem like an impressionistic string of semirelated concepts in English. As a phrase, "biidweweshin nitaa-miikodan" (as it would appear in modern orthography) might be better translated as "The one who always hits the center is heard walking here." Yet, such a translation would not retain the order of concepts as they appeared in the song, information Densmore likely thought more important for understanding its musical structure.

If Densmore's Japanese style was incidental, Vizenor's is purposeful, as each new iteration of the reexpressed nagamonan moves closer and closer to the openness of haiku. Take, for example, "The Song of the Crows," which appears in the 1965 version of *Summer* in a form almost exactly like the Densmore translation.

> The first to come
> I am called
> Among the birds.
>
> The rain I bring
> Crow is my name.[97]

In 1970's *Anishinabe Nagamon*, the same poem appears in an altered form, without a title, using more sophisticated—and polysemic—language.

> the first to come
> epithet among the birds
>
> bringing the rain
> crow is my name[98]

While the theme of the poem remains the same, the *Anishinabe Nagamon* version of "Song of the Crows" opens itself to a greater number of possible readings that had previously been foreclosed by the formal elements of punctuation and vocabulary. Where the punctuation in the 1965 version of the poem created enjambment that forced a linear relationship between one line and the next, Vizenor's removal of punctuation imparts each of the lines with an element of conceptual autonomy. Each line can now be read as an individual unit, a paratactical movement from one idea to another. Moreover, by dividing the text into two stanzas, Vizenor creates an ambiguous relation between the two halves of the poem—calling to mind haiku's aesthetic hallmark: the ambiguous juxtaposition of related images.

Vizenor's updated version of the poem also does not shy away from a more sophisticated vocabulary than is found in Densmore's translations. By using the semantically charged "epithet" rather than the explanatory "I am called," Vizenor creates an even greater indeterminacy in the poem, leading to several possible readings. The crow may be called "the first to come" as a name, or the name "crow" itself may be a term of abuse. At the same time, the use of a word of such cosmopolitan etymology as "epithet" allows Vizenor to address the conceptual limits of Densmore's transcriptions. For the sake of clarity and accuracy, Densmore's translations rely on a simplified English that made the expression of sophisticated thought all but impossible. By including complex language in his poems, Vizenor works against the construction of the Anishinaabeg as a primitive people incapable of understanding nuance.

All of these changes work to transform the Densmore transcription into an "open text," but the most explicit formal shift in Vizenor's revision of the poem is his effacement of the pronoun "I." As Patricia Haseltine has noted, throughout the post-1965 versions of the reexpressions, Vizenor "removed or deemphasized the first person pronoun," a change that she finds brings the poems "closer to the haiku."[99] Despite their many similarities, Nagamonan and haiku take fundamentally dissimilar approaches to the representation of subjectivity. As Vizenor observes, "ego in dream songs . . . is dominant; in haiku, of course, it's much more subtle."[100] Despite it being one of the defining thematic features of the nagamonan, Vizenor's reexpressions work in multiple ways to undermine the explicit subjectivity of the songs, often by representing the pronoun with a lowercase "i" or eliminating it altogether.

While *Summer in the Spring* (1965) and *Anishinabe Nagamon* (1970) are organized by Densmore's original categorizations (Love Songs, Mide Songs, etc.), the later editions of *Summer in the Spring* (1981, 1993) have no organizing principle other than Vizenor's artistic whim. Presented without titles or regularized line breaks, Vizenor arranges multiple songs in aesthetically and thematically interesting juxtapositions. In the 1981 version of *Summer*, for example, "Song of the Crows" (sans title) is paired with a shorter poem.

> the first to come
> epithet among the birds
> bringing the rain
> crow is my name
>
> my music
> reaching to the sky[101]

Vizenor includes nothing to indicate whether the reader should approach this text as separate poems or merely two stanzas of a single lyric. Juxtapositions such as this lend the text as a whole a greater sense of openness, as the reader is free to contemplate the implied relationship of the poems with one another, and, indeed, every other poem in the collection. Moreover, this change brings the poems even closer to haiku, the form of which is based partly on the unexpected juxtaposition of images.

The changes Vizenor makes to the nagamonan also brings them closer to his own idiosyncratic approach to the haiku form. Employed in this way, the Beaulieu stories act in a similar fashion to Vizenor's "haiku envoys," described as "a prose concentration and discourse on the images and sensations" of his haiku poems, which he uses to express the connections between "haiku sensations and tribal survivance." Vizenor explains, "practice combines my experiences in haiku with natural reason in tribal literature," creating "a new haiku hermeneutics."[102] Like his haiku envoys, Beaulieu's translations offer an important context for the poems of *Summer in the Spring*, connecting them, indirectly and imperfectly, to the tribal world from which they came. The Beaulieu texts (particularly the translations of Day-Dodge and Say-cose-gay's dibaajimowinan) offer a view into traditional Anishinaabe religious and social practice—such as the importance of dreams, the ability of animals to communicate with humans, and the great healing power of the Midewiwin—but without the limiting authority of an ethnographic footnote. We are not told what a song *means*, but are invited to imagine its potential meaning in the context of other traditional and contemporary practices.

We can see this process by returning to the "Initiation Song" as it appears in 1970's *Anishinabe Nagamon*. This new version of the poem appears without a title or punctuation, with its original wording significantly reworked.

> what is this i promise you
> he hi hi hi
> the sky
> will be bright and clear
> for you
> this is what i promise you
> ho ho ho ho[103]

The most apparent change to the poem is the inclusion of the vocables "he hi hi hi" and "ho ho ho ho," which were not included in Densmore's linear translation, Rothenberg's version of the song, or the 1965 edition of *Summer*. The vocalizations do appear, however, in Densmore's original musical transcription of the song, which she notes employs "[a]n unusual number of vowel syllables"[104] that "fill out the measures of the song," further noting, that "the syllables *ho ho ho ho*, ... indicate the conclusion."[105]

Vizenor's reinsertion of the vocables into the poem may be explained by the Beaulieu texts, which show that the sounds, although nonsemantic, do have a distinct religious and social meaning. One of Beaulieu's texts recounts the resurrection of a young child by a Midewiwin healer, who seems to draw power from the sound of the vocables.

> Upon entering the lodge he ran around to the left side of the lodge exclaiming *whe, whe, whe, whe*, at every step. In his hands he held a *mashkiki* pouch and when he had made a complete circle of the lodge he stopped and making a motion towards the body of dead child with the *mashkiki* pouch which he held in his hands, he exclaimed, *whay, ho, ho, ho*. The body of the child quivered and after this had been repeated the fourth time the dead child came to life.[106]

As Kimberly Blaeser notes, such untranslatable vocables play an important role in tribal literature, as they tie written expression back to the affective power of the oral tradition. As Blaeser argues, because "the remembered sounds themselves have power," they function "to place [Vizenor's] own writing in the oral tradition of the midewiwin songs."[107] It is important to note, however, that without preexisting knowledge of Midewewin religious practice, a reader would likely never make such a connection. The Beaulieu text does not help us to understand what the vocables meant (in an ethnographic sense) to nineteenth-century Anishinaabeg, only that they had meaning. Where Sarett and Rothenberg promise to re-create the affective and spiritual experience of Anishinaabe ceremony, Vizenor's poems offer only disjointed and fragmentary glimpses—reflecting a century's worth of missionary surveillance and legal censure of Midewewin religious practice.

The Oshkianishinaabeg

The formal changes Vizenor makes to the nagamonan not only create a sense of continuity between his poems and the original enunciation of the songs, but acts as an acknowledgment of the history that separates them. There is no return to the songs' original meaning, only what can be made of the translations from the retrospective position of a modern

Anishinaabe. The poems of *Summer in the Spring* represent Vizenor's attempt to make the Densmore texts relevant to his experiences as a modern Anishinaabe—one who also happens to speak English and has an appreciation for Japanese poetic forms. In short, Vizenor's poems do not seek to unlock the historical meaning of the nagamonan, they *impart* a meaning on them in the present.

In this way, we may see the way Vizenor's poetics reflect his political theory of "transmotion." Loosely defined, "transmotion" is the ability of indigenous communities to move freely, not only in space, but also time: to transform and adapt to new realities in ways informed by tradition, but not defined by it. For Vizenor, the political rights of Indigenous communities are inseparable from their ability to change as a community, saying that "Transmotion, that sense of Native motion and an active presence, is *sui generis* sovereignty."[108] In essence, indigenous sovereignty does not exist in spite of cultural change, but because of it. The indigenous community can change radically over time, like the Ship of Theseus, becoming almost completely different from how it once was. Yet, it is precisely the ability of the indigenous community to see itself as self-consistent with its previous incarnations that generates a claim to sovereignty.

The idea that cultural change represents an inherent aspect of Native sovereignty is critically important at a time in which indigenous political identity is being increasingly tied to knowledge of historical cultural practices. Due to its perception as the sine qua non of indigenous cultures, knowledge of the stories, songs, and histories that comprise a tribe's oral tradition have been increasingly linked to political status. In the past few decades, court decisions on indigenous land claims in Canada (*Delgamuukw v. British Columbia*, 1997) and Australia (*Mabo v. Queensland, Wik Peoples v. Queensland*, 1992) have recognized material from the oral tradition as a means of establishing native land title—but only if it is adjudicated as "authentic" by the (usually non-Native) courts. While the United States abandoned Termination policy by the 1970s, remnants of its recognitive logic remain a part of Federal Indian policy. The United States still conducts an assessment of authenticity in the process of federal recognition, in which applicant tribes are asked to "prove" their political and cultural continuity with a historical indigenous group. In 2013, U.S. Senator Dianne Feinstein introduced legislation intended to provide a fix for the calamitous *Carcieri v. Salazar* decision, which would make tribes prove a "Substantial, direct, aboriginal connection" to any land the tribe wishes to acquire and put into trust.[109] In each case, previously published ethnographic material, including tribal stories and songs, forms an implicit standard against which contemporary indigenous identity is held.

With each revision of the nagamonan, Vizenor disrupts the authority of the ethnographic text, creating another version of the nagamonan that is just as real (in terms of Anishinaabe creative expression) or just as fake (in terms of absolute authenticity) as any other. What is of primary importance to Vizenor is that no single version of a song or poem be understood as definitive. The poems, like the Anishinaabe themselves, transform over time—responding and adapting to new modes of address—almost to the point of unrecognizability. Yet, for all that, they remain Anishinaabe, reflecting something of their experience as a modern people, irreversibly marked by the colonial dispossession of the settler-state, the cultural pressures of global capitalism, and the simple passage of time. In a sense, Vizenor's poetics do not try to hide the scars of the Anishinaabeg, but make them public—offering a defiant assertion of survival in the face of colonization.

Nowhere is this process more apparent than in Vizenor's 1993 rendition of the Mide initiation song (fig. 3.3). In this version Vizenor presents

what is this i promise you

he hi hi hi

the sky

will be bright and clear

for you

this is what i promise you

ho ho ho ho

Figure 3.3. "Initiation Song" as reexpressed by Gerald Vizenor in *Summer in the Spring* (1993).

the text of the nagamon with a entirely unrelated pictograph: that of an animikii, or thunderbird. This particular juxtaposition of song and poem generates multiple possible interpretations. To the cultural outsider, the presence of the upward flying bird may seem like the ascending words of the Mide healer, sent up to clear the sky—a completely legitimate reading. To the cultural insider, however, the presence of the animikii is particularly relevant, as it profoundly changes the mood and tone of the poem. In the Anishinaabe oral tradition the animikiig brought lightning, floods, and tornadoes that threatened utter devastation. At the same time, the animikiig were also seen as agents of renewal, who rejuvenated the earth by bringing the rain. The juxtaposition of image and poem in this instance creates a narrative of destruction and the promise of renewal—an ominous thunderbank hovering over the eventual promise of clear skies.

Such a narrative is nowhere to be found in Densmore's original text, yet it has a profound relevancy to contemporary Anishinaabeg—those who Vizenor calls the "oshkianishinaabeg" or "new people." Faced with a long history of dispossession, it can be easy to think that these Anishinaabe, who no longer act as their ancestors did, have lost their way. Dominant narratives about the loss of land, of culture, of historical knowledge permeate our understanding about the lives of indigenous peoples, telling us that modern Anishinaabe are but shadows of who they once were. The flood of colonization, such narratives would have us believe, has washed away almost everything. The policy of termination relied on the acceptance of this narrative of cultural loss in order to strip indigenous peoples of their political rights—rights they had held for centuries. Vizenor's poem, however, acts as a reminder that even in the heaviest of rains, one has the power to imagine clear skies above. It is a promise that so long as the Anishinaabeg are capable of reimagining and reasserting who they are as a people—a continually new people—they will weather the storm.

Chapter 4

A Tribe of Pressed Trees

Representations of the State in the Fiction of Louise Erdrich

[O]nce the bureaucrats sink their barbed pens into the lives of Indians, the paper starts flying, a blizzard of legal forms, a waste of ink by the gallon, a correspondence to which there is no end or reason. That's when I began to see what we were becoming, and the years have borne me out: a tribe of filing cabinets and triplicates, a tribe of single-space documents, directives, policy. A tribe of pressed trees. A tribe of chicken-scratch that can be scattered by a wind, diminished to ashes by one struck match.

—Louise Erdrich, *Tracks*

PRINTED ABOVE IS ONE OF THE most widely cited passages from the oeuvre of Anishinaabe novelist Louise Erdrich. The moment comes near the end of *Tracks*, her 1988 novel set during the allotment era. Having lost his adopted daughter to a government boarding school, Nanapush, one of the novel's narrators, laments the enormity of the changes brought to his Anishinaabe community during the first years of the twentieth century. Critics seem drawn to this passage because it is such a "clear indictment of the United States,"[1] which reveals that "the white man's written promises are unstable texts."[2] Creating a symmetry between the ecological catastrophe of the timber industry's deforestation of Anishinaabe land and the cultural catastrophe of the U.S. government's assimilation programs (like the boarding school to which Lulu has been sent), this passage illustrates with remarkable lyricism the devastating effects of capitalist expropriation and state power. The passage is particularly good at showing, as Chadwick Allen puts it, "the subjugation of the Chippewa and the appropriation of their lands as the inevitable outcome of federal 'supervision and support.'"[3]

Very few critics, however, go on to quote the rest of the passage. Immediately after giving his dark prophecy, Nanapush tells the reader, "To become a bureaucrat myself was the only way that I could wade through the letters, the reports, the only place where I could find a ledge to kneel on, to reach through the loophole and draw [Lulu] home."[4] Given the context, Nanapush's decision to embed himself in the state seems to contradict not only his character, but a set of assumptions that have become common wisdom in our discipline. After decades of viewing the state as little more than a set of disciplinary institutions meant to break down tribal identity, literary critics may have trouble seeing Nanapush's decision as anything but the product of internalized colonialism. By choosing to be a part, however reluctant, of the institutional machinery by which traditional Anishinaabe life will be systemically attacked, Nanapush seems to willfully abandon his principles even as he laments their passing. The inconsistency of Nanapush's decision cannot help but undermine whatever rhetorical force his critique of state bureaucracy has, so it therefore goes quietly ignored.

Nanapush's rise to tribal chairman is hardly the only example in Erdrich's fiction of a character discovering agency in the blizzard of legal forms. In *The Bingo Palace*, Fleur Pillager, who once declared that "paper had no bearing or sense,"[5] spends her final years surrounding herself "with folders, with bundled envelopes and boxes of rippled cardboard that seem to hold still more files and newspapers and clippings."[6] In *The Round House*, a tribal enrollment form has the power to bring down the corrupt and racist governor of North Dakota. In *Love Medicine*, Nanapush's great-grandson, Lyman Lamartine, is kept from committing suicide by finding belonging in the "tribe of pressed trees."

> I could die now and leave no ripple. Why not! I considered, but then I came up with the fact that my death would leave a gap in the BIA records, my IRS account would be labeled incomplete until it closed. There would be minor confusion. These thoughts gave me a warm jolt. In cabinets of files, anyway, I still maintained existence. The government knew me though the wind and earth did not. I was alive, at least on paper. I was someone.[7]

Ambivalent and ironic as these examples are, they point to an important, and heretofore unacknowledged, theme that runs consistently throughout Erdrich's massive oeuvre: taking advantage of state and statelike institutions in order to reassert Anishinaabe political agency and cultural identity. In almost all of Erdrich's novels, at least one character (usually the protagonist) moves from alienated individualism to a profound sense of communal identity by embracing a degree of institutional authority. It is a narrative we see in Nanapush's rise to tribal chairman in *Tracks* and *Four Souls*, Lipsha's awakening to tribal political consciousness in *The Bingo Palace*, Agnes Dewitt/Father Damien's tireless advocacy as a parish priest, Judge Antone Bazil Coutts's judicial activism in *The Plague of Doves*, even Lyman Lamartine's ambivalent efforts to promote economic development in *Love Medicine* and *The Bingo Palace*. While one may credit the similarity of these stories to the plot of communal reintegration inherent in the comic mode, the fact that state and statelike institutions play a pivotal role in such narratives of reintegration marks an important and distinctive aspect of Louise Erdrich's fiction—one that has thus far been overlooked.

That Erdrich has an interest in the institutional life of the Anishinaabeg should hardly come as a surprise, given how deeply embedded her family has been within it. Like his fictional counterpart Nanapush, Erdrich's maternal grandfather, Patrick Gourneau, served as the tribal chairman of the Turtle Mountain Anishinaabeg during the tumultuous period between 1953 and 1959, leading the resistance to the government's efforts to terminate the tribe.[8] Erdrich's parents, Rita and Ralph Erdrich, were both employed by the BIA as teachers at an off-reservation boarding school in North Dakota.[9] While Erdrich pursued a career in writing, almost all of her siblings sought work in the public sector—most often working for tribal governments or the federal agencies that serve tribal communities. As Erdrich explained in a recent interview, her siblings' experiences working on behalf of tribal institutions have affected the way in which she thinks about literature, stating,

> I have six brothers and sisters, and nearly all of them work with Ojibwe or Dakota or other Native people. My youngest brother, youngest sister, and brother-in-law have worked with the Indian Health Service for a total of more than forty years. My second-oldest brother works in northern Minnesota sorting out the environmental issues for all of the Ojibwe Nations throughout the entire Midwest. Their experiences make magical realism seem ho-hum.[10]

Erdrich's insistence that magical realism pales in comparison with her siblings' day-to-day experience, to my mind, is more than a just jab at the critics who continue to misemploy the term to describe her own fiction.

The claim is both a statement of Erdrich's own generic sensibility, as well as an implicit argument about the nature of tribal bureaucracy. Rejecting the idea that the extra-rational aspects of her fiction are more than an accurate reflection of the everyday, Erdrich not only stakes a claim to writing in a realist mode, but also lends a degree of enchantment to what otherwise could be understood as the mundane work of tribal governance. Erdrich suggests that there is significance to the institutional life of tribal nations that is both profound and profoundly overlooked.

The literary scholar Amanda Claybaugh makes a similar claim about the overlooked importance of state institutions and the role literature may play in drawing attention to them. Claybaugh argues that state institutions suffer from a lack of visibility that makes them susceptible to neoliberal critique. "[W]e have trouble seeing that government is, in fact, good," Claybaugh argues, "because we have trouble seeing it at all." She continues,

> This is because the benefits that government provides become invisible as we become accustomed to them (we take the bridge for granted after it has been built); the benefits of government are often separated from its costs (we do not associate our visit to the park with the taxes we have paid); and the most significant benefits are often events that do not take place (the inspected building that does not collapse, the evacuation effected in time).[11]

One is only willing to defend what one can see, and the welfare state, so Claybaugh argues, is in vital need of defense. In a historical moment when the forces of neoliberalism are taking advantage of global economic instability to advocate for the dismantling of the welfare state—rendered as wasteful "entitlement" programs for the lazy and greedy—Claybaugh, following Michael Walzer, argues that literature may offer important counternarratives that make the work of the welfare state visible at a human level. Claybaugh and other critics argue that literature and other forms of narrative can play an important role in making these otherwise ignored benefits of government visible to readers by both dramatizing and humanizing their effects, bringing the operations of a vast institutional body to a more relatable scale by telling stories of the people who make up that institution as well as those who directly benefit from it.

In contradistinction to the observation of Claybaugh, the state does not suffer from a crisis of visibility in Indian Country—it suffers from a crisis of reputation. The daily lives of Natives are shot through with interactions with government institutions to such a degree that terms such as "HUD houses," "IHS clinic," "commods," "the BIA," and "CDIBs"—virtually unrecognizable to most Americans—are immediately and intimately familiar to most Natives. On most reservations governmental organizations (both tribal and federal) are the primary, if not only, sources of employment. Yet, if no other population in the United States is as exposed to the state as Native peoples, no other population has suffered more for it. Over the last five decades, whenever Natives erupted into wider public consciousness, it was almost always due to some fresh abuse at the hands of the state. Alcatraz, Wounded Knee II, the takeover of the BIA, the Oka crisis in Canada, all brought images of Native people, intensely angry at tribal and federal governments, into the living rooms of people around the world. Such anger is completely understandable. The legacy of state involvement in the lives of Natives, especially in the late nineteenth and early twentieth centuries, is an all-too-familiar litany of horrors: inadequate reservations, boarding schools, forced assimilation programs, full-scale war—a list of grievances known even to those with little other knowledge of Native peoples. What Vine Deloria observed in 1968 remains more or less true today: "People have found it hard to think of Indians without conjuring up the picture of a massive bureaucracy oppressing a helpless people."[12]

The problem with such a view, according to Deloria, is that it fails to acknowledge the existence of "early treaties and statutes by which Indians bargained and received . . . rights to services in return for enormous land cessions."[13] For those unaware of the history of treaty-making in the United States, the services provided to tribal nations may seem either like reparations for past harm or like rehabilitative welfare programs similar to those provided for the poor. Both of these models suggest that there can be a monetary value at which point whatever moral debts owed to Native people by the United States can be repaid, eventually absolving the federal government's trust relationship with Indian tribes. While this view is consistent with capitalist assumptions about the inherent fungibility of land and human life, it is inconsistent with the usufructuary paradigm historically assumed by many Indian tribes (including the Anishinaabeg) as the basis for the treaties they made with the United States. Simply put, tribal nations understand the resources they receive from the U.S. government to be compensation for the *use* of Native land, not its alienation. As long as the United States continues to occupy Native lands, treaties ensure that it bears a perpetual responsibility to provide health care, housing, food, and other resources to tribal nations.

In a certain sense, the services provided for by treaty act as a continual reminder of the United States' fundamental contingency as an occupying power. It is arguably this aspect of the treaty relationship that has made the United States anxious to free itself of its obligations since the late nineteenth century, when it first became apparent that Natives would not simply cease to exist as distinct peoples. With limited exceptions, lawmakers made a concentrated effort at ending treaty-mandated subsidies for most of the twentieth century, reaching a logical conclusion in the Termination policies of the 1940s–60s. What was at stake in this effort was not so much the costs of such subsidies (which were and remain a relatively tiny portion of the federal budget), but their symbolic power to reaffirm the existence of tribal nations' prior claims to the land—a power that Native protestors continue to draw on when they invoke a legacy of broken treaties.

Understanding the ambivalent history of state institutions in Indian Country, as well as the unique status of treaty-mandated subsidies, forces us to reformulate Amanda Claybaugh's contention about literature's relationship to state institutions as it applies to Native literature generally and the fiction of Louise Erdrich in particular. The majority of works by Native authors offer explicit (and explicitly negative) representations of state institutions. Novels such as *Ceremony*, *The Surrounded*, and *House Made of Dawn* all present the work of state institutions as being directly opposed to the tribal community—doing the important work of making visible the state's many abuses against Native people. Erdrich's work is, in many ways, the exception, in the sense that it shows state institutions working both against tribal interests and on their behalf. One may argue, as I will in this chapter, that Erdrich's work doesn't so much make the operation of state visible as much as it makes visible the principles by which the state operates, showing how the values and biases of those who carry out the day-to-day operations of the state inflect its activities for good or ill. The distinction, in Erdrich's fiction, lies in whether such institutions are administered by Euro-Americans or by Natives, showing how tribal control of the state's bureaucratic organs actually produces institutions that are not only more receptive to tribal cultures, but also (a little) more just.

On July 8, 1970, President Richard Nixon expressed a similar sentiment when outlining a new approach to federal Indian policy in a statement directed to both houses of Congress. In it, Nixon declared that, although the United States had ignored its treaty obligations for much of its history, "the special relationship between the Indian tribes and the Federal government which arises from these agreements continues to carry immense moral and legal force." Rejecting paternalism and termination as "two equally harsh and unacceptable extremes," Nixon declared his intent to usher in "a new era in which the Indian future is determined by Indian acts and Indian decisions." Nixon's solution was "to strengthen the Indian's sense of autonomy without threatening his sense of community" by delinking the positive benefits of state institutions from the bigoted drive to deracinate Natives.

> We must assure the Indian that he can assume control of his own life without being separated involuntary from the tribal group. And we must make it clear that Indians can become independent of Federal control without being cut off from Federal concern and Federal support.

Nixon proposed that such a task could only effectively be accomplished by allowing Native nations to administer state institutions for themselves, arguing that "the Indians will get better programs and that public monies will be more effectively expended if the people who are most affected by these programs are responsible for operating them."[14] Nixon's reforms strengthened tribal governments considerably by vesting in them the authority to administer their own education and health services. Subsequent court decisions and legal reforms have expanded the power of tribal nations even more, recognizing their ability to establish their own bureaucracies, generate revenue, and provide services directly to their constituencies. In the four decades since Nixon's reforms, Indian nations—including those of the Anishinaabeg—have begun to look less like federally administered ethnic enclaves and increasingly more like nation-states.

Taken as a whole, the entire Matchi Manitou series narrates the story of one Anisihnaabe community's effort to transform their reservation from a carceral institution to a stable nation-state. This change is effected not through rejection of federal influence, but through the ability of Natives—like Nanapush—to gain access to the management of the state institutions in order to limit their potential for racist abuse. The characters who most effectively work toward this change are those who have embraced a degree of upward mobility, most often presented as an assent to federal programs that are meant to make Native people more economically self-sufficient. While many such programs have been criticized as efforts to break the ties of communal reciprocity, in Erdrich's novels the privilege gained by upwardly mobile Natives tends to find its way back to the tribal community, either materially or in terms of expanded political power.

As Bruce Robbins theorizes, narratives of upward mobility in literature are politically significant because "by focusing on the passage *between* identities and how one gets from here to there, they reveal something interesting about power, which can never be located in one identity alone."[15] By presenting power as something between people of dissimilar social positions that is shared and withheld, lent, given, or taken, stories of upward mobility, according to Robbins, hold a mirror to the structures of feeling that guide the power of the state—in particular the welfare state. As characters in these novels rise in social standing, the reader sees how their rise is achieved only through the intervention and assistance of benefactors, patrons, wardens, and a host of others. Stories such as these create in the reader a sense that innate ability and self-sufficiency—heroic virtues in the ur-narrative of capitalism—are secondary to the democratic desire to aid others in achieving relatively more comfortable lives. The democratization of social responsibility that these narratives present reinforces and recapitulates the ideological assumptions that drive the welfare state, namely, that society as a whole bears some responsibility to improve the lives of those who are disadvantaged.

In this chapter, I will look at two of Erdrich's recent novels, *The Plague of Doves* (2008) and *The Painted Drum* (2005), examining the way in which they imagine the Anishinaabeg people's relationship to the state through symbolically charged scenes of upward mobility. In *The Plague of Doves*, the rise of Antone Bazil Coutts from deracinated lay-about to an activist tribal judge is brought about with by a years-long affair with a white racist, allegorically reflecting the ambiguous and contradictory effects of U.S. paternalism. In *The Painted Drum*, an Anishinaabe family is rescued from poverty and disaster through the efforts of both agents of the Anishinaabe nation-state and practitioners of traditional Anishinaabe religion—who are actually one and the same—showing the commensurability of state welfare institutions and the Anishinaabe philosophical ideal of mino bimaadiziwin. Showing the state to be both a source of trauma as well as identity, these narratives challenge our understanding of the way in which the state operates both in Native literature and Native nations. Paying attention to the ambiguities of the state's role in Native life in Erdrich's fiction, I argue, forces us to reconsider the purpose and intent of indigenous nationalism as it relates to the state-form of governance—especially in a time of increasing neoliberalism.

Erdrich's work suggests that the failures and abuses visited on Natives were never intrinsic to the structure of the state itself, but because its actions were (and often continue to be) guided by fundamentally racist attitudes that demean Anishinaabe cultural values. At the same time,

Erdrich's novels show how these same institutions, once brought under tribal control, can be made more consistent with Anishinaabe values—transforming them into an imperfect, but critically important, means of material and cultural survival. Showing the pressing need for the Anishinaabeg to control their own bureaucratic institutions in order to limit their potential for abuse, Erdrich's work reflects the political and philosophical assumptions that underwrite the self-determination policies that have governed U.S.-Anishinaabeg relations for the past half-century. At the same time, Erdrich's work shows how adherence to traditional Anishinaabe values makes one reconceive the project of ensuring the welfare of others as something that transcends (and even challenges) the boundaries of the nation.

Holding a Wolf by the Ear

In Erdrich's entire oeuvre, perhaps no character goes through a more paradigmatic upward mobility narrative than Antone Bazil Coutts in *The Plague of Doves*. Tracing the arc of Coutts's life from an apolitical border town youth to a tribal judge working to reassert Anishinaabe sovereignty, *The Plague of Doves* not only presents Coutts's mobility in terms of class, but also identity. Over the course of *Plague*, Coutts moves from the (literal) margins of Anishinaabe society to its center, becoming an important figure in both the secular and spiritual affairs of his community. Coutts's rise is primarily facilitated through his years-long affair with Cordelia Lochren, a white woman. Much older than Coutts, Cordelia met her future lover after curing him of mysterious, and potentially cancerous "head lumps" when he was a child. They begin sleeping together when Coutts is only seventeen, and continue their affair off and on for several years—even after Cordelia marries.

Throughout his narration, Coutts never refers to Cordelia by name, only by the initial "C.," a stylistic affectation that purposefully aligns his story with similar "older woman" narratives in the realist novels of the nineteenth century. Reading this trope in the novels of Balzac, Stendhal, and Dickens through the philosophical and biographical writings of Rousseau, Bruce Robbins suggests that such "older woman" narratives played an important role in the development of theories of social citizenship that laid the groundwork for the welfare state. In these stories of "erotic patronage," the relationship between a younger man and older woman is an example of "'unnatural' love—provisional, frustrating, often unconsummated matchups that do not aim at or end in marriage, reproduction, or heterosexual union of any sanctioned or enduring sort," which parallel "a story about the 'unnatural' emergence of the institutions of modern social democracy, institutions that could come into existence only by taking over some of the functions and responsibilities that used to be seen as natural to the individual and the family." Guided by an older woman who acts both as a lover (either platonic or romantic) and a surrogate mother, the young men in such stories are able to rise in social position because of their patron's benign desire to see a disadvantaged subordinate become an equal—the same kind of desire that lies at the heart of the political project of the welfare state.[16]

At first glance, the relationship between Coutts and Cordelia reflects this trope of erotic patronage well—at least in its structural aspects. At the beginning of their relationship Cordelia is successful and financially independent, while Coutts is directionless teenager from a once-important, but now poor, family of mixed-blood lawyers. Coutts draws attention to the disparity of their age and social positions by describing Cordelia as "slightly bigger" than himself, and as someone who moves her body "with the agility of a high school wrestler" while in bed.[17] Both sexually dominant and tenderly maternal, Cordelia "was a great believer in the restorative powers of milk and honey," feeding Coutts sandwiches and milk in order to sustain his energy during marathon sessions of love making (274). As one would expect from generic convention, this difference in social status becomes a goad to Coutts's desire for upward mobility, or as he puts it, "getting [him]self ahead" (280). In order to be nearer to Cordelia, Coutts takes his first job at the cemetery that abuts her property. As she begins to show interest in a wealthier suitor her own age, Coutts is driven to earn his law degree and pass the bar exam to prove his ability and his worth. Despite his rise in the world, Cordelia refuses to consider Coutts's multiple marriage proposals, citing their extreme difference in age.

In the historical tradition of the novel of erotic patronage, the difference in age between the young patron and his older benefactor correlates with the difference between their social classes. As the younger man rises in the world, the class distinctions separating him from his mistress begin to disappear, while their age difference remains. In the novels of Balzac and Stendhal, the erotic patronage between the older benefactor and the younger beneficiary comes to an end when the success of the younger partner instills in him the desire to start a family. Because of her age and position, the older woman cannot fulfill this desire, either because reproduction has become biologically impossible, or because doing so would lead to her social ruin. Almost invariably, the younger man abandons his mistress after finding a partner who is both his social equal and a match for him in age, with whom he may raise a family. Robbins reads this moment as symbolic of the goal of the welfare state, in which newly enfranchised citizens are filled with the desire to perpetuate the society in which they now have a stake.[18]

In *The Plague of Dove*'s erotic patronage narrative, however, class is not the only social determinate that separates the older woman from her younger counterpart—racial difference also plays a critical, if unacknowledged, role in the power imbalance of the relationship. The definitive end of Coutts and Cordelia's relationship comes when Coutts learns that Cordelia's refusal to publicly acknowledge their relationship has nothing to do with the difference in their ages, but because Cordelia harbors a strong hatred of Natives. Coutts is confronted with the depth of Cordelia's racism when he discovers that throughout her entire career as a border-town doctor, she always refused to treat Native people—even in emergencies. In light of this revelation, Coutts is forced to reassess the entire secret decades-long affair:

> I understood, then, that I'd known everything and nothing about the doctor. Only later did I realize; if I had been the same age as C., it would not have mattered. Even though she had treated my head bumps, become my lover, I'd always be her one exception. Or worse, her absolution. Every time I touched her, she was forgiven. (292)

Cordelia's racism is largely unconscious, making it ambiguous and unstable. Explaining why she rejected Indian patients in the final pages of the novel, Cordelia claims not to be "a bigoted person," explaining that her decision to deny treatment to Natives "shamed her." Rather, she explains that she experiences a "specific paralysis" when seeing Native people, an "unsteady weakness in their presence" (298). Given the confessional tone of the passage, we, as readers, have little reason to doubt the honesty of Cordelia's statement. The nature of Cordelia's "paralysis" and "weakness" before Natives speaks to a kind of fear based (as all racist beliefs are) on the perpetuation of a false narrative. Indeed, Cordelia was allowed to believe, well into adulthood, that her family was massacred by a group of Anishinaabeg, even though there was evidence enough to implicate a local white man (307). By the time she learns the truth, however, her mistrust and fear of Indian savagery has hardened into unconscious habit. Cordelia's feelings about Native people lack the force of genocidal disgust, but are still strong enough to compel her to treat them as social inferiors, and refuse them access to medical care.

If, as Robbins argues, erotic patronage narratives reflect the same structures of feeling that inform the relationship between subject and the state, then we may read Cordelia and Coutts's relationship as paralleling that of the United States and the Anishinaabeg—a relationship historically defined by two conflicting desires: a humanitarian desire to promote Native welfare, and the racist desire for Native land and resources. Cordelia's unstable, ill-defined prejudice is similar to that espoused by those who advocated for the expansion of state involvement in Indian life during the assimilation era of the late-nineteenth and early-twentieth centuries. As Beth Piatote notes, such advocacy marked a distinct shift in the character of anti-Indian racism in the United States, stating, "To these advocates, policies of assimilation—that is the systematic conversion of communal Indian land and cultural practices into individuated 'civilized' forms amenable to market capitalism and liberal democracy—were preferable to the policies of bloody annihilation."[19]

Like Cordelia, the architects of the assimilation era were able to denounce bigotry, even as their policies were structured by the racist assumption that white culture and economic privilege were norms to which Natives failed to conform. As Piatote and others have capably argued, the push to "improve" the material lives of Native people during this period was inextricably linked with processes of dispossession. In the nineteenth and early twentieth centuries, the U.S. state tied access to material welfare (food, clothing, education) to the proper performance of cultural, religious, and economic activities that reinforced the supremacy of both capitalism and white culture. The result was a system where upward mobility was predicated on the explicit rejection of a tribal identity, both in terms of culture as well as any communal economic practice not aligned with capitalism. Breaking down the cultural and economic cohesion of the tribal community eased the way for capitalist interests to alienate tribal lands and extract labor from Native bodies.

Given the parallels between this history and the narrative of Cordelia and Coutts's affair, it is unsurprising that the crisis that definitively ends their relationship revolves around an act of dispossession. In order to pay off the costs of law school, Coutts is convinced to sell his family's home to Cordelia's land-speculating husband, Ted, who wants to tear it down. Immediately after the sale, Coutts realizes that the house is not just his property, but his identity, telling the reader, "I could feel myself chopped into, gutted, chipped out, destroyed . . . reduced to bones or beams" (287). The degree to which Coutts identifies with his family's home not just as a place of fond memories, but as a part of his physical body has obvious resonances with traditional Anishinaabe beliefs about the sacredness of the land, but more than that, it suggests a dawning recognition on the part of Coutts that his path to upward mobility has not been without significant personal cost. In selling his home, Coutts has, in a sense, surrendered his understanding of his family's history and his own identity as an Anishinaabe. That Cordelia allows Ted to go through with the demolition forces Coutts into the painful realization that Cordelia has demanded such sacrifices the entire time they had been together. Adding the factor of race to a narrative trope that historically has been concerned only with class difference, Coutts and Cordelia's story of erotic patronage illustrates the ways racism adds an unexpected complication to the upward mobility story. Just as Cordelia's racism will not allow her to consider marrying Coutts (and admit their social equality), so too is mere economic upward mobility incapable of producing true social equality between Natives and whites. No amount of economic success can fully insulate the Native subject from racism (although it may mitigate its effects considerably), a situation that will always foreclose the possibility of attaining true social citizenship even for upwardly mobile Natives.

The arc of Coutts's narrative is echoed in *The Plague of Doves* in the palimpsestic presence of Louis Riel, as he is remembered by the character Mooshum. Like Coutts, Riel was an educated and urbane mixed-blood with legal training, who returned to his people in order to help them resist the aggressions of the Canadian state. While many remember Riel as separatist revolutionary, Mooshum characterizes him as committed to democratic inclusion—fighting for the integration of Natives and the Métis into Canadian society as political and social equals. As Mooshum declares, Riel's conflict was not a "rebellion" (32), as a white character describes it, but "an issue of rights" (33).

> Getting their rights recognized when they had already proved the land—the Michifs and the whites. And [the Cree leader] old Poundmaker. They wanted the government to do something. That's all. And the government pissed about this way and that so old Riel says, 'We'll do it for you!' Ha! Ha! Howah! 'We'll do it for you!' (33)

In Mooshum's telling, the real roots of the conflict between Riel and Canada had everything to do with the Canadian government's failure to live up to its own democratic mandate, excluding indigenous peoples from meaningful participation in the nation-state in order to dispossess them of their lands. Riel's uprising, Mooshum suggests, was as much about resisting racist exclusion from the state as it was about resisting imperial incorporation into it.

The parallels *The Plague of Doves* draws between Coutts and Riel suggests that Euro-American racism toward Natives has the unintended effect of redirecting upwardly mobile Natives' sense of social citizenship back toward their own communities. Prior to the demolition of his home, Coutts saw himself entering private legal practice, hoping to make money once he'd "hung out [his] shingle" (286). Like the historical Riel, Coutts's dispossession galvanizes his resolve to use his legal education to work on behalf of his people: "I got some land back for one tribe, went to Washington, helped with a case regarding tribal religion, one thing and another, until I jumped at the chance to come back. Only not to Pluto, but to the reservation" (289).

Coutts's narrative invites the reader to see how Euro-American racism acts the centripetal force that keeps upwardly mobile Natives from being propelled into assimilation. Cordelia's feelings for Coutts are not predicated on his qualities as an individual, but on his ability to represent a constellation of conflicting emotions she has toward all Natives. As such, Coutts is forced to reimagine his subjectivity in the context of their romantic relationship, as well as his place in society, as being defined by his Anishinaabe identity—something he had never seriously considered before. By being reduced to a mere representative of a social group, Coutts is forced to identify with members of his own tribe in ways he may not have otherwise. The social surplus of this identity forces Coutts to recognize the degree to which his relationship with Cordelia came at the expense of his own people—he was the "exception" given special treatment denied to others. Seeing himself as unfairly privileged causes Coutts to assume a portion of responsibility for Cordelia's mistreatment of his people. The novel confirms as much when Coutts describes his ignorance of Cordelia's racism as evidence of his "off-reservation" mind-set (291). He had no knowledge of the harm being caused by Cordelia's bitter feelings toward other Natives because he didn't imagine himself as being part of a larger Anishinaabe community.

Using another upward mobility narrative in which Coutts becomes the benefactor to a young Anishinaabe man, *The Plague of Doves* shows how an upwardly mobile Native in a position of institutional authority is able to limit the state's abuse. Several years after the end of his affair with Cordelia, Coutts has become the tribal judge for the reservation, hearing the case of Corwin Peace, a troubled youth that some in the community consider as having "no redeeming value whatsoever" (197). Coutts tells the reader that he takes a particular interest in Corwin because he believes he "was fated from the beginning to witness the full down-arcing shape of [Corwin's] life's trajectory" (198). Surely enough, Corwin comes under Coutts's jurisdiction when he is arrested for tying up his elderly uncle, Shamengwa, and stealing his priceless violin. In deciding what to do with Corwin, Coutts tells the reader:

> I have a great deal of latitude in sentencing. In spite of my conviction that he was probably incorrigible, I was intrigued by Corwin's unusual treatment of the instrument. I could not help thinking of his ancestors, the Peace brothers, Henri and Lafayette. Perhaps there was a dormant talent. And perhaps as they had saved my grandfather, I was meant to rescue their descendant. These sorts of implications are simply part of tribal justice. I decided to take advantage of my prerogative to use tribally based traditions in sentencing and to set precedent. Then I sentenced Corwin to apprentice himself with the old master. . . . He would learn to play the violin, or he would do time. (209)

This passage shows how the operations of the state fundamentally change when an Anishinaabe is able to direct them. The judgment Coutts renders onto Corwin understands him as one part of a complex system of mutual obligation and social history (indicative of a deeply Anishinaabe worldview, as I shall discuss later on)—instead of a mere criminal in need of discipline. Instead of inflicting on Corwin a jail sentence that would remove him from his community, Coutts uses his legal "prerogative" to enmesh Corwin more deeply in it. Coutts's experiment works, and Corwin, under Shamengwa's guidance, becomes a successful violinist. After Shamengwa passes, Corwin inherits the same priceless violin he had previously tried to steal. Out of grief for his uncle and mentor, Corwin has it buried with Shamengwa—choosing to honor the memory of a kinsman than profit from his passing.

In his ability to renegotiate the state's response to Corwin's criminal activity, Coutts is engaged in a process of cross-cultural translation that makes the values of his community apprehensible to the institutions of the liberal state. According to the Anishinaabe political philosopher Dale Turner, such translation is an essential strategy for indigenous communities in liberal settler-states, saying, "As *a matter of survival*, Aboriginal intellectuals must engage the non-Aboriginal intellectual landscapes from which their political rights and sovereignty are articulated and put to use in Aboriginal communities."[20] For Turner, this work is done by those, like Coutts, who translate "Indigenous philosophies . . . rooted in oral traditions" into "the discourses of rights, sovereignty, and nationhood" on which the liberal state is structured.[21] At once articulating communal values into the discourse of individual rights, while simultaneously questioning the universality of liberal individualism, Turner suggests that such intellectuals "broaden the intellectual landscape from which the normative language of rights can evolve,"[22] creating the opportunity for "indigenous voices to help determine the normative language used for defining the meaning and content of Aboriginal rights discourse."[23]

What is important about Coutts's judgment is not just the way it reflects Anishinaabe values, but also how it communicates those values back to the state in a language that it understands. Coutts intimately understands that the legal framework in which he is embedded is incommensurate, if not hostile, to Anishinaabe values—recalling the Robert Burton quote Coutts gives early on in the novel, "He who goes to law holds a wolf by the ear" (114). Therefore, Coutts decides to "takes advantage of [his] prerogative to use tribally based traditions in sentencing," in order to "set precedent," giving Anishinaabe traditions the force of recognized juridical value. In so doing, he challenges the entrenched cultural assumptions of white supremacy by showing that an Anishinaabe value system has the intellectual coherence to form the basis of a functioning, modern society. Coutts's ability to do this work requires his understanding of both sets of cultural traditions, along with a willingness to find value and commonalities between them—not a rejection of one set for another. Ultimately, *Plague of Doves* suggests that the potential for Anishinaabe communities to continue to exist means breaking down the corrosive ideology of white supremacy embedded within the state by challenging the normativity of Euro-American cultural values while simultaneously articulating the intellectual and moral coherence of Anishinaabe cultural values back to Euro-American society. In so doing, the Anishinaabeg are able to shape policy on their own behalf, but also meaningfully challenge the normativity of white supremacy and its ideological basis, capitalism.

This critical process of resistance and translation is one that Erdrich's novels do not just depict, but participate in. In their positive representations of tribal government, Erdrich's novels work toward two distinct but ideologically related goals. First, to present the Anishinaabe nation-state and its institutions as an imperfect but critically important means of protecting Native life, and to show how such protection is not necessarily antithetical to traditional Anishinaabe cultural identity. In so doing, Erdrich's fiction speaks to two different audiences with differing perceptions about the state's involvement in Indian affairs: Natives who experience the ambiguously positive effects of tribally administered programs, as well as non-Natives who are largely unaware that they hold an enormous amount of power to ensure that such programs continue. In speaking to both audiences simultaneously, Erdrich's fiction strikes a balance between acknowledging the undeniable history of state institutions' devastating assaults on Native peoples and cultures, and the critical importance of defending many of these same institutions from contemporary efforts of neoliberal interests to defund and dismantle them.

An Almost Painful Happiness

On November 1, 2011, the journalist Mark Trahant (Shoshone-Bannock) stood before the gathered tribal government leaders at the annual conference of the National Congress of the American Indian and announced that the Self-Determination Era was over. Indian nations now faced what Trahant called the "Era of Contraction." According to Trahant, the series of economic crises that has gripped the world after 2008 had fundamentally changed the relationship between the United States and tribal nations. Pointing out that the policies that most threatened tribal sovereignty (allotment, removal, termination) came during times of economic instability and government contraction, Trahant argued that current efforts on the part of the U.S. and state governments to enact austerity measures would have a disastrous effect on the prosperity and political rights of tribal nations.

> [T]he policy of contraction puts Indian Country at risk of a total economic collapse. It's as if policy makers want to see how bad things can get on reservations and in native communities where the economy is already bleak. The policy recipe being advocated is to significantly reduce government funding; reduce or eliminate the only good paying jobs available, and hope for the best. In the larger economy the mantra is that the private sector will pick up the pieces. But that is total fiction in remote Alaska villages or on Indian reservations because there is no significant private sector. The vast majority of jobs are government, either tribal or federal.[24]

While acknowledging that specific cuts to programs directly benefiting Natives had yet to be made, Trahant pointed out that much of the federal money that comes into Indian Country actually comes from national-level welfare initiatives—like Medicaid and Medicare, social security, and food assistance programs—that were major targets of proposed austerity measures.

The years have largely borne out Trahant's prediction. Since 2011, the budget of the BIA has faced yearly cuts that have made it increasingly difficult for the agency to provide contract costs for tribally administered services. An internal budget document produced by the BIA in 2015 presented the effects of these cuts in uncharacteristically dire language for a bureaucratic organization.

> The FY 2013 sequestration cuts of 5.04%, on top of an additional 8% in permanent rescissions since FY 2000, has caused immediate and severe damage to tribes' abilities to protect human life. If sequestration cuts are not restored, the safety and living standards of tribal members living in Indian communities will further diminish. It will require decades to reverse the third world living standards that sequestration and permanent rescissions have imposed on Indian Country.[25]

As noted above, the latest round of cuts are but one instantiation of a longer trend of divestment stretching back at least two decades. Even as tribal nations have assumed greater authority to manage their own institutions, the funding on which those institutions rely has been steadily shrinking, despite the fact that such funding is oftentimes mandated by treaty. Some tribes have been able to make up for budget shortfalls by developing their own revenue streams—sometimes by pursuing less-than-sustainable forms of resource extraction.

This turn of events was likely welcome news for Chris Edwards, a neoliberal economist at the Cato Institute who has openly called for "Repealing Indian subsidies and closing down the BIA," declaring such policies to be the "logical end goal of the Indian self-determination movement."[26] Arguing that "The government has taken many actions depriving Indians of their lands, resources, and freedom," Edwards has suggested that tribal nations should prevent such abuses in the future by ending their reliance on institutions that have "exploited, coddled, and micromanaged Indians."[27] According to Edwards, "As the tribes move further toward self-governance, the trust responsibility becomes less relevant," since tribes should be able to support their own people by "maximiz[ing] the returns from their lands and resources."[28] Outlining his vision for the future of Indian Country, Edwards calls for the privatization and development of all remaining trust land, and redefining "Indian sovereignty" as "the autonomy of the Indian person."[29]

Edwards's position, though extreme, points to the uncomfortable way in which the rhetoric of tribal self-determination and sovereignty has become imbricated with the ideology of liberalism. Rather than understand self-determination as a pragmatic response to U.S. mistreatment and mismanagement, Edwards sees absolute autonomy as the ultimate end-point of tribal politics—even to the point at which the very idea of a tribe becomes antithetical to the attainment of an individual's sovereignty. In calling the end of federal subsidies the "logical end goal" of self-determination, Edwards neatly elides the historical import of the trust relationship and the critical role treaty-mandated subsidies play as a perpetual reminder of tribal nation's prior claims to the land on which the United States exists. What makes Edwards's argument particularly insidious is in the way it uses the United States' brutal treatment of Natives as an excuse for Natives to abandon the treaty relationship and turn, instead, to the free market—cynically obscuring capitalism's motivating role in the history of Native dispossession.

Despite what one might think of Edwards's conflation of tribal sovereignty with austerity, his argument reveals a fundamental, if unfortunate, truth. If tribal nations are to continue to ensure their people's health and welfare without having to engage in capitalist exploitation of labor or natural resources, then they must communicate the necessity of their funding to those who hold de facto power over it: the American people. Despite the obvious injustice of the situation, it remains a pragmatic necessity to convince non-Natives that treaty-mandated subsidies are necessary to the existence of tribal nations (at least until such time as the relationship between tribal nations and the United States can be significantly reformed). This is the political work that I see Erdrich's fiction carrying out—communicating the social and historical importance of the United States's trust responsibility to non-Natives who may not understand the role their tax dollars and their votes play in maintaining it. By employing the rhetoric of cultural persistence, Erdrich's fiction works to show how treaty-mandated subsidies, when disseminated via tribal nation-states, serve to protect and even strengthen traditional tribal values. In so doing, Erdrich's novels offer a robust defense of the United States's trust responsibilities from neoliberal efforts to end them.

Nowhere is this more clear than in Erdrich's 2005 novel, *The Painted Drum*, which explicitly shows state institutions working not only to strengthen Anishinaabe cultural practices, but to save Anishinaabe lives. In the novel's most memorable section, readers are presented with a dire scenario: three young Anishinaabe children have been left alone in a remote cabin—without food, electricity, or heat—after their desperate mother attempts to earn money by prostituting herself at a local bar. As a severe blizzard rolls in from the north, the children struggle to stay warm. As a last resort, the eldest child, nine-year-old Shawnee, starts a fire on the floor of their living room that quickly spreads to the rest of the house. The children barely escape the fire with their lives, only to find themselves exposed to the freezing night. Shawnee and her siblings struggle through the blizzard for hours, until finally reaching the safety of their neighbor's house three miles away. The bulk of the narrative takes place after this harrowing event, focusing on the children's recovery in an Indian Health Service hospital, where it becomes increasingly clear how the children's current and future survival is predicated on the existence of imperfect, but functioning, welfare institutions.

The Painted Drum's positive depiction of two of these institutions may come as a surprise to readers knowledgeable about Native history. The reputations of the Indian Health Service (IHS) and Indian Child Welfare services are checkered at best, with both programs implicated in multiple human rights violations during the twentieth century. Over the past four decades, however, both the IHS and Indian Child Welfare have been the subject of massive reforms—carried out in large part by the Natives who took over their administration—eventually becoming important (if imperfect) resources for tribal nations and their peoples. Never well funded to begin with, both the IHS and Indian Child Welfare have recently come under great political pressure to be defunded and disbanded—with most strident criticism coming from non-Native lawmakers from the conservative right. Using many of the same critiques Native reformers launched at these dysfunctional institutions over the past century, neoliberal interests have embraced a rhetoric of government abuse and dysfunction as an excuse to abolish treaty-mandated services to tribal communities altogether.

The Painted Drum is, to my mind, in direct conversation with those who would seek to defund services such as the IHS and Indian Child Welfare, showing how both can work for the benefit of a Native family in distress. Doing so requires overcoming their historical legacy of violence and abuse in order to convince readers that such institutions can be trusted to do right. The novel does so not only by making visible the work of these programs (in the sense that Amanda Claybaugh uses the term), but by showing how they do not necessarily conflict with the values that inform traditional Anishinaabe communal identity. Instead, *The Painted Drum* shows how, in an idealized form, an Anishinaabe nation-state can not only provide adequate care for it citizens, but that doing so can be an extension of traditional Anishinaabe values. By presenting this idealized version of the Anishinaabe nation-state, *The Painted Drum* works against the antistatist rhetoric of neoliberal interests who would seek to defund treaty-mandated subsidies, while offering a sustained critique of neoliberalism's rhetoric of heroic individualism and personal responsibility.

Given the larger theme of rehabilitating the image of state's function in Indian Country, it makes sense that the majority of "The Little Girl Drum" focuses on the work of the Indian Health Service. Founded in 1955 as the only federally funded health-care provider for civilians in the U.S., the IHS has come under repeated criticism for its outdated facilities, inept employees, and rationed care. Despite acting as the primary source of medical services for many tribal people, especially those in remote reservation communities, the IHS has been chronically underfunded for its entire existence. As late as 2009, the average yearly expenditure by the IHS on Indian health care was only slightly more than half that spent on health care for inmates of federal prisons, per capita.[30] Stories of waiting for long periods in IHS waiting rooms, only to be misdiagnosed or mistreated by inexperienced or indifferent doctors—or be turned away without seeing any doctor at all—are all too familiar to many Natives (myself included).[31] This negative reputation has become so entrenched that even the woman who was responsible for the oversight of the IHS during the Obama administration, Secretary of Health and Human Services Kathleen Sebelius, publicly described the Service as a "historic failure."[32]

Even more damning are the accusations of human rights abuses carried out by doctors working under the auspices of the IHS. In 1972, a physician and activist named Constance Redbird Pinkerton-Uri brought public attention to the case of a Native woman who had been sterilized by IHS doctors without full understanding of the consequences of the procedure. A subsequent investigation by the Government Accountability Office that found that 3,406 Native women had been sterilized in the four years between 1973 and 1976. A number of these women, the GAO found, were coerced by IHS doctors who had not fully explained the procedure or claimed that the women's welfare services would be withheld if they were not sterilized. The same report also found that the IHS had participated in medical experiments that used tribal populations as test subjects, as well. While these experiments were found to be unlikely to cause health impacts, the GAO reported that experimenters had neither provided adequate information, nor obtained clear consent, from those Natives used as test subjects.³³ These incidents, in addition to the Service's other failings, have led some to characterize the IHS's treatment of Natives as not just ineffective, but actively genocidal.³⁴

This representation of the IHS has worked its way into the popular imagination, where its emotionally compelling claims are repeated and strengthened in works of art. Take, for example, Sherman Alexie's depiction of the IHS from the opening paragraph of *Indian Killer* (1996).

> The sheets are dirty. An Indian Health Service hospital in the late sixties. On this reservation or that reservation. Any reservation, a particular reservation. Antiseptic, cinnamon, and danker odors. Anonymous cries up and down the hallways. Linoleum floors swabbed with gray water. Mop smelling like old sex. Walls painted white a decade earlier, now yellowed and peeling. . . . Twenty beds available, twenty beds occupied. Waiting room where a young Indian man sits on a couch and holds his head in his hands. Nurses' lounge, two doctor's offices, and a scorched coffee pot. . . . Donated newspapers and magazines stacked in bundles, months and years out of date, missing pages. In one of the examining rooms, an Indian family of four, mother, father, son, daughter, all coughing blood quietly into handkerchiefs.³⁵

In Alexie's deliriously imaginative introduction, the IHS hospital literally becomes a front in a war the U.S. government still wages with Natives—a place where Indian babies are kidnapped after delivery and loaded into military helicopters that "strafe the reservation with explosive shells."³⁶ While this representation of the IHS as a staging ground in a campaign of genocide is obviously hyperbolic, the history of the institution lends the scene an understandable emotional plausibility.

Compare this with a similarly expositive description of an IHS hospital in *The Painted Drum*.

> The nurse tucked the digital thermometer underneath Shawnee's arm and she swam up from her dream to half-wakefulness. She heard the *woosh* of the pump on the blood pressure cuff, and heard it again as the nurse stood over Alice. An hour ago, Shawnee's hands had throbbed and itched, but now that the medicine the nurse had given her had kicked in, she was comfortable. The nurse went out of the room, but Shawnee did not return entirely to sleep. The door was open a crack

and she could hear the nurses talking at their big round station in the middle of the ward. It was comforting talk.... As the room and its safety surrounded her, she was flooded by a startling and almost painful happiness.[37]

The Painted Drum's idealized depiction of the IHS hospital is no less hyperbolic than that in Indian Killer, but it too contains a kernel of truth. In its best incarnation, the IHS hospital can act as a space of safety, security, and community—just as in its worst it can be a place of despair, dispossession, and abuse. The Painted Drum presents the IHS hospital as a safe space in which Shawnee and her mother, Ira, can go through a process of both physical and emotional healing without having to worry about how to meet their needs. Indeed, members of the IHS staff not only care for the children, but go out of their way to provide Ira with extra food, clean clothes, and a place to sleep. Although we are constantly reminded of the utter destitution of Ira's family, the cost of her children's health care is never addressed as an issue. The routine kindness shown toward Ira and her children by anonymous IHS doctors and nurses are not the charitable acts of individuals, but representative of a larger therapeutic institution where care for community members is the operating norm.

This sense is disrupted, however, by Ira's cousin, Honey, who provides a stark contrast to the anonymous benevolence of the hospital. A nurse at the hospital, Honey is the only member of the medical staff to be identified by name. Described as "round and cute, and full of satisfaction about her house and children and hard-working husband," Honey talks to Ira's children "because they made her feel so much better about her own children and her situation in this life" (239). When Honey tries to convince Shawnee that her mother is responsible for the fire, her unprofessional manner causes Shawnee to wonder "if Honey went to school or just practiced until she got the job of nurse" (239). The moment is telling in its ability to illustrate how, in the context of an otherwise functional institution, a single negative interaction is enough to sow distrust for the entire hospital. In an environment where care is a norm, one can become conditioned to notice only the failure to live up to that norm. In this sense, just as Honey stands out from an otherwise anonymous hospital staff due to her unprofessional manner, the history of IHS's systemic accomplishments (rendered difficult to see by their scale) are often ignored in favor of stories about the agency's dysfunction—limiting the political will to defend the IHS from defunding and privatization.

At the time of *The Painted Drum*'s publication in 2005, the political support for the IHS was indeed at an all-time low. The automatic appropriation measures of the Indian Health Care Improvement Act (IHCIA) had long expired, forcing Congress to reauthorize spending for IHS operations every year. According to a 2004 report from the U.S. Commission on Civil Rights, such appropriations had "failed to account for medical inflation rates and increases in population," leading to spending rates far below the national average in health care expenditure.[38] Opposition to the reauthorization of IHCIA was spearheaded by then Oklahoma Senator Tom Coburn, who had consistently blocked prior attempts to increase funding for the IHS. Declaring that "Indian health care is the worst,"[39] Coburn proposed that funds already appropriated for the IHS instead be allocated individually, forcing Natives to buy health care à la carte or purchase private insurance on the open market—despite the fact that per capita spending on the IHS was (and remains) far below average health care costs.[40] In an effort to gain support for his proposal, Coburn publicly recounted the graphic details of incidents of Indian patients receiving substandard care.

> Rhonda Sandland couldn't get help for her advanced frostbite until she threatened suicide. Though her hands were purple and she could not dress herself, she could not get an appointment at the Indian health clinic. When she finally got one, the clinic decided to remove five of her fingers. Fortunately, a visiting doctor intervened and gave her drugs instead—saving her fingers.[41]

Coburn argued that incidents like this were the result of a "broken system" that "rations health care services on a 'life or limb' basis" not because of chronic underfunding, but because it is "insulated from any competition."[42]

In the face of these attacks, many prominent Native Americans rose to defend the IHS. In a speech before Congress, Jefferson Keel, then vice president of the National Congress of the American Indian, testified: "the IHS has been characterized over the past decade as a 'broken' system. The truth is that the IHS system is not so much broken as it is 'starved.'"[43] Mark Trahant went even further, stating in an editorial that, "with sufficient resources, the Indian Health Service could be the model for reform," due to its investments in "in education, sanitation and preventative care."[44] An internal report on the history of the IHS confirms Trahant's point, finding that the Service had a profound impact on the public health of Native people.

In the first 25 years of the [IHS] program, infant mortality dropped by 82 percent, the maternal death rate decreased by 89 percent, the mortality rate from tuberculosis diminished by 96 percent, and deaths from diarrhea and dehydration fell by 93 percent. The improvement in Indians' health status outpaced the health gains of other disadvantaged U.S. populations. For example, between 1980 and 1992 infant mortality was nearly halved for Indians, whereas it decreased by 25 percent among African Americans.[45]

The report also found that, while the life expectancy for Native people in 1955 was a full nine years lower than that of the general population, the difference had been more than halved by 1999. These figures encouraged the coauthors of the report (one of whom was Dr. Angela Erdrich, IHS physician and younger sister of Louise) to conclude that the IHS is one of the "few bright spots . . . in the shared history of the American Indians and the federal government."[46]

As compelling the statistics may be, they do little to counteract the emotional impact of anecdotes of botched care, long lines, and mistreatment. The resulting imbalance makes the failures of the IHS highly visible while its successes remain obscure. *The Painted Drum* works to counteract this perception by simply presenting an IHS experience in which Indian children are saved from a life-threatening situation with effective medical treatment and nothing goes wrong. Although it would be absurd to think that Erdrich's novel had any real impact on the congressional debates leading up to the reauthorization of IHCIA in 2009, *The Painted Drum* does reflect the structure of feeling that guided Native activists, tribal leaders, and their allies who worked toward its passage—making it an important document for understanding the ambiguous attachment contemporary Native communities have to an institution that was not only a historical site of abuse, but continues to be, in many ways, inadequate to their needs.

We Live Because We Live

The Painted Drum does more, however, than simply present the work of state institutions in a positive light. Embedded in Ira's narrative is a pointed critique of a liberal concept of individualism and its attendant emphasis on personal responsibility—which the novel presents as antithetical to both the work of the welfare state and traditional Anishinaabe culture. The novel posits that desperate situation in which Ira finds herself is the product of a misguided conflation of Native identity with individual autonomy. Seeing subsistence and self-sufficiency as the most important aspect of Native identity, Ira has cut herself off from her tribal community out of fear that it is no longer culturally pure. We see this fear early on in the narrative, when Ira takes great offence at John String's suggestion that she may be in need of "spiritual help." Ira tells John that the mere mention of ceremony at a bar is hypocritical, saying, "You can be either a drunk or a spiritual person. Not both if you're an Indian. I'm sorry. That's the way it is" (202). For Ira, being Indian (N.B. *not* Anishinaabe) means that one either follows a path of traditional behavior, or falls into a failed state of authenticity—represented in this instance by the use of alcohol. The moral implications of either side of the binary are clear: the only good Indian is a traditional Indian. When John String asks Ira who came up with such a definition, she retorts, "Oh come on . . . the Shawnee Prophet. You ever heard of the Shawnee Prophet? That's who said" (202).

Invoking the memory of Tenskwatawa, Ira reveals a complex moral system in which personal responsibility, religious belief, and Native identity are made synonymous with one another. The Shawnee religious leader Tenskwatawa (1775–1836) founded a charismatic movement that would allow his brother, Tecumseh, to politically unite the various tribes of the Great Lakes region in common purpose during the first decade of the nineteenth century. In 1812, Tecumseh would draw this new religious coalition into war with the United States as allies of the British. Tenskwatawa's teachings, like those of Popé and other Native revitalizationist charismatics, were highly moralistic. Whites, so Tenskwatawa argued, were sent to earth by an evil spirit in order to punish Indian sinfulness. In order to return to the good graces of the Great Spirit, Tenskwatawa's followers were asked to make radical changes to their behavior—changes aimed almost entirely at ridding Native life of any shred of Euro-American influence. Some of these changes, like the prohibition of alcohol, no doubt were addressing the very real negative consequences of Euro-American colonialism, but Tenskwatawa's injunctions went beyond intoxicants. Followers were exhorted to abandon the use of any Euro-American technologies, including metal utensils, manufactured cloth, flint, steel, and domestic animals (even, ironically, dogs). It was only by rejecting the trappings of modernity and embracing historical subsistence practices that Tenskwatawa's followers could ameliorate the Great Spirit, who would eventually reward the faithful by ridding the continent of white interlopers.[47]

Seemingly having internalized Tenskwatawa's Manichean worldview (even going as far as to name one of her daughters Shawnee), Ira has spent the last several years attempting to adhere to what she perceives to be a traditional Indian lifestyle. Ira lives in the remote cabin of her late father, a "true-life bush Indian" (211). Ira remembers her father as a self-sufficient traditionalist who stubbornly supported himself through hunting and trapping despite the fact "there wasn't a living in it" (211), and who built his rustic cabin "by hand" (201) rather than accept the "cheap miracle" of tribally subsidized housing (201). In an attempt to emulate her father's self-sufficiency, Ira tries to support her family through beading—a high-skill occupation with historical resonances to traditional Anishinaabe women's labor—but has trouble selling her work due to the remoteness of her cabin. Ira eventually recognizes this irony, admitting, "If I moved into town, I guess I could do pretty well" (211). Ira's heroic image of her father is not only false (we later learn that he supported both himself and Ira with social security and a veteran's pension), it also reflects an emotionally charged ideology, derived from Tenskwatawa, which makes Native identity conditional on the performance of certain subsistence practices

The Painted Drum parodies this ideology through the character of Kit Tatro—a white wannabe from New England. Tatro strongly desires to be a Native person, going as far as to live in a tipi, harvest hides from roadkill, and wearing an array of charms that include "a bear's claw, a small tusk of some sort, a brown leather pouch that looks like it contains herbs, or maybe human knuckle bones" (52). Tatro pursues this lifestyle out of "the firm conviction that he is an American Indian" despite the fact that he "cannot decide which kind," his tribal affiliation a matter of subjective feeling, prone to change day-by-day (51). For all the humor we are meant to find at Tatro's expense, he acts in *The Painted Drum* as a very serious reminder of the impossibility of tribal identity as a set of discrete practices carried out by individuals. As the Anishinaabe character Fay Travers puts it, since "the point is to have a tribe and belong to a specific people," Tatro's actions can be nothing more than "a lonely obsession" in support of a "fantasy" (53). What makes Tatro into a figure of comedy is the same thing that makes Ira's story tragic: both fail to understand that traditional material practices are important not because of a spiritual quality inherent in their performance, but because they represent the literal subsistence of the tribal community. Outside of a communal context, the act of beading, trapping, or hunting has no significance other than appealing to the individual's sense of their own authentic experience. For both Ira and Tatro, the performance of subsistence activities is not the assertion of a tribal identity, but an inadequate substitution for it, meant to solace their own persistent feelings of inauthenticity and isolation.[48]

One of the most clearly didactic moments in *The Painted Drum* illustrates the way in which an insistence on individualism is antithetical to traditional Anshinaabe philosophy. The scene comes in the form of a story told by Bernard Shawaano, a janitor at the hospital. According to Bernard's story, Ira's father had once attempted suicide. Driven by despair, Ira's father goes to a frozen lake where he knows a pack of wolves congregates, sits on the ice, and asks the wolves "to sink their teeth into his heart" (119). After several days, one of the wolves—clearly a powerful manidoo (spiritual being)—approaches Ira's father and asks if he wants to die. Unsure of his answer, Ira's father asks the wolf, in turn: "How is it that you go on living with such sorrow? How do you go on without turning around and destroying yourselves, as so many of us Anishinaabeg have done under similar circumstances?" The wolf's answer is simple: "We live because we live" (120).

Behind this seemingly simple tautology lies a complex moral philosophy by which traditional Anishinaabeg life was, and continues to be, largely defined. Although there have been several recent attempts to do so, the concept of mino bimaadiziwin remains difficult to define—especially in brief. The term itself translates roughly to "the good way of living," being the nominalized form of the verb "mino bimaadizi" meaning "he or she lives well," or, perhaps better, "well-being." In one sense mino bimaadizi is a very simple idea, expressing one's ability to exist without hardship, starvation, and disease, but one could only achieve such a life through a complex relational process. As Michael McNally argues, "Ojibwe tradition values the cultivation of an awareness of one's interdependence in the web of life," allowing for an individual to achieve "a good life lived well in proper relationship with human and nonhuman persons."[49] The maintenance of relationships of interdependency formed a critical aspect of Anishinaabe philosophy, as Cary Miller explains.

> The only way to ensure *mino-bimaadiziwin* in all seasons was through establishing relationships of interdependency as widely as possible—including extended family in neighboring communities, and spiritual entities. In obtaining human assistance through the expansion of social networks to new families and communities, one also allied with those other-than-human persons who aided them.[50]

As such, achieving mino bimaadizi relied on the individual's ability to open themselves as widely as possible to relationships of interdependency in order to secure well-being for both themselves and those with whom they maintained relations. Such networks of interdependence were reciprocal, as those who received aid would be expected to offer it to others—and not just those who had helped them in the past. The opportunity for one to lend aid assistance to those who were not yet related was a chance to extend that person's own network of interdependency even further. The resulting networks of aid tied together disparate families into a doodem (clan), and doodemag into a tribe, but also created kin relationships with animals, natural phenomena, and the elements of the landscape itself—all considered to have an agentive existence in the form of manidoog whose aid could also be called on in times of need.[51]

This relational aspect of mino bimaadiziwin distinguishes it from Eurocentric conceptions of eudaemonia, through the way it imagines the role of individual in achieving the good life. With its emphasis on self-knowledge and personal virtue, the ideal of eudaemonia inherited from Aristotle takes the individual as a discrete ethical actor, whose quality of life is determined by the ability to master (in the widest possible sense of the word) his or her place in the world. For Aristotle, the goal of eudaemonia was as much about the care of soul (the *daimon*) as the body, focusing the individual's attention inward to attend to matters of rationalism, knowledge, and virtue in an effort to master the self. Although its negative connotations in Western society unfairly overburden the term, "patheticness" is a likely the best way to describe the optimal moral state for an individual in pursuit of mino bimaadizi, as it means a radical openness to assistance from others. Historically such a state was achieved through acts of ritual fasting, self-impoverishment through gift giving, and other displays of humility meant to elicit pity (and therefore aid) from both human and other-than-human people.

Traditional conceptions of mino bimaadiziwin, on the other hand, articulated a much more permeable idea of the individual, who was seen not only as an ethical actor but also as something to be acted on. As such, the concept of mino bimaadiziwin offered very little in the way of explicit moral injunctions or set practices. As Scott Richard Lyons explains, "For *Anishinaabeg*, what we now call culture was always geared toward the production of *more life*, not political theology."[52] Under the ideal of mino bimaadizi, the health, happiness, and contentment of an individual were influenced by external forces as much as, if not more than, the efforts of the individual themselves. When disaster, in the form of famine, disease, or other difficulty presented itself, it was due to a breakdown of these relationships of interdependency, rather than the failure of individuals to live up to codified moral behaviors. Unlike eudaemonia, which made happiness and fulfillment an individual pursuit (albeit one that took place in a social context), mino bimaadiziwin's emphasis on establishing and maintaining relationships of interdependency made the good life an explicitly collective practice. In short, as the wolf manidoo of Shawaano's story puts it, "We live because *we* live" (emphasis mine, 120).

Tenskwatawa's moral philosophy, in its insistence on self-sufficiency and rejection of modern technologies, is much more aligned with the concept of eudaemonia, than it is with mino bimaadiziwin. Although the concept of negative behavior somewhat resembling sin existed in Anishinaabe communities prior to Tenskwatawa, his moral teachings transformed it from a teleological system (behavior that impeded mino bimaadizi is a sin) to a deontological one (behavior that made use of foreign technologies to achieve mino bimaadiziwin is a sin). In his restructuring of the indigenous moral universe, the misfortune that had been seen before as the lamentable breakdown of reciprocal relationships was refigured as a punishment from the Great Spirit for personal sin.

Tenskwatawa's teachings led to a massive breakdown of mino bimaadiziwin for the Anishinaabeg in the nineteenth century. According to Tenskwatawa's contemporary, John Tanner, the teachings of the Shawnee prophet failed "to unite [the Anishinaabeg] in the accomplishment of any human purpose," and only served to expose the Anishinaabeg "to much inconvenience and suffering." Not only were Tenskwatawa's followers forbidden from using Euro-American–made goods, they were also instructed to maintain a constant fire in their lodges as a sign of their commitment to their new religion. These fires had to be continuously maintained, but only by the individual to whom the fire belonged, as Tenskwatawa's followers were taught that "no man should give fire to another." More distressingly, Tenskwatawa's Anishinaabe followers were forced to dispose of their medicine bags—a material symbol of their dependency on the manidoog—essentially forbidding them from asking for spiritual aid in times of trouble. Living in an environment in which cooperation was all but required for survival, Tenskwatawa's injunctions put an incredible strain on the Anishinaabeg's already precarious life. By the time he wrote his memoir in 1830, Tanner (who Erdrich has described as "a man of instinctive principle") reported that the Anishinaabeg's opinion of the Shawnee Prophet had become damningly dismissive, saying that he was "looked upon by the Indians as an imposter and a bad man."[53]

Ira goes though a similar process of disenchantment in *The Painted Drum*, learning to see her insistence on self-sufficiency to be at odds with both her well-being and her Anishinaabe identity. Ira's investment in an individualistic view of morality has caused her to place an enormous amount of responsibility on herself as both an Indian and a mother—far more than a single person can actually bear. Ira thinks she must provide for her children alone, just as she thinks she must expose herself to unnecessary hardship in order to prove her Indianness. Because Ira conceives of self-sufficiency as an ethical imperative, she equates asking for help with moral failure, even to the point that she chooses prostitution before pity (an uncomfortable reminder of the ideological overlap of liberal individualism and capitalist commodification). In order to accept the kind of aid that will benefit herself and her children, Ira must overcome her overinvestment in autonomy and reimagine herself as a deserving recipient of help. Essential to this process is Ira's acceptance that the situation that nearly claimed the lives of her children was not her fault, despite her choice to leave them alone. As Ira begins to see how the circumstances leading to the fire were outside of her control, she begins to recognize the degree to which her insistence on personal autonomy is actually false-consciousness.[54]

This process begins with Ira's confrontation with Seraphine String, an Indian Child Welfare officer sent to interview her. The moments leading up to the interview are incredibly tense, as Ira worries that String will take her children away. Ira's anxiety (as well as our own as readers) is understandable. Over the course of the twentieth century, Child Welfare officers regularly used questionable interpretations of parental negligence as a pretext to remove Native children from their communities and place them in non-Native households.[55] Moreover, Ira discovers that String is a religious leader and traditional healer in her community, making her even more threatening to Ira, who fears that String will "act all spiritual" and publicly shame her from a position of cultural authority (226). Most distressingly, Ira also discovers that she has already personally wronged String—who is also the wife of the man in the bar she tried to solicit for sex. For a person with a strong investment in personal responsibility, String can only represent the sum of Ira's fears—an authority capable of rendering judgment on Ira's fitness as a mother, an Anishinaabe, and a moral being.

It comes as something of a shock to both Ira and the reader when String finally appears. Described as "quietly matter of fact" (225), String is "more interested in where Ira thought she might stay while she applied for emergency housing" than in interrogating Ira about her decision to leave her children alone or about her flirtation with String's husband (227). Ira has been so consumed with fear of being punished—for her transgression against String, for neglecting her children, for not being a properly spiritual person—that she hadn't even considered the question of how she will care for herself and her family. The thought catches Ira off guard, sending her into an apoplexy of defensive self-consciousness.

> The red cotton placket-front blouse she was wearing, the too large bra, the baggy black pants, and the hospital slippers made her feel poor and beggarly. But I am poor and beggarly, she thought. Everything I have is burnt. She remembered Shawnee's school pictures. Her breath caught. And now this woman is going to ask me if I had sex to get the money. But I can honestly tell her that I did not, though I would have, but would have doesn't matter. (226)

The confusion and contradiction of Ira's internal monologue reveals that her prior assumptions are beginning to break down and be remade. Ira imagines herself as a mother willing to do anything for her children, but String, as a representative of both the state and her Anishinaabe community, reminds her of the myriad social services and community resources that she never thought to take advantage of. String's presence forces Ira to honestly confront the desperation of her situation, to see being "poor and beggarly" not as the sign of personal failure, but in the positive sense (foundational to mino bimaadiziwin) of being open to spiritual and material aid.

As a character, Seraphine String illustrates, in an idealized manner, the degree to which the political practice of social welfare shares a considerable degree of philosophical overlap with mino bimaadiziwin. Through String, we see how Ira's insistence on a self-sufficiency is not only at odds with mino bimaadiziwin's emphasis on interdependency, but with the "no fault" philosophy of the welfare state, in which the causes of poverty, substance abuse, and other social ills lie in larger processes of economic exploitation and dispossession. Although there are differences between the two moral systems, the welfare state and mino bimaadiziwin share a particular emphasis on the collective nature of responsibility. In an idealized state, both mino bimaadiziwin and the welfare state do not conceive of the individual as solely responsible for their circumstances; rather, it is society (either the cosmological society of Anishinaabe philosophy or the merely human society of the welfare state) that bears the burden.

The Painted Drum reinforces the connection it draws between the philosophies of the welfare state and mino bimaadiziwin by alluding to a well-known dibaajimowin through the name of Ira's youngest child, Apitchi. Recorded multiple times by ethnographers and Anishinaabe writers since the early nineteenth century, the dibaajimowin of the apichi speaks to the danger of choosing pride over pity. It concerns a young man about to embark on his first gii'igoshimowin, a ceremonial fast in which he will solicit the manidoog for aid in achieving a good life. The young man's father (like many an ambitious parent) wishes for his son to achieve greatness, and therefore pressures him to fast for far longer than normal—twelve days, in most versions. The father believes that by fasting for such a long period, his son will amass a huge amount of spiritual power, allowing him to become a celebrated warrior, gifted healer, or lead his people as an ogimaa. After nine days, the father goes to check on his son, who begs his father to give him food. The father refuses, leaving his son alone for another three days. When the father eventually returns, he finds his son preparing himself to die, having painted his chest red and singing his death song. With his last bit of strength, the boy tells his father that the manidoog have taken pity on him and will indeed give him great power. Before his father's eyes the boy is transformed into a robin ("apichi" in Anishinaabemowin), which then flies away, singing its distinctive song.

That the boy was transformed into a tiny robin rather than an ogimaa or warrior is not an ironic reversal of the father's wishes, but a reconfirmation of the Anishinaabe conception of power that the father had forgotten. Dibaajimowinan such as this convey an understanding of power fundamentally different from that expressed in a Western philosophical traditions, as Cary Miller explains.

> Ojibwe oral tradition instructs that survival is such a precarious and dangerous business that only with the aid of spiritual power given by manidoog could the individual expect to achieve a long and successful life. . . . Such help was perceived as so essential that no performance of any task, whether in the service of subsistence, war, peace, or even love, was interpreted as due to an individual's own abilities or efforts.[56]

Whereas Eurocentric traditions understand power largely in terms of an individual's capacity to control the external world around them, traditional Anishinaabe ideas of power are largely defined by the ability to sustain life. Where a Eurocentric tradition imagines humanity's ability to shape the world around it as second only to that of the gods (or nothing at all), the Anishinaabe tradition takes a more measured view of human power—especially that of the individual. With our dependency on the natural world to provide us with food, shelter, clothing, and almost everything else necessary for the maintenance of human life, people are considered to be relatively powerless.

The dibaajimowin of the apichi achieves its allegorical value by showing how the ambitious father has lost sight of this understanding of power. In pushing his son to become powerful through performing a feat of individual resilience, the father mistakenly thinks of power as a resource that can be amassed and hoarded, rather than something that circulates through relationships of aid and interdependency. In such a conception, those who receive the most aid from others hold the greatest amount of power. Despite being transformed into small, frail bird, the boy has become very powerful indeed because, as Jane Johnston Schoolcraft writes in her version of the story, his needs would be "spontaneously furnished by the mountains and fields," freeing him "from the cares and pains of human life."[57]

Like the father in the dibaajimowin, Ira has developed a similarly misguided understanding of spiritual power, thinking of it, as Tenskwatawa did, as a matter of personal devotion rather than openness to outside aid. It is only by almost losing her son, Apitchi, that Ira's insistence on individual autonomy begins to fully break down. Late in Ira's narrative, Apitchi suffers a pneumonia-induced seizure while in his mother's arms—forcing her to call for help. Lacking the training to know what to do, Ira is forced to stand back as the medical professionals attempt to save her son: "They kept working on him, calling for things she didn't know the names of. Nobody noticed her. He couldn't be dead, she thought, as long as there was so much activity. She fixed on the bustling of the nurses. The low key, businesslike voices of the doctors reassured her. If the doctors were giving orders there was hope" (241). Unnoticed by the doctors, Ira's invisibility finally frees her to see beyond her own self-conscious guilt.

By experiencing a moment of true helplessness, Ira is forced to recognize the precariousness of her position. Unlike the dibaajimowin of the robin, Ira does not lose her son—although the doctors would like to spirit Apitchi away, the ongoing blizzard keeps the medevac helicopter grounded. Looking at an unconscious, but stabilized Apitchi, Ira critically reflects on the desperation of her situation, coming to a painful realization.

I don't know. And I don't know either about myself as a mother. No good, maybe. I know I love them. I know I give up things for them. I don't have men. I don't have lots of things. But why did I go in that bar on this one night of all fucking nights instead of going home? How did all of this get set into motion? Was it the oatmeal? The last pan of fucking slop? How come I didn't walk to Bernard's then, and borrow some food and catch a ride in and out with a trustworthy person? Was it because I never thought of it, or was it because I wanted—just for a moment, or one night, just an evening, really—to get away from the kids? (252–23)

Having repeatedly told herself that she had gone to the bar as an act of heroic self-sacrifice, Ira confronts the fact that she has neglected to care for herself (a burden, she realizes, that she has inadvertently passed down to Shawnee). However painful it may be, Ira's admission that she put her own needs ahead of those of her children is the first step in recognizing that her needs and desires have validity—that she too is deserving of assistance, care, and love. That she can make this admission honestly and free of guilt is a testament to the degree to which her investment in personal autonomy has broken down, allowing her to see how—in the words of one character—"Some mistakes had bigger outcomes than they deserved" (248).

The paradoxical nature of Ira's realization—that she made decisions that led to fire, but is not responsible for it—is an important one for her ability to put her life back together with the help of others. As Bruce Robbins argues, "it does not seem haphazard that . . . the upward mobility story should place this rejection of individual responsibility at its decisive turning point." He goes on to explain,

> "It's not your fault" is a proposition that a society of proudly rugged individualists will resist. The genre seems intent on breaking down this resistance. To do so is not merely to release the individual from misguided guilt, but to win agreement to a counterposition: that, because society is interdependent, what the individual is and does is neither entirely his fault nor—as the doctrine of self-reliance had insisted—his achievement.[58]

No longer saddled with a crippling sense of guilt, Ira is able to reach out and ask others for help—asking her neighbor, Bernard Shaawano (who happens to be a janitor at the hospital), if she and her children can live with him. Lonely after his elderly wife moved into town a few months earlier, Shaawano is more than happy to oblige. The decision is a fortuitous for both parties, with Shaawano gaining company and Ira and her children gaining the benefit of Shaawano's vast traditional knowledge.[59] In the novel's coda, Shaawano reports that Ira and the children have not only been reintegrated into the tribal community, but that their house has been rebuilt, saying, "Our housing authority did come through there pretty good" (269). Ira, once quick to dismiss such assistance as a "cheap miracle," has finally come to see that a good life is only possible with the help of others.

Drawing a Line

It would be easy for an unsympathetic reader to dismiss the idea of seeing the welfare state as ethically consistent with Anishinaabe values as a way of rationalizing "domestic dependent sovereignty" and its supposedly assimilationist ends. Let me be clear, my reading of *The Painted Drum* does not suggest that the U.S. government should be immune from Natives' criticism, or that there is no value in resisting federal intervention in Indian Country, or even that the nation-state, as a form of governance, is always and invariably beneficial. The simple observation of history shows the absurdity of such a position. I am, however, interested in the role literature plays in the construction and defense of what Scott Richard Lyons has called "actually existing Indian nations."[60] Through a mixture of compulsion and chance, the majority of tribal nations in existence today organize themselves into forms that resemble the nation-state, with a set of institutions meant to ensure the health, education, and welfare of tribal peoples. What we are to make of this state of affairs can be (and should be!) a matter of debate, but as long as tribal nations continue to operate in a state-like manner, it is worth our time to take tribal institutions as objects of serious scholarly study—especially for those of us for whom the nation has a particular political importance.

Critical consensus has it that Erdrich's fiction has little or no interest in the promotion of indigenous nationalism—a reputation due, at least in part, to these uncritical representations of bureaucracy's expansive role in Anishinaabe life. As early as 1988, Erdrich's fiction came under fire for its apparent lack of dedication to anticolonial resistance. The most notable criticism came from fellow Native novelist Leslie Marmon Silko, who accused Erdrich of being a "self-referential" writer who pandered to a non-Native readership. Silko argued that Erdrich's prose has "an ethereal clarity and shimmering beauty because no history or politics intrudes to muddy the well of pure necessity contained within language itself."[61] This line of criticism was repeated—more forcefully—by the public intellectual Elizabeth Cook-Lynn, who argued that Erdrich not only fails to coherently criticize the colonial domination of Natives, she was also indirectly complicit in it, because her fiction reflected the "tastes and interests of the dominant culture" instead of participating in the "defense of a coherent national mythos."[62] Even more sympathetic readers of Erdrich locate the politics of her fiction somewhere in the continuum of a cosmopolitanism, as seen in Alan Velie's assessment that critics should "honor [Erdrich's] wish" to be seen as "an American writer" who "usually (though not always) writes about members of her tribe, the Chippewa."[63] Summing up two decades of critical reception to Erdrich's work, Arnold Krupat and Michael Elliot argue that Erdrich's novels present an "understanding of community that sometimes resembles nationalism" but is not nationalist itself, because it lacks "the political force of an exclusive national sovereignty."[64]

What interests me about these assessments of Erdrich's work has to do with a fundamental assumption made visible in Krupat and Elliot's formulation of *exclusive* national sovereignty as the primary goal of Native American nationalism. Krupat and Elliot make it clear that, for them and many others, the only logical telos of Native nationalism is separatism: "To undo [the] paradoxical or oxymoronic status as 'dependent sovereigns'—to resist colonial limitations on their *sovereign* rights—is the foremost concern of Native nations today."[65] I specifically choose this formulation because it comes from a critic (Arnold Krupat) whose attitude toward the project of Native separatism is ambivalent at best, showing how deeply rooted this assumption is in the criticism of Erdrich that it can bring two critics as ideologically divergent as Krupat (a cosmopolitanist) and Cook-Lynn (a separatist) together in tacit agreement about the nature of Native nationalism. For Erdrich's writing to support the project Anishinaabe nationhood, these critics agree, it must articulate an unequivocal claim to absolute Anishinaabe sovereignty. Anything less becomes a promotion of integrationist multiculturalism at best, and an apology for colonization at worst.

In such an interpretative framework, the attempts of characters like Seraphine String, Nanapush, and Judge Antone Bazil Coutts to control the state's influence on Anishinaabe life through greater *involvement in it* instead of *resistance to it* works against the best interests of their own nation. Such a reading forces the reader to engage with Erdrich's work as the tragic history of the slow diminishment and disappearance of Anishinaabe identity, of the kind prophesized by Nanapush in *Tracks*. Yet any such tragic reading of the Matchi Manitou novels is foreclosed by the novels themselves, which are (with the possible exception of *Tracks*) unerringly comic. Each one of these novels ends with a strong reassertion of community into which previously alienated characters are reintegrated—the structural definition of the comic mode. Indeed, one could easily read the continued coherence of Anishinaabe identity and community in Erdrich's fiction as a kind of nationalism, though one different than that articulated by Krupat, Cook-Lynn, and others. The nationalism of Erdrich's fiction is one that shows how the social and economic needs of Anishinaabe community can be met, if imperfectly, by an organized Anishinaabe nation-state that seeks to maximize both its ability to self-govern *and* the resources it can draw from federal authorities (working within what Kevin Bruyneel calls the "third space of sovereignty").[66]

In Erdrich's work, sovereignty is most certainly seen as a long-term goal, but Anishinaabeg also have pressing concerns of basic welfare that demand immediate attention. As the pioneering scholar of federal Indian law Rennard Strickland once observed: "*Sovereignty!* The word slides melodically from our lips, but sovereignty alone doesn't put food on tables, clothes on backs, or heat in houses."[67] More often than not, attaining the resources necessary to address these needs effectively has meant that tribal nations have had to form closer ties to the federal government—not distance themselves from it. Indeed, most tribal nations in the United States devote large amounts of time and resources to engaging with government institutions in order to bring more federal services and money into their communities. At the same time, Strickland suggests, self-determination isn't antithetical to tribal welfare, but intrinsic to it, stating, "Our challenge . . . is to forge the sword of sovereignty into a weapon capable of attacking the basic human problems of Indian people."[68]

This, to my mind, is the value of Erdrich's fiction: it forces us to attend to the way in which tribal nations organize their institutional bodies to meet the needs of their people, a project with profound implications for the ongoing project of indigenous nationalism. By their nature, state institutions instill a set of values in their citizens that will cause them to feel personally invested in the continuity of the state.[69] Rather than see tribally administered institutions as mere adjuncts to the "true" tribal nation (most often understood not as a population, or a territory, but as a set of cultural ideals), Erdrich's fiction demands that we see the pivotal role such institutions play, for both good and ill, in defining the ideologies by which tribal nations operate, and which they impart on their citizens. Such scrutiny is needed now more than ever, as tribes gain greater levels of economic, jurisdictional, and institutional autonomy even as federal authorities lose both the funding and the political will to maintain their trust responsibilities properly. In short, if we are to take seriously the project of tribal nationhood, Erdrich's fiction reminds us that we must also think about the state.

Presenting state-run institutions not as monolithic sites of discipline and domination, but as sites at which dominant ideas about the definition of power, subjectivity, and community can be contested and changed, Erdrich's fiction has presented a strong case for importance of self-determination over the past thirty years. More importantly, in showing how the welfare state and mino bimaadiziwin share similar understandings of collective responsibility and a fundamental right to a decent life, Erdrich's fiction asks us to see a continuity between traditional Anishinaabe cultural practices and the contemporary tribal nation-state—as well as the threat posed to both by the ideology of neoliberalism. Despite the fact that the state-form has been historically used as a tool of Native dispossession by capitalist interests, Erdrich's fiction posits that it can also be a powerful means of protecting the Anishinaabe people from future abuse, and ensuring them mino bimaadiziwin.

At the same time, Erdrich's fiction suggests that the Anishinaabeg's continued pursuit of mino bimaadiziwin may entail a set of political commitments that transcend the boundaries of the nation-state. Observing the changes brought about to his community after decades of self-determination policy, Judge Antone Bazil Coutts remarks on a curious irony. Even as the reservation has become a place of "slight stability and even occasional prosperity" at the end of the twentieth century, Coutts notes that the non-Native communities that surround it continue to "empty out and die" (91).

> It's a shame to see them go, but Geraldine and I agreed that we were not about to waste our sympathies. In the winter of our great starvation, when scores of our people were consumed by hunger, citizens of Argus sold their grain and raffled off a grand piano. (92)

In their failure to recognize their obligation to the Anishinaabeg in their time of need, the non-Natives of Argus and Pluto showed an implicit rejection of mino bimaadiziwin—letting Anishinaabe people die because of a racist conviction in their own cultural superiority. That such an existence proved unsustainable therefore seems like just desserts, especially given the callousness of selling their grain in order to buy a grand piano—an impractical object heavy with classist and Eurocentric implication—while their neighbors starved. In treating land and people as fundamentally expendable, the Euro-Americans of Argus and Pluto consigned themselves to their fate, doomed to vanish once their extractive productivity inevitably declines.

Yet, even as Coutts refuses to mourn the death of Pluto, he is forced to consider the way in which the separation he feels from his home town is predicated on an emotional investment in an unstable, and ultimately transitory, ideal.

> As I look at the town now, dwindling without grace, I think how strange that lives were lost in its formation. It is the same with all desperate enterprises that involve boundaries we place on the earth. By drawing a line and defending it, we seem to think we have mastered something. What? The earth swallows and absorbs even those who manage to form a country, a reservation. (Yet there is something to the love and knowledge of the land and its relationship to dreams— that's what the old people had. That's why as a tribe we exist to the present.) It is my job to maintain the sovereignty of tribal law on tribal land, but even as I do so, I think of my grandfather's phrase for the land disease, town fever, and how he nearly died of greed, its main symptom. (115)

In his ambivalence Coutts gives voice to an irresolvable dichotomy in Anishinaabe nationalism to which I have, until this point, only alluded. For more than a century, nationalism has provided a powerful means for the Anishinaabeg to defend their cultural traditions, and more importantly the values those traditions encode. At the same time, the separatism on which the very idea of nationhood is founded seems fundamentally irreconcilable with those values. Coutts's association of such boundaries with "the land disease"—capitalism's terminal tendency to see the natural world as little more than a set of resources to be exploited for human consumption—is apt. Even as nationalism protects Anishinaabe people from the devastating effects of Euro-American racism, it has the potential to blind us to even greater threats to mino bimaadiziwin presented by the global effects of industrial pollution, labor exploitation, and climate change. Setting artificial boundaries between what belongs to the nation, and what does not, the logic of nationalism is at odds with mino bimaadiziwin's radically expansive idea of interdependency—which stretches the idea of social obligation beyond the mere humans to plants, animals, manidoog, and everything else that comprises the natural world. As Stuart Hall suggests, "An ecological understanding of the world is one that challenges the notion that the nation-state and the boundaries of sovereignty will keep things stable because they won't. The Universe is coming!"[70] Once we shift our focus, as Coutts does, from the abstraction of the nation to this universal reality, we may begin to see ourselves embedded in a web of relations that extends far beyond any arbitrary political borders. We may even find that the pursuit of mino bimaadiziwin may eventually mean leaving behind the idea of nationhood altogether for a more expansive and inclusive understanding of what it means to lead a good life.

Conclusion

More than a century after George Kabaosa premiered *Hiawatha, or Nanabozho* on the shore of Lake Huron, a new generation of Anishinaabe writers continue to grapple with the complicated legacy of Longfellow's epic poem. In "Of Hereafter Song," Anishinaabe poet Liz Howard returns to *The Song of Hiawatha*, using it to meditate on the effects of Euro-American colonialism, the environmental destruction caused by the mining industry, and her own mixed identity. The poems of "Of Hereafter Song" are written in the form of pastiche, combining lines taken from *The Song of Hiawatha* with technical terminology from government assessments of the ecological health of the Great Lakes and excerpts from Howard's own journal—written in the informal patois of the Internet. Describing "Of Hereafter Song" as a "remix," Howard imparts the term with an uncomfortably biological literalness, as each of the poems share a common fascination with the idea of interrelation, and its troubling corollary, contamination. Howard writes:

> the women of the bitumen looked over tailing ponds
> like a cloud-rack of a tempest
> rushed the pale canoes of wings and thunder
> to kill the wilderness in the child
> sweeping westward our remnants
> sulphur infinite, sorrow extracted tuberculosis[1]

According to Howard, the experimental form of "Of Hereafter Song" is meant to reflect the threat that ongoing mining projects pose to the Anishinaabeg and their lands: "As I write this a mining company is positioning to mine in/near Anish[i]naabe territory in my hometown. I'm deeply concerned about what environmental/health effects may result from this. Climate is blood. Earth is blood. The delicate membranes of the human system are all too permeable. Verse, then, is also so permeable."[2] In "Of Hereafter Song," the desire for Anishinaabewaki's mineral resources is a reflection and extension of Longfellow's appropriation of Anishinaabe narrative material, as Howard writes, "I, Minnehaha, a small LOL / fiction antecedent / to quarry a nation" (47). Longfellow's quarrying of Anishinaabe culture in the nineteenth century is a literary antecedent to the open pit mines of today. In both cases, the act of taking threatens to leave a lasting mark—on the environment, on Anishinaabe bodies, and even on poetry.

In Howard's poems, individual subjectivity (the supposed sine qua non of lyric poetry) is constantly troubled by processes of exchange—genetic, chemical, economic—that occur at scales both too large and too small for the individual to comprehend. The world that "Of Hereafter Song" describes is one in which the capitalist world-system and mino bimaadiziwin's networks of mutual dependency exist in an uneasy tension with one another. It is a world in which communication can be instantaneous and demand for copper and iron in far-off places can have immediate and lasting impacts on the Anishinaabeg and their lands. A world in which the cruel north-wind manidoo communicates not through ice and snow (as he does in Longfellow's poem), but by "skyping / the real of consumer goods" (41).

Howard's critical reappropriation of *The Song of Hiawatha* in "Of Hereafter Song" puts her work in conversation with a body of Anishinaabe writing that stretches back more than two centuries. As I have endeavored to show throughout this book, Anishinaabe authors have used writing to imagine a relationship with the United States that was neither separate, nor integrated, but instead transnational in nature. They did so by taking technologies of expression from sources outside their own cultural tradition—the novel, lyric poetry, and drama—and adapting them to their own uses. By speaking to non-Natives on a cultural register that they could understand, writers such as Theo Beaulieu and Louise Erdrich have presented their nation as having an equitable legitimacy as that of the United States, even as that status was continually undermined and denied by it. I have argued that acts of appropriation, adaptation, and resistance to the rhetoric of authenticity have played just as important a role in the pursuit of Anishinaabe sovereignty as expressions of cultural and political difference. I have done so with the hope that our understanding of indigenous nationalism might be complicated and enlarged to include forms of resistance that have gone unexamined. This project has also been an effort to recover what I believe to be a much-needed narrative of indigenous agency. The stories of the Anishinaabeg authors

I have discussed over the course of this book do not fall easily into well-worn narratives of assimilation, self-betrayal, and decline, nor do they insist on a static vision of Anishinaabe cultural identity. Instead, they show the incredible ability for a community to adapt to rapidly changing circumstances by drawing on the strength of their traditional values while simultaneously embracing new ways to express those values.

In many ways, *Our War Paint* was conceived of as an attempt to knit together the insights that have emerged in both American and Native American literary criticism over the past twenty years. By combining an emphasis on the particularities of indigenous literary nationalism with a critique of the settler-colonial ideology latent in Euro-American writing, I hoped to articulate a mode of comparative criticism that might allow a more nuanced understanding of the settler/indigenous conflict as a local phenomenon. To be sure, the Anishinaabeg's use of translation, appropriation, and adaptation as strategies of resistance is, in many ways, a product of their unique circumstances. Early economic contact with the French, a relative lack of Euro-American settlement pressure until the late nineteenth century, and a culture that did not prohibit the sharing of stories with outsiders all contributed to the establishment of an indigenous literary tradition unlike any other. Given this project's emphasis on the local and particular, what insights it offers may not have direct application outside the small (but growing) subfield of Anishinaabe studies. What was true in the experience of the Anishinaabeg will not necessarily be true for other tribal nations. Just as tribal nations have cultures and literary traditions particular to themselves, so too do they have particular responses to the threat of colonization—a set of strategies unique to themselves. By tracing the dialogic that emerges from a particular relationship between a tribal nation and the settler-state, we stand to gain a better understanding of the history of indigenous resistance, and perhaps discover strategies that have been especially effective at disrupting settler authority. Over the course of this project I have come up with several recommendations that might help direct such studies.

First, more attention ought to be paid to issues of form and genre. As I have explained elsewhere in this book, there is a need for more work that theorizes the process by which Euro-American genres are indigenized by Native writers. It is not enough to say Native writing is "inspired," "influenced," or "reflects" oral traditions without articulating how those traditions operate at the level of form. While some of this work was carried out in the early years of Native literary criticism, there was too much emphasis on the universal nature of such narratives rather than their particularity. We need more substantive engagement with the formal logic of specific tribal narrative traditions, including research into indigenous concepts of genre. I have begun to do this work through my analysis of the difference between the chronotopic conventions of the epic and aadizookaanag in chapter 1, and (in a more cursory manner) by looking at the way in which the syntax of Anishinaabemowin impacted the translation of the nagamonan in chapter 3. While these efforts should only be considered first steps at best, I hope that they show the degree to which our understanding of Native literature can be enriched by paying more attention to issues of form.

Second, I see a need to engage with what Scott Richard Lyons has called "actually existing Indian nations"[3] as they are represented in literature. This means, in part, paying more attention to the ways in which the institutional life of indigenous communities is reflected in writing, as well as how it, in turn, inflects the work of Native writers. To be clear, this does not mean conflating tribal nations with tribal governments, but recognizing the degree to which Native life is affected by organizational forces beyond those often seen as cultural. Another necessary aspect of this work is a better accounting for the diversity of Native experience without reducing difference to a set of insider/outsider dichotomies that prioritize certain kinds of indigenous experiences over others. Decades ago, Vine Deloria articulated an understanding of tribal nationhood that saw the differences of politics, religion, economics, and cultural practice within tribal communities as a source of conflict but also strength.[4] If our goal is to show how literature supports the project of indigenous nationhood, we should be building on this insight—not dismissing the heterogeneity of tribal communities as evidence of assimilation or cultural loss. More specifically, much more attention must be paid to the issue of class disparity within and between indigenous communities as tribal nations continue their economic development.

Last, I hope to see more comparative work done between settler and Native literatures—especially work that complicates and historicizes our understanding of settler-colonialism and indigenous resistance. Rather than make generalizations about the differences between Native and non-Native authors, we need to look at the way writers responded to one another in an ongoing dialogue that helped to shape public policy over the centuries. While the work to unpack the settler-colonial ideology of Euro-American writing has been a very important and fruitful endeavor in Americanist criticism, there is a distinct need to incorporate more Native voices into these critiques. I am confident that contemporaneous indigenous responses to settler literature (like those offered in the

Progress) remain to be discovered in the archive. With regard to Native literary criticism, a major aspect of this work should be more engagement with the critique of recognitive politics being made by theorists such as Glen Coulthard and Elizabeth Povinelli.[5] In an era in which public expressions of indigenous cultural difference have the potential to reinforce—rather than challenge—the authority of multicultural settler-states, literature seems to occupy a particularly privileged position in the political discourse. Capable of shaping perceptions of cultural authenticity in a way few other forms of expression can, literature's ambivalent role in both the promotion of, and resistance to, the politics of recognition remains to be adequately theorized.

My sincere hope is that this book can offer the first steps toward a model for assessing texts, like "Of Hereafter Song," that do not seem to fit comfortably into a single literary or cultural tradition, but nonetheless make strong political claims on behalf of indigenous peoples who find themselves embedded in the cultural and political contexts of settler society. Indeed, in "Of Hereafter Song," the threat of contamination cuts both ways. Calling on Longfellow's devastating prophecy in "The White Man's Foot" of "wild and woful" nations scattered "Like the withered leaves of Autumn,"[6] Howard's poems suggest that it is not just the Anishinaabeg who are in danger of destruction. Instead, the entire world is brought together by the threat of ecological disaster, as Howard warns: "*sweet reconciliation spoke in / mercury, arsenic, lead, and cadmium*" (37). In "Of Hereafter Song," the threats of industrial contamination, labor exploitation, and climate change bind "all nations in a night / terror" (41).

Howard's gesture toward internationalism reflects an unacknowledged assumption that has guided this book from its beginning. My own nationalism is of the Fanonian sort: a desire to preserve those beliefs that might someday help us build a more inclusive, more balanced understanding of humanity and its place in the world. That the Anishinaabe nation is worthy of sustaining not because of cultural tradition or an abstract sense of justice, but because the values held and defended by the Anishinaabeg for centuries—a faith in the interconnectedness of the natural world and a resolute love of living for its own sake—might help us to heal the damage wrought by racism, industrialism, and the unchecked expansion of capitalism. The Anishinaabeg's struggle to overcome colonization and assert their place in modernity is, in a sense, a struggle to preserve and articulate a set of beliefs to a world in desperate need of their message. The values that the Anishinaabeg hold allowed them to survive centuries of almost unimaginable challenges as a distinct people. If humanity is to survive the coming centuries, Liz Howard's poetry suggests, we must listen to what the Anishinaabe people have to say,

> and now the world
> has ended and we have not ascended
> into heaven
>
> here comes the future
>
> let it in (46)

Notes

Ozhibii'ige

1. "Ogimaa" is the Anishinaabemowin word for a hereditary political leader, that is, "chief." Please note: I do not italicize Anishinaabemowin words in this book because I do not want them to be glossed over, or worse, be seen as somehow "foreign." In this, I am following a well-established tradition in Native literature and Indigenous Studies.

2. The terminal "g" of "Anishinaabeg" makes the animate noun plural in Anishinaabemowin. Throughout this book, I have attempted to use "Anishinaabe" when referring to individuals or as an adjective modifying another noun, and "Anishinaabeg" when referring to groups of Anishinaabe people. I do the same in the case of other plural animate nouns (e.g., "ogimaa" and "ogimaag") and I have appended a terminal "n" to plural inanimate nouns (e.g., "nagamon" and "nagamonan"), following the conventions of Anishinaabemowin.

3. William Whipple Warren, *History of the Ojibway People* (2nd ed.). St. Paul: Minnesota Historical Society Press, 2009, pp. 53–54.

4. Jean Paul le Jeune, "Of the Hope We Have for the Conversion of Many Savages." In *The Jesuit Relations and Allied Documents*, ed. by Reuben Gold Thwaites. Cleveland: Burrows Bros. Co., 1896–1901. Vol. 18, p. 231.

5. Gerald Vizenor, *Touchwood: A Collection of Ojibway Prose*. Moorhead, MN: New Rivers Press, 1987, Preface, v.

Introduction

1. "The Ojibways Play 'Hiawatha' Again," *Minneapolis Journal*. August 31, 1901.

2. Kate Flint, *The Transatlantic Indian, 1776–1930*. Princeton: Princeton University Press, 2009, p. 135.

3. Michael McNally, "The Indian Passion Play: Contesting the Real Indian in Song of Hiawatha Pageants, 1901–1965." *American Quarterly* 58, no. 1 (2006): 105–36.

4. Margot Francis, *Creative Subversions: Whiteness, Indigeneity, and the National Imaginary*. Vancouver: University of British Columbia Press, 2011, p. 138.

5. Alan Trachtenberg, *Shades of Hiawatha: Staging Indians, Making Americans, 1880–1930*. New York: Hill and Wang, 2005, p. 95.

6. McNally, p. 108

7. Ibid., p. 131.

8. A curious omission, given that the script is held by multiple libraries across the United States and Canada.

9. L. O. Armstrong, *Hiawatha, or Nanabozho*. Montreal: Desbarats Press, 1904. All proceeding citations will be given parenthetically.

10. In modern orthography: "*Hiawatha, or Nanabozho*, Iw Ojibwe Anishinaabe Inakamigiziwin (Odaminowin)."

11. Raymond McBride, "The Play of 'Hiawatha'—the Indian Epic. *Theatre Magazine* 8 (1908): 253.

12. Alice Longfellow, "A Visit to Hiawatha's People," *The Song of Hiawatha*, Boston and New York: Houghton Mifflin, 1902, p. 318.

13. Henry Rideout, *William Jones, Indian, Cowboy, American Scholar, and Anthropologist in the Fields*. New York: Frederick A. Stokes Company, 1912, pp. 96–97.

14. "Patriarch of Ojibways Meets Violent Death," *Winnipeg Evening Tribune*, June 12th, 1929.

15. William Edgar, "'Hiawatha,' as the Ojibways Interpret It." *American Monthly Review of Reviews* 30 (1904): 693.

16. "The Ojibways Play 'Hiawatha' Again," *Minneapolis Journal* (August 31, 1901).

17. Henry Wadsworth Longfellow, *The Song of Hiawatha*. Boston: Tricknor and Fields, 1856, pp. 188–89.

18. Ibid.

19. Joshua Bellin, *The Demon of the Continent: Indians and the Shaping of American Literature*. Philadelphia: University of Pennsylvania Press, 2012, p. 181.

20. Longfellow, p. 189.

21. Ibid., p. 190.

22. Bellin, p. 181.

23. Henry Rowe Schoolcraft, *Personal Memoirs*. Philadelphia: Lippincott, Grambo and Company, 1851, p. 109.

24. Ibid., p. 655.

25. See Bellin, chapter 7.

26. Christoph Irmscher, *Public Poet, Private Man: Henry Wadsworth Longfellow at 200*. Amherst: University of Massachusetts Press, 2009, p. 127.

27. Longfellow, p. 3.

28. Ibid., p. 4.

29. Ibid., p. 300.

30. Birgit Rasmussen, *Queequeg's Coffin: Indigenous Literacies and Early American Literature*. Durham: Duke University Press, 2012, p. 42.

31. Mikhail Bakhtin, *Speech Genres and Other Late Essays*. Austin: University of Texas Press, 1986, p. 163.

32. Trachtenberg, p. 71.

33. Ibid., p. 74.

34. Roy Harvey Pearce, *Savagism and Civilization*. Berkeley: University of California Press, 1988, p. 192.

35. This interpretation and translation of Kabaosa's text is ultimately my own—as are any mistakes. However, I received much guidance in my effort to translate this text from Anton Treuer, for which I am very grateful.

36. This way of writing out Anishinaabemowin is not standard, even for its time. Anishinaabe translations of the gospels produced in the Garden River community around the time of *Hiawatha, or Nanabozho*'s production present words of Anishinaabemowin as complete semantic units—often of great length. The use of hyphenated Anishinaabemowin in *Hiawatha, or Nanabozho* appears to have been meant to accommodate nonspeakers.

37. For more on the temporal implications of the epic form in *Hiawatha*, see chapter 1 of this book.

38. Francis, p. 133.

39. Kevin Bruyneel, *The Third Space of Sovereignty: The Postcolonial Politics of U.S.-Indigenous Relations*. Minneapolis: University of Minnesota Press, 2007, p. 25.

40. Ibid., p. xvii.

41. Ibid., p. 8.

42. Ibid., p. 2.

43. Ibid. p. 2.

44. Pearce, p. 4.

45. According to Williams, literature has often been a space in which emergent, prepolitical forms of belief can be articulated within the structuring confines of established cultural, economic, and legal norms. Although lacking the definitional force of ideology or law, such "structures of feeling," Williams argues, "exert palpable pressures and set effective limits on experience and on action." In this sense, we can understand literary writing not just as a mere reflection of the social context in which it was produced, but as a force working—in minor and very circumscribed ways—to shape it. Raymond Williams, *Marxism and Literature*. Oxford: Oxford University Press, 1977, p. 132.

46. Craig Womack, *Red on Red: Native American Literary Separatism*. Minneapolis: University of Minnesota Press, 1999, p. 14.

47. Jace Weaver, "Splitting the Earth: First Utterances and Pluralist Separatism." In *American Indian Literary Nationalism*, ed. Warrior, Weaver, and Womack. Albuquerque: University of New Mexico Press, 2006, p. 15.

48. Scott Richard Lyons, *X-Marks: Native Signatures of Assent*. Minneapolis: University of Minnesota Press, 2010, passim.

49. Bruyneel, p. 6.
50. Ibid., p. 215.
51. Ibid., p. 217.
52. Ibid., p. xvii.
53. Ibid., p. xvii.
54. Bakhtin, p. 170.

55. In this, I seek to extend and complicate a similar argument made by David Treuer about Native American fiction. While I do not agree with Treuer's insistence that literature can only ever express "the longing for culture" (199), I do think there is something to the idea that the representation of culture in Native literature can be a self-conscious act on the part of the author, who may choose to shape their representation of culture for reasons beyond authenticity. See David Treuer, *Native American Fiction: A User's Manual*. Minneapolis: Graywolf Press, 2006.

56. The idea that non-Indians represent the implied audience for most works of Native literature may be seen as a controversial assertion, but evidence certainly suggests it to be the case. In terms of style and content, works of Native literature almost always come with an interpretive apparatus meant to shepherd non-Natives readers through an unfamiliar cultural context, either appended to the text (in the form of introductions, appendices, glossaries, etc.) or embedded in it (inline translations, explanations of unfamiliar historical or cultural information as exposition, the structure of so-called homing narratives). At the level of simple economics, the publishing industry has had little interest in producing books targeted at Natives, a proportionally tiny population with relatively low buying power. By and large, the popularity of figures like Sherman Alexie, Louise Erdrich, and Joseph Boyden has been a product of their ability to render aspects of Native life intelligible to the widest possible audience, while writers less invested in such explication (like Gerald Vizenor, Stephen Graham Jones, or LeAnne Howe) remain marginal in market terms.

57. Philip Deloria, "American Indians, American Studies, and the ASA." *American Quarterly* 55, no. 4 (December 2003): 672.

58. Joseph Bauerkemper and Heidi Kiiwetinepinesiik Stark, "The Trans/National Terrain of Anishinaabe Law and Diplomacy." *Journal of Transnational American Studies* 4, no. 1 (2012): 6.

59. Rebecca Kugel, *To Be the Main Leaders of Our People: A History of Minnesota Ojibwe Politics, 1825–1898*. East Lansing: Michigan State University Press, 1998, p. 199.

60. In Minnesota alone, for example, there are seven different Anishinaabe reservations: Bois Forte, Leech Lake, Fond du Lac, Mille Lacs, White Earth, Red Lake, and Grand Portage—not to mention a substantial population of urban Anishinaabe in Minneapolis (indeed, many of the Anishinaabe nations in Minnesota have offices in Minneapolis in order to serve their off-reservation citizens). Of these seven tribal nations, six make up the Minnesota Chippewa Tribe, an umbrella organization that manages each of the six member reservations under a single constitution. The seventh, Red Lake, is independent (and fiercely so,

having never ceded its land to the U.S. government). Each of these reservations constitutes their own nation—with its own government, laws, and leaders—yet each recognizes the others as part of the larger community of Anishinaabe. Some even extend the same rights to citizens of the other Anishinaabe nations as they do their own.

61. Rachel Adams, *Continental Divides: Remapping the Cultures of North America*. Chicago: University of Chicago Press, 2009, p. 35. Adams warns, however, that such an understanding of transnationalism must take into account "the vexed condition of contemporary Native American politics in which a desire for solidarity across national lines rests uneasily against the nationalist assumptions underlying tribal claims to land and sovereignty" (35).

62. Take, for example, my family, who has kinship ties to several Anishinaabe tribal nations. Although they are enrolled at White Earth, my family traces their ancestry back to the Lake Superior Band Anishinaabe at the Lac Du Flambeau reservation in Wisconsin. During the Great Depression, my great-grandfather's brothers left White Earth to work with the CCC's Indian Division on the Grand Portage reservation in the Arrowhead region of Minnesota, and their families have been there ever since. My aunt married a man from the Bad River Anishinaabe reservation in Wisconsin, so my cousins claim affiliation there. These sorts of complex networks of affiliation are hardly unique among Anishinaabe families and serve to tie various Anishinaabe communities together.

63. David Scott, *Conscripts of Modernity*. Durham: Duke University Press, 2004, p. 19.

64. Lyons, p. 131.

65. Eric Cheyfitz, "The (Post)Colonial Construction of Indian Country: U.S. American Indian Literatures and Federal Indian Law." In *The Columbia Guide to American Indian Literatures of the United States since 1945*, ed. Eric Cheyfitz. New York: Columbia University Press, 2006, p. 8.

66. Gerald Vizenor, *Fugitive Poses: Native American Scenes of Absence and Presence*. Lincoln: University of Nebraska Press, 1998, p. 15.

67. Ibid., p. 182.

68. Ibid., p. 183.

Chapter 1

1. Advertisement, *The Tomahawk*, May 14, 1903, p. 1.

2. Daniel F. Littlefield and James W. Parins, *American Indian and Alaska Native Newspapers and Periodicals: 1826–1924*. Westport: Greenwood Press, 1984, p. xiv.

3. United States Senate Committee on Indian Affairs, *Testimony in Relation to Affairs at the White Earth Indian Reservation, Minnesota: Hearings before the United States Senate Committee on Indian Affairs, Fiftieth Congress, first session and Forty-Ninth Congress, second session, on Mar. 8, 9, 11, 12, May 23, June 1, 1887*. Washington, DC: U.S. GPO 1887, p. 49.

4. Clement Beaulieu Jr., "Salutatory," *Progress*, March 25, 1886, p. 1.

5. "Memorials of Deceased Members, 1909–14." *Collections of the Minnesota Historical Society, Vol. XV*. Saint Paul: Minnesota Historical Society, 1915, pp. 844–45.

6. Gerald Vizenor, *The People Named the Chippewa: Narrative Histories* Minneapolis: University of Minnesota Press, 1995, p. 87.

7. *Testimony*, p. 113.

8. Qtd. in Vizenor, *The People Named the Chippewa*, p. 79.

9. Gerald Vizenor, "Constitutional Consent." In *The White Earth Nation: Ratification of a Native Democratic Constitution*, ed. Vizenor and Doerfleur. Lincoln: University of Nebraska Press, 2012, p. 40.

10. *Testimony*, p. 67

11. Ibid., p. 85.

12. "A Half Breed Has Rights." *New York Times*, July 18, 1887, p. 1.

13. "Sheehan Sat Down." *St. Paul Daily Globe*, August 29, 1887.p. 1.

14. Theo Beaulieu, "Getting Things Mixed." *Progress*, October 29, 1887, p. 4.

15. Theo Beaulieu, "Is It an Indian Bureau?" *Progress*, June 9, 1888, p. 1.

16. Theo Beaulieu, "The Great Sioux Reservation," *Progress*, December 17, 1887, p. 4.

17. For an in-depth history of the history of allotment at White Earth, see Melissa Meyers, *The White Earth Tragedy: Ethnicity and Dispossession at a Minnesota Anishinaabe Reservation*. Lincoln: University of Nebraska Press, 1994.

18. Gus Beaulieu, "Why He Objects to the Treaty," *Progress*, December 3, 1887, p. 1.

19. Alexandre Jeanotte and Louis Lenoir, "Might Is Right," *Progress*, April 27, 1889, p. 4.

20. Theo Beaulieu, "Gabriel Dumont," *Progress*, April 27, 1889, p. 4.

21. Ibid.

22. Theo Beaulieu, "Prejudicial Vagaries!" *Progress*, December 17, 1887, p. 1.

23. Ibid.

24. Wah-Boose, "Race Prejudice," *Progress*, June 23, 1888, p. 1.

25. Hippolyte Taine, *History of English Literature*. Translated by H. Van Laun. New York: Holt, 1885, p. 21. Proceeding citations from Taine are given parenthetically.

26. Theodore Beaulieu, "What Do We Want?," *Progress*, July 13, 1889.

27. Theodore Beaulieu, "Detroit Record vs. Nelson," *Progress*, April 14, 1888.

28. Theodore Beaulieu, "Indian Traditions and Legends," *Progress*, October 22, 1887, p. 1.

29. An example of this function of the dibaajimowinan is seen in the *Progress* in the account of a young man who becomes a robin after being compelled by his father to fast for too long, despite his protests. Dibaajimowinan, however, are not always allegorical, but often times also anecdotal—as can be seen in Beaulieu's addendum to the robin story in which he relates a missionary's

account of a robin warning off potential thieves. Both stories, one fictional, the other historical, are meant primarily to instruct.

30. Theo Beaulieu certainly seemed to have had a sense of the ritualized nature of the aadizookaanag when publishing his translations in the *Progress*. Stories featuring Wenabozho only appear during the months of March, April, and early May—still a wintry time in northern Minnesota. The last story appears in the same issue as a note on the first sugar-maple harvest of the year, marking the traditional beginning of spring in the Anishinaabe seasonal round.

31. Theo Beaulieu, "Indian Traditions and Legends," *Progress*, October 22, 1887.

32. Other short stories, poems, and items of curiosity, including traditional stories from other tribes, usually appeared on pages three or four of the *Progress*.

33. Elizabeth McNiel, " 'The Game Never Ends': Gerald Vizenor's Gamble with Language and Structure in *Summer in the Spring*." *American Indian Culture and Research Journal* 19.2 (1995): 91–92.

34. Qtd. in Vizenor, *The People Named the Chippewa*, p. 11.

35. Theo Beaulieu, "The Ojibwas," *Tomahawk*, May 7, 1903, p. 1.

Please note: This quotation comes from a reprinting of the Beaulieu translations made several years after they had been printed in the *Progress*. I've had to cite this version because the issue of the *Progress* in which it had originally appeared was not preserved. The other Beaulieu stories reprinted in the *Tomahawk* appear exactly as they had in the *Progress*, leading me to believe it highly likely that this quotation would have appeared this way in 1888.

36. James Ruppert, *Mediation in Contemporary Native American Fiction*. University of Oklahoma Press, 1995, p. 26.

37. Alan Velie, "The Trickster Novel." In *Narrative Chance: Postmodern Discourse on Native American Indian Literatures*, ed. Gerald Vizenor. Norman: University of Oklahoma Press, 1993. pp. 126, 128.

38. McNiel, p. 97.

39. Theo Beaulieu, "The Ojibwas," *Tomahawk*, May 7, 1903, p. 1. Please see note 35 for an explanation of my use of this source.

40. Velie, p. 127.

41. Velie, p. 124. In many ways, making any claim that oral narratives *are equivalent*, in any uncomplicated sense, to a form of written genre is a proposition that betrays a certain Eurocentrism.

42. David Treuer, *Native American Fiction: A User's Manual*. Graywolf Press, 2006, p. 55.

43. Vizenor, *People Called the Chippewa*, p. 3.

44. Joe Auginaush, "Gii-pakitejii'iged Wenabozho." Trans. Anton Treuer. *Living Our Language: Anishinaabeg Tales and Oral Histories*. St. Paul: Minnesota Historical Society Press, 2001, pp. 162–63.

45. Mikhail Bakhtin, *The Dialogic Imagination: Four Essays*. Austin: University of Texas Press, 1981, p. 17.

46. Ibid., p. 13.

47. Ibid., p. 14.
48. Theo Beaulieu, "The Ojibwas," *Tomahawk*, May 7, 1903, p. 1.
49. Henry Wadsworth Longfellow, *The Song of Hiawatha*. Boston: Ticknor and Fields, 1856, p. 31.
50. See Roy Harvey Pearce, *Savagism and Civilization*, pp. 191–94; Joshua Bellin, *The Demon of the Continent*, pp. 171–87, Janet Lewis, *The Invasion*, pp. 226–27, Kate Flint, *The Transatlantic Indian*, pp. 124–34, and Alan Trachtenberg, *The Shades of Hiawatha*, passim.
51. Longfellow, p. 283.
52. Ibid.
53. Ibid., p. 293
54. Theo Beaulieu, "The Ojibwas," *Tomahawk*, May 7, 1903, p. 1.
55. Theo Beaulieu, "The Ojibwas, Part XI." the *Progress* May 12, 1888, p. 1.
56. Victor Barnouw, *Wisconsin Myths and Tales: And Their Relation to Chippewa Life*. Madison: University of Wisconsin Press, 1977, p. 78.
57. Benedict Anderson, *Imagined Communities: Reflections on the Origin and Spread of Nationalism*. New York: Verso, 1991, pp. 9–46. Anderson's theory of print capitalism's production of the modern nation has come under critique for both the chicken-and-the-egg-like relationship between the print culture and nationhood (after all, one could argue that the temporality represented in the novel was the effect, and not the cause, of heightened nationalism) and for the very homogeneity of Anderson's idea of "empty homogenous time" (see Chatterjee's "Nation in Heterogeneous Time," *Indian Economic Social History Review* 38 [2001]: 399). Neither of these critiques necessarily affect my reading of Beaulieu's stories, however, because I am describing Beaulieu's self-conscious attempt to emulate already existing forms of nationhood—not the spontaneous development of Anishinaabe nationhood.
58. Theo Beaulieu, "The Ojibwas," *Tomahawk*, May 7, 1903, p. 1.
59. Scott Richard Lyons, *X-Marks: Native Signatures of Assent*. Minneapolis: University of Minnesota Press, 2010, p. 123.
60. Ibid., p. 127.
61. The geographies present in Beaulieu's translations are so ill-suited to the chronotope of the novel, in fact, that they become difficult to assimilate into the representation of time, as we can see in Wenabozho's journey to the "fourth fold of the skies," the otherworldly realm of the manidoog.
62. The only major change Beaulieu does make to the stories' traditional portrayal of space is a telling one. Unlike most aadizookaanag, which begin with Wenabozho wandering out in the world, each episode of Beaulieu's translation begins and ends in Nookomis's wigwam, a place that is repeatedly represented as comforting, safe, and regenerative—Wenabozho's *home*. The constant circularity of Wenabozho's travels work in the stories to reinforce the rootedness of the stories in a particular landscape, a way of making the Anishinaabeg's claim to their land all the more distinct in the minds of Beaulieu's Euro-American readers.
63. Theo Beaulieu, "The Ojibwas, Part IX." *Progress*, March 24, 1888, p. 1.

64. As James Ruppert argues, mediation in contemporary Native literature is a product of writing to multiple audiences—both Native and non-Native—simultaneously, a process which, by necessity, forces both implied readerships to renegotiate their relationship to each other.

> As the reader's language is translated, his or her self-conception and cultural code become translated; conceptions of Native and Western discourse and identity are then seen through someone else's system. The implied Native reader sees through the non-Native; the implied non-Native reader sees through the Native. . . . An implied reader of the mediational text must conclude by the end of a text that his or her understanding is complete and adequate even though it has been challenged and is now altered. In that sense, the Otherness has been illusory. The mediational world of the text may supply a place to assimilate the Other where the physical world may not. However it is not a world divorced from the political realities of contemporary Native American experience . . . A mediational text attempts to maneuver readers into taking a series of regenerated socio-political positions. An ideological translation takes place, though not a physical transmutation, but, real readers may be ready to act because they perceive things differently. (Ruppert, p. 15)

65. A point that will be important for my discussion of Vizenor's translation of the Anishinaabe nagamonan (songs) in a later chapter.

66. Qtd. in Craig Womack, "The Integrity of American Indian Claims." In *American Indian Literary Nationalism*, ed. Warrior, Weaver, and Womack. Albuquerque: University of New Mexico Press, 2006, p. 117.

67. Jace Weaver, "Splitting the Earth." In *American Indian Literary Nationalism*, eds. Warrior, Weaver, and Womack. Albuquerque: University of New Mexico Press, 2006, p. 32.

68. Theo Beaulieu, "Announcement." *Progress*, July 13, 1889, p. 4.

69. Melissa Meyers, *The White Earth Tragedy: Ethnicity and Dispossession at a Minnesota Anishinaabe Reservation*. Lincoln: University of Nebraska Press, 1994, passim.

70. "Chippewa Indian Chief Is Honored by Men He Protected." *New Ulm Review* 26 (August 1914): 1.

71. "White Earth Reds Hold Grand Pow Wow." *Saint Paul Globe*, June 21, 1903, p. 28.

72. "Local and Personal." *Tomahawk*, April 16, 1903, p. 4.

73. Gerald Vizenor, *A Brief Historical Study and General Content Description of a Newspaper Published on the White Earth Indian Reservation in Becker County, Minnesota*, 1965.

74. Vizenor, Gerald. *Native Liberty: Natural Reason and Cultural Survivance*. Lincoln: University of Nebraska Press, 2009, p. 36.

75. Ibid., p. 36.
76. Ibid., p. 42.
77. Vizenor, Gerald. *Summer in the Spring: Anishinaabe Lyric Poems and Stories, New Edition*. Norman: University of Oklahoma Press, 1993, p. 13.

Chapter 2

1. One notable rail operator was Thaddeus Pound, future lieutenant governor of Wisconsin, and grandfather of Ezra Pound, who made a small fortune as president of both the Chippewa Falls and Western as well as the St. Paul Eastern Grand Trunk Railways. After Thaddeus passed away in 1914, his grandson wrote a (fairly poor) imitation of *The Song of Hiawatha*, titled "Legend of Chippewa Spring and Minnehaha, the Indian Maiden."

2. See James Kates, *Planning a Wilderness: Regenerating the Great Lakes Cutover Region*. Minneapolis: University of Minnesota Press, 2001.

3. As the historian Charles Cleland explains, access to such work (the only kind available to Anishinaabe at the time) was already tenuous.

> At the turn of the twentieth century, the natural resources of northern Michigan were almost depleted and complex machinery was already reducing labor requirements in mining and agriculture. Indians were ill-prepared to compete with whites in this diminishing labor market. Lack of language skills, little formal training in the use of mechanical equipment, and their nonaggressive demeanor were practical disadvantages. But more depressing was the fact that Indian[s] . . . had to face intense hostility and racial prejudice from the competing white majority. As never before, Indians were forced even further to the margins of the American economy.

Charles Cleland, *Rites of Conquest: The History and Culture of Michigan's Native Americans*. Ann Arbor: University of Michigan Press, 1992, pp. 256–67.

4. See Kates, *Planning a Wilderness*, passim.
5. See Aaron Shapiro, *The Lure of the North Woods: Cultivating Tourism in the Upper Midwest*. Minneapolis: University of Minnesota Press, 2013.
6. Madeleine Hemingway Miller, *Ernie: Hemingway's Sister "Sunny" Remembers*. Holt, MI: Thunder Bay Press, 1999, p. 17.
7. Ibid., p. 28.
8. Ernest Hemingway, Sean Hemingway, and Patrick Hemingway. *Hemingway on Hunting*. New York: Simon and Schuster, 2012, p. 181.
9. Qtd. in Constance Cappel Montgomery, *Hemingway Michigan*, New York: Fleet, 1966, p. 60.
10. Ernest Hemingway, *The Complete Short Stories*. New York: Scribner, 1987, p. 69.

11. Jeffrey Meyers, "Hemingway's Primitivism and 'Indian Camp.'" *Twentieth Century Literature* 34, no. 2 (1988): 219.
12. Ibid., p. 217.
13. Ibid., p. 219.
14. William Churchill, "The Golden Bough," Review, *Bulletin of the American Geographical Society*. American Geographical Society of New York, 1912, p. 544.
15. Christopher Schedler, *Border Modernism*. New York: Routledge, 2013, p. 72.
16. Philip Melling. "'There Were Many Indians in the Story': Hidden History in Hemingway's 'Big Two-Hearted River.'" *Hemingway Review* 28, no. 2 (2009): 49.
17. Ibid., p. 62.
18. Katalin Kállay, "The Bark Peelers of the North: A Reading of Ernest Hemingway's 'Indian Camp.'" In *Indigenous Perspectives of North America*, ed. Sespi, Nagy, Vassányi, and Kenyeres. Newcastle: Cambridge Scholars, 2014, p. 212.
19. Ernest Hemingway, *Death in the Afternoon*. New York: Scribner, 2002. pp. 153–54.
20. Hemingway, *Complete Short Stories*, p. 372.
21. Kállay, p. 210.
22. James M. McClurken, "Wage Labor in Two Michigan Ottawa Communities." In *Native Americans and Wage Labor: Ethnohistorical Perspectives*, ed. Littlefield and Knack. Norman: University of Oklahoma Press, 1996.
23. Theodore J. Karamanski, *Blackbird's Song: Andrew J. Blackbird and the Odawa People*. East Lansing: Michigan State University Press, 2012, pp. 193–94.
24. McClurken, p. 93.
25. One of the most brutal episodes of in this history of dispossession came on October 15, 1900, when a timber speculator named John McGinn claimed, and then leveled, an entire village on the shore of Burt Lake. Brandishing a deed of forfeiture and backed by a posse of armed sheriff's deputies, McGinn forcibly removed the Anishinaabeg from their homes, before dousing the structures in kerosene and setting them alight, one by one. Because it was payday for the lumber companies in Cheboygan, most of Burt Lake's men were away from the village—as McGinn would have been well aware. The evictees, largely women, children, and the elderly, were forced to leave the property. Taking what possessions they could carry, they walked more than twelve miles to the Odawa mission at Cross Village. The Burt Lake Burnout, as it came to be known, drew immediate and widespread condemnation among the people of Michigan, but McGinn never faced criminal charges, and was ultimately found to have acted within his rights by a Federal District Judge in 1917. The Hemingways, having already spent two summers in the area at the time of the conflagration, were likely aware of the event—especially given its proximity (the site of Burt Lake village was only about twenty miles away), as well as the publicity surrounding the subsequent trial.

26. While it is impossible to say exactly how much Ernest knew of this history, its effects certainly had a profound impact on his own experiences in Michigan. One of the new homesteaders who flooded into Emmet County during the 1875 land rush was an Anglo-Canadian named Henry Couch, who claimed 135 acres on a peninsula on the north shore of Walloon Lake—likely former Indian land. A few months into his residency, Couch was killed while clearing timber off the homestead. Understanding the potential value of the property, Henry's sister, Elizabeth Bacon, her husband (also named Henry) left Canada to take over the homestead. After clearing the land and improving it with a small farm, they were granted patent in 1883. The Bacons split their waterfront into lake lots, three of which they sold to Clarence and Grace Hemingway in 1898, who built Windemere on it a few years later. The memory of the land's previous occupants was commemorated with the bucolic name the Bacons gave to the peninsula, "Indian Garden Point."

27. Ernest Hemingway and Carlos Baker. *Ernest Hemingway Selected Letters 1917–1961*. Simon and Schuster, 2003, p. xii.

28. Mark Rifkin, *Settler Common Sense: Queerness and Everyday Colonialism in the American Renaissance*. Minneapolis: University of Minnesota Press, 2014, p. 7.

29. James H. Cox, *Muting White Noise: Native American and European American Novel Traditions*. Norman: University of Oklahoma Press, 2006, p. 207.

30. The name, O-Non-E-Gwud (Onaanigwad) is a verb meaning "to rejoice."

31. Letter to Janet Lewis from Molly Johnstone, September 13, 1920. The Yvor Winters and Janet Lewis papers, 1906–1982 (M352), Box 6, Folder 12. Stanford University Library Archives.

32. Brigitte Hoy Carnochan, "Interview with Janet Lewis." Unpublished transcript. Brigitte Hoy Carnochan Papers relating to research on Janet Lewis. Box 4, Folders 23 and 26, n.p. Stanford University Library Archives.

33. Ibid.

34. Ibid.

35. John Macdougall Johnstone added an "e" to the family name after another family of Johnstons settled at the Sault.

36. Importantly, when the written accounts (almost all of which were produced by Euro-Americans) contradicted the family's version of historical events, Lewis privileged the oral history as more accurate. (See Carnochan papers.)

37. Patrick Wolfe, *Settler Colonialism*. Continuum International Publishing Group, 1999, p. 163.

38. John Chamberlain, "A Chronicle of the Old Northwest: The Invasion. By Janet Lewis." *New York Times*. October 2, 1932, p. BR7.

39. Dorothea Brande, "Four New Novelists." *Bookman* 75, no. 5 (September 1932): 518.

40. Morton Dauwel Zabel, "The Northwest Passage." *Nation* 135, no. 3517 (November 30, 1932), pp. 537–38.

41. Fanny Butcher, "Janet Lewis Pens Epic of Soo Country." *Chicago Daily Tribune*, September 15, 1932, p. 13.

42. Carnochan papers, n.p.

43. Ibid.

44. Indeed, Lewis's claim is strikingly similar to one made by James Fenimore Cooper in the 1826 preface to *The Last of the Mohicans*, in which he declares: "The reader who takes up these volumes, in expectation of finding an imaginary and romantic picture of things which never had existence, will probably lay them aside, disappointed. The work is what it professes to be in its title-page—a narrative." James Fenimore Cooper, *Last of the Mohicans*. Paris: A. & W. Galignani, 1826, p. i.

45. Doris Sommer, "Foundational Fictions: When History Was Romance in Latin America." *Salmagundi* 82/83 (1989): 111–41, p. 114.

46. Ibid.

47. Gregg Crane, *The Cambridge Introduction to the Nineteenth-Century American Novel*. Cambridge University Press, 2007, p. 35.

48. Ezra Tawil, "Domestic Frontier Romance, or, How the Sentimental Heroine Became White." *Novel: A Forum on Fiction* 32, no. 1 (Autumn, 1998): 118–19.

49. Cary Miller, *Ogimaag: Anishinaabeg Leadership, 1760–1845*. Lincoln: University of Nebraska Press, 2010, pp. 65–111.

50. Richard White, *The Middle Ground: Indians, Empires, and Republics in the Great Lakes Region, 1650–1815*. Cambridge University Press, 2010, p. 52.

51. Brenda J Child, *Holding Our World Together: Ojibwe Women and the Survival of Community*. New York: Penguin, 2012, p. 32.

52. White, p. x.

53. Lewis departs from both of her sources on Waub-ojeeg's speech. Thomas McKenney presents it in the language of a transaction between the two men—leaving out Waub-ojeeg's insistence on Johnston and Ozah-guscoday-wayquay's marriage as legally binding: "White man, I have noticed your behavior. It has been correct. But, white man, *your colour is deceitful*. Of you, may I expect better things? You say you are going to return to Montreal—go; and if you return, I shall be satisfied of your sincerity, and will give you my daughter." McKenney, Thomas. *History of the Indian Tribes of North America*. Carlise, MA: Applewood Books, 2010, pp. 154–55.

Anna Jameson maintains Waub-ojeeg's criticism of white hypocrisy, but undercuts Waub-ojeeg's authoritative tone.

> White man! [. . .] your customs are not our customs! You white men desire our women, you marry them, and when they cease to please your eye, you say they are not your wives and you forsake them. Return, young friend, to Montreal; and if there the women of the pale faces do not put my child out of your mind, return hither in the spring, and we will talk farther [sic]; she is young, and can wait.

Anna Jameson, *Winter Studies and Summer Rambles in Canada*. London: Saunders and Otley, 1838, pp. 210–11.

54. "Doodem" is an Anishinaabemowin word usually translated to "clan" or "family," and is the source of the English-language word "totem"—which has unfortunately taken on a range of meanings in psychology and anthropology that have obscured the term's original emphasis on kin relations. Doodemag were usually identified by a crest depicting an animal or supernatural being that was used to mark property, territory, or grave sites. Early ethnographers (including Schoolcraft) mistook the importance of these images, thinking the figures represented gods worshiped by the Anishinaabeg instead of the kinship networks they relied on for survival. This original mistake created an interesting malapropism later on, when ethnographers insisted on describing the clan markers of the Pacific Northwest as "totem poles"—not realizing that that term's original meaning perfectly described the importance of the markers to the indigenous peoples that made them.

55. Robert Bieder, a historian of the Sault, explains that although the fur trade "mimicked a seigneurial world," he asserts that "it was also compatible with the Ojibwa society, which was characterized by heavy kinship obligations and responsibilities. Indeed, in many ways, Sault society was more Ojibwa than European and proved superbly adapted [sic] to the severe environment and precarious economic situation." Robert E. Bieder, "Sault Ste. Marie and the War of 1812: A World Turned Upside Down in the Old Northwest." *Indiana Magazine of History* 95, no. 1 (1999): 1–13.

56. Carnochan papers, n.p.

57. Ibid.

58. The symbolic connection Lewis makes between Schoolcraft's desire to exploit Indian cultural material and his work to dispossess the Anishinaabeg of their land and natural resources has been corroborated by a raft of recent criticism. Robert Dale Parker observes that "Just as Henry worked with Jackson Democrats to support the 'removal' of Indian people from their land, so he sometimes seems to try to remove Indian people from their own stories" (61). Like Lewis, Joshua Bellin also links Schoolcraft's dual roles of geologist and ethnographer, arguing, "Schoolcraft's work finally reveals (or conceals) that at the heart of ethnology lies not mental but material speculation, conflict over America's ground" (152). The harshest criticism comes from Maureen Konkle, who refuses to mince word by saying "Schoolcraft's transformation of the knowledge provided by his wife's family into evidence of Indians' difference, inferiority, and impending disappearance quite literally supported colonial control" (167). That Lewis could come to a similar conclusion in 1932 is almost astounding, given the high degree of historical reverence with which Schoolcraft was treated at the time. For example, Chase Osborn, the source of much of Lewis's historical information, wrote of him in 1942, "To the Indians Henry Rowe Schoolcraft was a sun god" (558).

Robert Dale Parker, *The Sound the Stars Make Rushing through the Sky: The Writings of Jane Johnston Schoolcraft*. Philadelphia: University of Pennsylvania Press, 2007.

Joshua Bellin, *The Demon of the Continent: Indians and the Shaping of American Literature*. Philadelphia: University of Pennsylvania Press, 2012.

Maureen Konkle, *Writing Indian Nations*. Chapel Hill: UNC Press, 2005.

Chase Osborne and Stellanova Osborne, *Schoolcraft, Longfellow, Hiawatha*. Lancaster, PA: Jaques Cattell Press, 1942.

59. Originally written as a short story and published in the *Bookman* as "At the Swamp" in 1928, this scene was, in many ways, the nucleus around which the rest of *The Invasion* would form.

60. Rifkin, p. 193.

61. Johnston Family Papers 1822–1936, Box 1, Bentley Historical Library, University of Michigan, Ann Arbor.

62. Letter to Janet Lewis from William M. Johnstone, April 10, 1931. The Yvor Winters and Janet Lewis papers, 1906–1982 (M352), Box 6, Folder 12. Stanford University Library Archives.

63. Charles Cleland, *The Place of the Pike*. Ann Arbor: University of Michigan Press, 2000, p. 70.

64. Several other Anishinaabeg bands that were signatories to the Treaty of 1855, including the survivors of the Burt Lake Burnout, are still seeking recognition.

65. Lorenzo Veracini, *Settler Colonialism: A Theoretical Overview*. New York: Palgrave and Macmillan, 2010, p. 110.

Chapter 3

1. Matthew Weiner, "Mayham," *The Sopranos*, season 6, episode 3, directed by Jack Bender, aired March 26, 2006.

2. Frances Densmore, *Chippewa Music I*. Washington, DC: Government Printing Office, 1910, p. 118.

3. Frances Densmore, "She Heard an Indian Drum." In *Frances Densmore and American Indian Music*, ed. Hoffman, Charles. New York: Museum of the American Indian Heye Foundation, 1968, p. 2.

4. Qtd. in Joan M. Jensen and Michelle Wick Patterson, *Travels with Frances Densmore*. Lincoln: University of Nebraska Press, 2015, p. 33.

5. Densmore, "She Heard an Indian Drum," p. 2

6. Biographical information about Mary English taken from a short sketch written by her sister, Julia Spears, published in *A Pioneer History of Becker County Minnesota*, ed. Alvin Wilcox. St. Paul: Pioneer Press, 1907, pp. 253–55.

7. See the *Tomahawk*, April 5, 1917 and Michael McNally, *Ojibwe Singers*, p. 136.

8. Densmore, *Chippewa Music I*, p. 3.

9. Frances Densmore, "Notes on the Indians' Belief in the Friendliness of Nature." *Southwestern Journal of Anthropology* 4, no. 1 (Spring 1948): 94.

10. Densmore, *Chippewa Music I*, p. 8.

11. Ibid., p. 2.
12. Ibid., pp. 14–15.
13. Frances Densmore, "Selected Letters." In Hoffman, p. 61.
14. Krystyn R. Moon, "The Quest for Music's Origin at the St. Louis World's Fair: Frances Densmore and the Racialization of Music," *American Music* 28, no. 2 (2010): 191–210.
15. Qtd. in Jensen and Patterson, *Travels*, p. 44
16. Densmore, *Chippewa Music I*, p. 175.
17. Densmore, *Chippewa Music I*, pp. 172–73.
18. Sandburg, Carl. "Aboriginal Poetry." *Poetry Magazine*, February, 1917, p. 255.
19. George Cronyn, ed. *The Path on the Rainbow*, New York: Boni and Liverlight, 1918, p. xv.
20. Ibid., p. 16.
21. Ibid., p. xvi.
22. Louis Untermeyer, "The Indian as Poet," *Dial* 66, no. 785 (March 8, 1919): 240.
23. Thomas Stearns Eliot, "War Paint and Feathers," reprinted in *Primitivism and Twentieth-Century Art: A Documentary History*, ed. Jack Flam and Miriam Deutch. Berkeley: University of California Press, 2003, pp. 121–22.
24. Ibid., p. 122.
25. Alice Corbin Henderson, "Buffalo Dance," *Poetry Magazine*, February 1917, pp. 235–36.
26. Alice Corbin Henderson, "Aboriginal Poetry," *Poetry Magazine*, February 1917, p. 256.
27. Frances Densmore, *Chippewa Music II*. Washington, DC: Government Printing Office, 1913, p. 102.
28. Henderson's creative interpretative strategy was likely inspired, in part, by the work of her one-time frequent correspondent, Ezra Pound. Pound had articulated an entirely new approach to the idea of poetic interpretation in his widely celebrated collection, *Cathay* (1913), in which he offered "translations" of Chinese poetry based not on the original texts, but the fragmentary interpretive notes of the late Orientalist, Ernest Fenallosa. Despite containing many additions, substitutions, and inaccuracies, *Cathay* was celebrated as a masterwork of poetic translation.
29. Henderson, "Aboriginal Poetry," p. 256.
30. Frances Densmore, *Poems from Sioux and Chippewa Songs*. Washington, DC: self-published, 1917, n.p.
31. Ibid.
32. Ibid.
33. Lew Sarett, *Many, Many Moons*. New York: Henry Holt and Company, 1920, p. 120.
34. Lew Sarett, *The Box of God*. New York: Henry Holt & Company, 1922, p. 10.

35. Harriet Monroe, "A Contrast," *Poetry Magazine*, March 1923, p. 330.

36. Qtd. in Herbert S. Case, "Lone Cairbou, Michigan's Poet." *Michigan Chimes* 3, no. 6 (March 1922): 12.

37. Qtd in Lynn Miller Rein, *A Rhetorical Study of Lew Sarett*, dissertation, Northwestern University, ProQuest Dissertations Publishing, 1978, p. 38.

38. Sarett, *Box of God*, p. 78.

39. Sarett, *Many, Many Moons*, pp. vii–viii.

40. Ibid., p. 7.

41. Ibid., p. viii.

42. For instance, see Michael Castro's insufficiently problematized use of the term "Native American Consciousness" when discussing the poetry of Jerome Rothenberg and Gary Snyder in *Interpreting the Indian: Twentieth-Century Poets and the Native American*. Norman: University of Oklahoma Press, 1991.

43. Sarett, *Many, Many Moons*, p. 80.

44. Yvor Winters, *The Uncollected Essays and Reviews of Yvor Winters*, ed. Francis Murphy. Chicago: Swallow Press, 1973, p. 42.

45. Ibid., p. 36.

46. Yvor Winters, *The Magpie's Shadow*. Chicago: Musterbookhouse, 1922, p. 20.

47. Ibid., p. 27.

48. Ibid., p. 30.

49. Yvor Winters, *Forms of Discovery*. Chicago: Swallow Press, 1967, p. 356.

50. "Tribal religions are actually a complex of attitudes, beliefs, and practices fine-tuned to harmonize with the lands on which the people live. It is not difficult to understand that the Hopi people, living in the arid plateau and canyonlands of northern Arizona, had need of a rain dance to ensure the success of their farming. Here place and religion have such an obvious parallel that anyone can understand the connection." Vine Deloria, *God Is Red*. Golden: Fulcrum Publishing, 2003, p. 69.

51. Winters, *Uncollected Essays*, pp. 40–41.

52. Ibid., p. 43.

53. William Carlos Williams, *Pictures from Brueghel and Other Poems*. New York: New Directions Press, 1967, p. 1.

54. Margot Astrov, *The Winged Serpent*. Boston: Beacon Books, 1992, p. 3.

55. Kenneth Rexroth, *Assays*. Norfolk, CT: J. Laughlin, 1961, p. 57.

56. Francis Paul Prucha, *Documents of United States Indian Policy*. Lincoln: University of Nebraska Press, 2000, p. 234.

57. Ibid.

58. Francis Paul Prucha, *The Great Father: United States Government and the American Indians*. Lincoln: University of Nebraska Press, 1995, p. 351.

59. Donald Lee Fixico, *Urban Indian Experience in America*. University of New Mexico Press, 2000, p. 25.

60. Densmore, *Chippewa Music II*, p. 268.

61. Densmore, *Chippewa Music I*, p. 127.

62. Gerald Vizenor, *Summer in the Spring: Lyric Poems of the Ojibway*. Minneapolis: Noodin Press, 1965, p. 55.

63. Ibid., p. 15.

64. For a comprehensive overview of these translators' work and philosophy, see Arnold Krupat's very good essay, "On the Translation of Native American Song and Story: A Theorized History." In *On the Translation of Native American Literatures*, ed. Brian Swann. Washington, DC: Smithsonian Institution, 1992, pp. 3–32.

65. Jerome Rothenberg, "Total Translation: An Experiment in the Presentation of American Indian Poetry." *Pre-Faces & Other Writings*. New York: New Directions, 1981, p. 91.

The idea that poetry's representational power went beyond mere language was built upon the work of a previous generation of poets such as William Carlos Williams, Louis Zukofsky, and, importantly, Charles Olson—who proclaimed the influential dictum, "FORM IS NEVER MORE THAN AN EXTENSION OF CONTENT."

66. Densmore, *Chippewa Music I*, p. 77.

67. Jerome Rothenberg, *Shaking the Pumpkin*. Garden City: Doubleday & Company, 1972, p. 332.

68. Ibid., p. 403.

69. Williams Bevis, "American Indian Verse Translations." *College English* 35, no. 6 (March 1974): 700.

70. Ibid., 694.

71. William Clements, "Faking the Pumpkin: On Jerome Rothenberg's Literary Offenses." *Western American Literature* XVI, no. 1 (Spring 1981): 194.

72. Ibid., 203.

73. Ibid., 195.

74. Neal Bowers, Charles Silet, Gerald Vizenor. "An Interview with Gerald Vizenor." *MELUS* 8, no. 1 (Spring 1981): 49.

75. Gerald Vizenor, *Summer in the Spring: Anishinaabe Lyric Poems and Stories, New Edition*. Norman: University of Oklahoma Press, 1993, pp. 3–4.

76. Vizenor, a vocal critic of essentialist thinking, certainly would not believe that the historical contingency of his being born Anishinaabe entitles him to a better understanding than Rothenberg of the cultural material both present.

77. Vizenor, *Summer in the Spring* (1965), p. 14.

78. Densmore, *Chippewa Music I*, p. 82.

79. Vizenor, *Summer in the Spring* (1965), p. 73.

80. Ibid., p. 25.

81. Rothenberg, *Pumpkin*, p. 332.

82. Densmore, *Chippewa Music I*, p. 17.

83. Rothenberg, *Pumpkin*, p. 405.

84. Elizabeth Povinelli, *The Cunning of Recognition: Indigenous Alterities and the Making of Australian Multiculturalism*. Duke University Press, 2002, p. 39.

85. Ibid., p. 49.

86. As a minor example of this phenomenon, take Minnesota's former-governor Jesse Ventura, who declared in 1999 that if the Anishinaabeg of Minnesota wished to maintain their treaty rights to subsistence fishing, "then they ought to be back in birch-bark canoes instead of 200-horsepower Yamaha engines with fish finders" (qtd. in Bruyneel, xii). Note how it is the Anishinaabeg who must satisfy *Ventura's* standards for proper cultural behavior in order to retain their treaty rights.

Kevin Bruyneel, *The Third Space of Sovereignty: The Postcolonial Politics of U.S.-Indigenous Relations*. Minneapolis: University of Minnesota Press, 2007.

87. Gail Guthrie Valaskakis, *Indian Country: Essays on Contemporary Native Culture*. Wilfrid Laurier University Press, 2005. pp. 184–85.

88. Ibid., p. 195.

89. Ibid., p. 195.

90. Take, for example, "The Song of Manabozho," which appeared in 1965, as follows:

> Do not look
> Or your eyes
> Will always
> Be red. (72)

In 1970, the poem appeared simply as "manabozho song."

> dance and sing
> across the water
> if you open your eyes
> they will turn red (103)

91. Vizenor, *Summer in the Spring* (1993), p. 13.

92. Ibid., p. 4.

93. Vizenor, *Summer in the Spring* (1965), p. 12. This is very similar to what Robert Dale Parker describes as the motivation for non-Natives, such as Dell Hymes and a Jerome Rothenberg, to present Native song as poetry. "The real purpose of presenting traditional Indian oral narrative as poetry or verse," Parker explains, "is polemical and canonizing."

> In the social ideology of genre, verse and poetry have canonical status and even an elite class status. If their elite status can be claimed for traditional Indian oral narrative, then the status of traditional narrative (and those who study it) can be raised, but at the cost of complicity with a discourse of colonizing appropriation. (85)

I modify Parker's argument with the proviso that attempting to claim an elite status for tribal oral materials need not always be complicit with "the discourse of colonizing appropriation," but can instead be seen as a self-conscious effort (as it seems to be in Vizenor) to articulate a tribal history of 'high' cultural production. Robert Dale Parker, *The Invention of Native American Literature*. Ithaca, NY: Cornell University Press, 2003.

94. Blaeser, *Writing in the Oral Tradition*, p. 119.
95. Ibid., p. 110.
96. Densmore, *Chippewa Music II*, p. 283.
97. Vizenor, *Summer* (1965), p. 19.
98. Vizenor, *Anishinabe Nagamon*, Minneapolis: Nodin Press, 1970, p. 43.
99. Patricia Haseltine, "The Voices of Gerald Vizenor: Survival through Transformation." *American Indian Quarterly* 9, no. 1 (Winter 1985): 32.
100. Bowers, Silet, and Vizenor, "An Interview," 42.
101. Gerald Vizenor, *Summer in the Spring: Ojibwe Lyric Poems and Tribal Stories*. Minneapolis: Nodin Press, 1981, p. 25.
102. Gerald Vizenor, "The Envoy to Haiku," *Chicago Review* 39, no. 3 (1993): 60.
103. Vizenor, *Anishinabe Nagamon*, p. 72.
104. Densmore, *Chippewa Music I*, 81.
105. Ibid., 106.
106. Gerald Vizenor, *Anishinabe Adisokan*. Minneapolis: Nodin Press, 1970, p. 74.
107. Blaeser, *Writing in the Oral Tradition*, p. 23.
108. Gerald Vizenor, *Fugitive Poses: Native American Scenes of Absence and Presence*. Lincoln: University of Nebraska Press, 1998, p. 15.
109. S.477 (113th). *Tribal Gaming Eligibility Act*.

Chapter 4

1. Daniel Cornell, "Woman Looking: Revis(ion)ing Pauline's Position in Louise Erdrich's *Tracks*." *Studies in American Indian Literature* 4, no. 1 (Spring 1990): 62.
2. Nancy J. Peterson, *Against Amnesia: Contemporary Women Writers and the Crises of Historical Memory*. Philadelphia: University of Pennsylvania Press, 2001, p. 31.
3. Chadwick Allen, "Postcolonial Theory and the Discourse of Treaties." *American Quarterly* 52, no. 1 (2000): 77.
4. Louise Erdrich, *Tracks*. New York: Harper Perennial, 2004, p. 225.
5. Ibid., p. 174.
6. Louise Erdrich, *The Bingo Palace*. New York: HarperCollins,1994, p. 134.
7. Louise Erdrich, *Love Medicine* (rev. ed.). New York: HarperCollins, 2005, pp. 300–1.
8. Henry Louis Gates Jr., *Faces of America: How 12 Extraordinary People Discovered Their Pasts*. New York: New York University Press, 2010, p. 81.

9. Lisa Halliday, Interview. "Louise Erdrch, The Art of Fiction No. 208." *Paris Review* 195 (Winter 2010). http://www.theparisreview.org/interviews/6055/the-art-of-fiction-no-208-louise-erdrich.

10. Ibid., n.p.

11. Amanda Claybaugh, "Government Is Good." *Minnesota Review* 70 (Spring/Summer 2008): 70.

12. Vine Deloria Jr., *Custer Died for Your Sins: An Indian Manifesto*. Norman: University of Oklahoma Press, 1969, p. 125. Even though Deloria originally made this observation in 1968, I believe very little about the situation has changed.

13. Ibid.

14. Richard Nixon, "Special Message to the Congress on Indian Affairs." July 8, 1970. Online by Gerhard Peters and John T. Woolley, *The American Presidency Project*. http://www.presidency.ucsb.edu/ws/?pid=2573.

15. Bruce Robbins, *Upward Mobility and the Common Good: Toward a Literary History of the Welfare State*. Princeton: Princeton University Press, 2007, p. xii.

16. Robbins, pp. 22–54.

17. Louise Erdrich, *The Plague of Doves*. HarperCollins, 2008, p. 274. All proceeding citations are given as parentheticals.

18. Robbins, pp. 23–24.

19. Beth H. Piatote, *Domestic Subjects*. New Haven: Yale University Press, 2013, p. 2.

20. Dale Turner, *This Is Not a Peace Pipe*. Toronto: University of Toronto Press, 2008, p. 90.

21. Ibid., p. 81.

22. Ibid., p. 121.

23. Ibid., p. 120.

24. Mark Trahant, "Tribes Deal with Another Brutal Federal Policy." *Indianz.com*. November 1, 2011. http://www.indianz.com/News/2011/003563.asp.

25. Bureau of Indian Affairs. "Indian Affairs/Tribal Interior Budget Council Budget Subcommittee Meeting." 2015. http://www.bia.gov/cs/groups/xasia/documents/document/idc1-030539.pdf.

26. Chris Edwards, "Indian Lands, Indian Subsidies." *Downsizing the Federal Government*, February 1, 2012. http://www.downsizinggovernment.org/interior/indian-lands-indian-subsidies.

27. Chris Edwards, "What Do American Indians Deserve: Name Changes or Policy Changes?" *Cato Institute*, April 2, 2014. http://www.cato.org/publications/commentary/what-do-american-indians-deserve-name-changes-or-policy-changes.

28. Edwards, "Indian Lands," n.p.

29. Ibid.

30. Mark Trahant, "The Indian Health Service Paradox." *Kaiser Health News*. September 6, 2009. http://www.kaiserhealthnews.org/Columns/2009/September/091709Trahant.aspx.

31. There even exists a Facebook group titled "I just spent 6 hours at IHS just for them to give me Tylenol," dedicated to sharing stories about negative

experiences with the service. Mark Trahant, "I Just Spent Six Hours at IHS Just for Them to Give Me Tyenol." *Seattle Post Globe*, March 8, 2010. http://seattlepostglobe.org/2010/03/08/why-facebook-complaints-about-the-indian-health-service-are-important/.

32. Mary Clare Jalonick, Interview. "AP Interview: Sebelius to Boost Indian Health Care." *Seattle Times*, June 16, 2009. http://seattletimes.com/html/politics/2009344224_apussebeliusindianhealthcare.html.

33. Government Accounting Office. "Investigation of Allegations Concerning Indian Health Service." HRD-77-3. 1976. http://www.gao.gov/assets/120/117355.pdf.

34. Around the same time as the GAO report, Pinkerton-Uri began making startling accusations that the prevalence of sterilization among Indian women was much higher, claiming that at least 40 percent of Native American women of child-bearing age had already been sterilized by the IHS without their knowledge. Claiming to have conducted a study of IHS's sterilization practices, Pinkerton-Uri predicted that 25,000 Native women would be sterilized in 1975 alone—a number representing significant portion of the population of American Indian women at the time. Despite never publishing her findings, Pinkerton-Uri's claims took hold in the public imagination—especially after they were picked up and aggressively reported by anti-abortion organizations in the pro-life movement. Some academics continue to cite Pinkerton-Uri's claims, repeating the figure of 25,000 forced sterilizations taking place in 1975 as a proven historical fact rather than her prediction (see, for example, Jane Lawrence. "Indian Health Service and the Sterilization of Native American Women." *American Indian Quarterly* 24, no. 3: 410).

It is doubtless that the IHS doctors who coerced Native women into sterilization were acting out of an adherence to either explicit or unconscious belief in white supremacy, but there is no evidence that the IHS purposefully carried out a campaign of genocide. Somewhat ironically, continued fear of forced sterilization subsequently became a commonly stated reason for Natives to avoid seeking medical care, doubtlessly leading to otherwise preventable cases of death and disease. It is also worth noting that the IHS actually withheld reproductive health services from many Native women well into the late 1960s, largely to avoid being accused of committing genocide, only changing their policies after sustained protest from Native women's groups (Grossman, Bergman, Erdrich, et al. "A Political History of the Indian Health Service." *Millbank Quarterly* 77, no. 4: 582).

35. Sherman Alexie, *Indian Killer*. New York: Atlantic Monthly Press, 1996, pp. 3–4.

36. Ibid., p. 6.

37. Louise Erdrich, *The Painted Drum*. New York: HarperCollins, 2005, p. 247. All subsequent citations from this novel will be given in parenthetical notation.

38. M. Berry, et al. "Broken Promises: Evaluating the Native American Health Care System." U.S. Commission on Civil Rights, Office of the General Counsel (2004), p. 87.

39. Kathy Parker, "Coburn Health Care Bill Not a Fix." *Pryor Times*, April 2, 2010. http://pryordailytimes.com/local/x1612523842/Coburn-Health-care-bill-not-a-fix/print.

40. Indian Health Service. "IHS Year 2014 Profile." January 2014. https://www.ihs.gov/newsroom/index.cfm/factsheets/ihsyear2014profile/.

41. Tom Coburn, "Don't Get Sick after June." *Fox News Online*. November 5, 2009. http://www.foxnews.com/opinion/2009/11/05/tom-coburn-public-option-indian-health-service/.

42. "Coburn Amendment 4034 Empowers Tribal Members to Choose for Themselves How They Get Their Health Care." February 14, 2008. http://www.coburn.senate.gov/public/index.cfm?a=Files.Serve&File_id=d9e5a73c-d177-4f42-aa29-932221f0bfd7.

43. Jefferson Keel, Testimony to the Senate Subcommittee on Indian Affairs. *Hearing on Reforming the Indian Health Care System*. June 11, 2009. http://www.indian.senate.gov/public/_files/JeffersonKeeltestimony.pdf.

44. Mark Trahant, "The Double Standard of Government-Run Health Care: The Indian Health Service." *News from Indian Country*. July 2009. http://www.indiancountrynews.com/index.php?option=com_content&view=article&id=7030:trahant-the-double-standard-of-government-run-health-care-the-indian-health-service&catid=287&Itemid=108.

45. Grossman, Bergman, Erdrich, et al., p. 573.

46. Ibid., p. 571.

47. John Tanner, *The Falcon: A Narrative of the Captivity and Adventures of John Tanner*. London: Penguin Classics, 2003. pp. 144–47.

48. Such a sense of personal failure, one can argue, is the very source of the intergenerational trauma that runs throughout *The Painted Drum*. Anaquot's brutal sacrifice of her own daughter in order to save herself, the elder Shawaano's drinking and abusive treatment of Bernard and his siblings, even Elsie Traver's willingness to turn a blind eye to her husband's sadistic treatment of his own children—in each case an individual is compelled to inflict pain on their children because of a sense of powerlessness and personal failure in the face of massive dispossession.

49. Michael McNally, *Ojibwe Singers: Hymns, Grief, and a Native Culture in Motion*. St. Paul: Minnesota Historical Society Press, 2009, p. 61.

50. Cary Miller, *Ogimaag: Anishinaabe Leadership, 1760–1845*. Lincoln: University of Nebraska Press, 2010, p. 25.

51. It is important for me to note that I make absolutely no claims to a personal understanding of mino bimaadiziwin's spiritual or religious connotations. My treatment of mino bimaadiziwin as a philosophical ideal in the context of this book is simply an attempt to understand it as a coherent *modus vivendi* that

has structured, and continues to structure, Anishinaabe social and cultural life. Some may object to this approach as a secularization of an idea with profoundly important religious connotations, and indeed such objections may be well-founded, but I would rather stand accused of impiety than pretend to have insight into a spiritual tradition that I—by both chance and choice—do not participate in. As my predecessor, the Anishinaabe historian William Warren, once wrote, "I frankly acknowledge that I stand as yet, as it were, on the threshold of the Me-da-we lodge." This note is meant to act as an invitation to those with a more spiritually oriented understanding of mino bimaadiziwin to criticize my theorization of the concept—may they do so with all the authority their belief grants them. I can say with confidence that in my attempt to understand the meaning of the term, I have tried my best to listen to their voices. I cannot, in good conscience, raise my own to join them.

52. Scott Richard Lyons, *X-Marks: Native Signatures of Assent*. Minneapolis: University of Minnesota Press, 2010, p. 90.

53. Tanner, p. 147.

54. *The Painted Drum* offers an interesting inversion of a trope so prevalent in contemporary Native American literature that it has almost ossified into generic convention. This trope can be seen in Leslie Marmon Silko's *Ceremony*, Louis Owen's *Sharpest Sight*, Linda Hogan's *Power*, Joseph Boyd's *Three Day Road*, and—in some respects—in Erdrich's earlier novel *The Bingo Palace*, to name but a few. In each of these novels, the troubled protagonist, alienated by modernity, can only find the cultural tools to reintegrate into his or her tribal society by fleeing to a remote place and becoming self-sufficient. This is often accomplished through apprenticing under a traditional elder who lives alone and forces the protagonist to give up the trappings of modern life and assume aspects of a historically traditional lifestyle. This apprenticeship both heals the psychic wounds of the protagonist and allows him or her to bring traditional values back to a fragmented tribal community that has lost sight of what it means to be truly Indian. (Incidentally, at least three of these novels, *Ceremony*, *Power*, and *Three Day Road*, represent the hospital as a space of compromising, dangerous social control over Indian bodies.)

55. The passage of the Indian Child Welfare Act in 1978 strongly curtailed (but did not completely end) the "adopting out" of Native children. Despite the strides made over the past forty years, the figure of the Child Welfare officer, like the IHS hospital, is one that has not fared well in Native American literature or the public imagination. Novels such as Joseph Bruchac's *Skeleton Man* (2001) and Barbara Kingsolver's *Pigs in Heaven* (1993), along with Erdrich's own early short story, "American Horse" (1983), present the figure of the Child Welfare officer as ill-informed, at best and outright hostile to the concept of Native motherhood at worst. In each case, the figure of the Welfare officer is presented as a kind of state-sponsored kidnapper, almost always conceptually linked to Indian boarding schools—a figure who can only threaten Native cultural identity with grim, totalizing bureaucracy.

56. Miller, p. 23.

57. Henry Roe Schoolcraft, *Algic Researches*. New York: Harper & Brothers, 1839, p. 225. Note: the version of the robin story that appears in, *Algic Researches*, is nearly identical to one published under Jane Johnston Schoolcraft's pen-name in the journal *Muzzeniegun*.

58. Robbins, p. 89.

59. It is worth pointing out here that "Shawnee" is an English corruption of the Anishinaabemowin word "Shaawano."

60. Scott Richard Lyons, "Actually Existing Indian Nations: Modernity, Diversity, and the Future of Native American Studies." *American Indian Quarterly* 35, no. 3 (2011): 294.

61. Leslie Marmon Silko, "Here's an Odd Artifact for the Fairy-Tale Shelf." Reprinted in *Studies in American Indian Literatures* 10, no. 4 (Fall 1986): 177–84.

62. Elizabeth Cook-Lynn, *Anti-Indianism in Modern America: A Voice from Tatekeya's Earth*. Champaign: University of Illinois Press, 2001, p. 35. Interestingly, Cook-Lynn's apparent animus against Erdrich may have something to do with Erdrich's (misguided) agreement with her late husband Michael Dorris's suggestion that pregnant Indian women suffering from alcoholism be imprisoned to reduce the chances that their children be born with fetal alcohol syndrome. Cook-Lynn rightfully criticizes Dorris for the misogynistic underpinnings of this argument, which couched the incarceration in terms of legal punishment for moral wrongdoing on the part of women suffering from a debilitating disease. Dorris, as Cook-Lynn also rightly points out, does not take into account the economic, cultural, and historical factors involved in alcoholism.

63. Alan Velie, "Louise Erdrich and American Indian Literary Nationalism." In *Studies in the Literary Achievement of Louise Erdrich Native American Writer: Fifteen Critical Essays* ed. Brajesh Sawhney. Lewiston, NY: Edwin Mellen Press, 2008, p. 45.

64. Michael A. Elliot and Arnold Krupat, "American Indian Fiction and Anticolonial Resistance." In *The Columbia Guide to American Indian Literatures of the United States Since 1945*, ed. Eric Cheyfitz, New York: Columbia University Press, 2006, p. 149.

65. Ibid., p. 127.

66. Kevin Bruyneel, *The Third Space of Sovereignty*. Minneapolis: University of Minnesota Press, 2007, p. xvii.

67. Rennard Strickland, *Tonto's Revenge: Reflections on American Indian Culture and Policy*. Albuquerque: University of New Mexico Press, 1997, p. 52.

68. Ibid.

69. This is what Althusser has ominously called "the reproduction of the relations of production." Louis Althusser, *On Ideology*. New York: Verso, 2008, p. 22.

70. Stuart Hall, "Ethnicity: Identity and Difference." *Radical America* 23, no. 4 (1989): 14.

Conclusion

1. Liz Howard, *Infinite Citizen of the Shaking Tent*. Toronto: McClelland & Stewart, 2015, p. 37. All proceeding citations given in parentheses. I am not the first to recognize the continuity between Howard's poetry and the translational work being done in *Hiawatha, or Nanabozho* more than a century earlier. Here, I follow Fenn Elan Stewart, who first made the connection in her essay "Hiawatha/Hereafter: Re-appropriating Longfellow's Epic in Northern Ontario," *ariel: A Review of English Literature* 44, no. 4 (October 2013): 159–80.

2. "Jillian Harkness Interviews Liz Howard." *The Town Crier*, February 20, 2015. http://towncrier.puritan-magazine.com/interview/liz-howard/.

3. Scott Richard Lyons, "Actually Existing Indian Nations: Modernity, Diversity, and the Future of Native American Studies." *American Indian Quarterly* 35, no. 3 (Summer 2011): 294–312, passim.

4. See chapter 17 of Vine Deloria and Clifford Lytle's *The Nations Within: The Past and Future of American Indian Sovereignty*. New York: Pantheon Books, 1984.

5. See, Glen Coulthard, *Red Skins, White Masks: Rejecting the Colonial Politics of Recognition*. Minneapolis: University of Minnesota Press, 2014. See also Elizabeth Povinelli, *The Cunning of Recognition: Indigenous Alterities and the Making of Australian Multiculturalism*. Durham: Duke University Press, 2002.

6. Henry Wadsworth Longfellow, *The Song of Hiawatha*. Boston: Ticknor and Fields, 1856, p. 283.

Index

Page numbers followed by an f refer to figures.

aadizookaanag (trickster): vs. chronotopic conventions of the epic, 184, 193n41; and connection to political struggles, 47–48; legendary stories appeared in the Progress from 1886–1889, 23–24; as outside of time, 51; sacred space of, 59–60; take on novelistic form, 49–54

aadizookaan narratives (legendary), 44, 46–48, 193n41

aadizookewin ("sacred storytelling"), 14

aboriginal verse, 108

acculturation, 127

An Act for the Restoration to Market of Certain Lands in Michigan (1872), 73

Adams, Nick (Hemingway character), 69–70, 71

Adams, Rachel, 22, 191n61

address, modes of, 61, 130, 137f

Adult Vocational Training Program, 118

agency. See indigenous agency

Alcatraz protests, 121, 143

Alcoff, Linda Martin, 65

Alexie, Sherman, 190n56

Algic Researches (H. R. Schoolcraft), 8–9, 90

Allen, Chadwick, 139–140

allotment policy: ended upon IRA passage in 1934, 96; invoked at White Earth with Nelson Act in 1889, 62–63; in late '60s Indians emerge from dark days of, 119; opened Odawa land in Michigan to homesteading, 73; primary architect of, Alice Fletcher, sought out by Densmore, 103; as pushing Anishinaabe toward self-governance, 23–24; tribal nations receive resources from U.S. occupiers of Native land, 143; to usher Anishinaabeg into modernity via private property, 34, 59–60; as U.S. official policy upon Dawes Act passage, 34–35; White Earth implementation of given 1867 treaty, 42–44

"American Horse" (Erdrich, 1983), 210n55

American Indian Employment and Guidance Center (Minneapolis), 119

American Indian Literary Nationalism (Womack, Weaver, and Warrior), 17

American Indian Movement, 119

American Indian Studies, 20–21

American themes, 54, 69, 127. *See also* capitalism, global
Anderson, Benedict, 58, 194n57
Anglo-Saxon culture, 40–41, 50
animacy, 47
animals, 134, 167
animikiig (thunderbirds), 102, 137f–138
Anishinaabe bands. *See* bands, Anishinaabe
Anishinaabe communities, 22, 191n62
Anishinaabe cultural values: vs. commodification of, 5; as counternarrative to liberal individualism, 153–155, 163–164; as creative expression, 137f; including a love of living for its own sake, 185–186; of interdependency and collective responsibility, 166–168, 177; and racist attitudes toward, 146–147; as sensibility submerged in Hemingway's writing, 71; of separatism and nationhood, 178
Anishinaabeg (of Michigan), 34, 65–66, 76, 95–98
Anishinaabeg (of Minnesota), 34–35, 37–38, 190–191n60
Anishinaabeg (people): as cohesive bands and factions, 43–44; contemporary, 137f–138; dispossessed into increasingly marginal existence, 196n3; and Garden River community, 2, 3, 5; migration by, xviii; and modernity, xix, 4–5; and natural world, 59–60; as oppressed, not conquered, 41–42; and relationships with, xviii, xx; scars of, 137f; sophisticated sense of territorial rights by, xviii, xix, 84–86; survival of, xiv, 5; treaty-based alliance with U.S. by, xix; and U.S. relations, 146–147, 150. *See also* traditional Anishinaabeg life; White Earth Reservation
Anishinaabeg deterioration, 78–82
Anishinaabe identity. *See* identity, Anishinaabe
Anishinaabe kinship networks: as clan markers relied on for survival, 200n54; as a complex relational process in the web of life, 166–167; with heavy obligations and responsibilities, 200n55; of mutual dependency, 182; as reciprocal-communalist system, 87–92; tie various Anishinaabe communities together, 191n62; by which nationhood is maintained, 22
Anishinaabemowin (language), 12–13, 90–91, 131–132, 187n2, 189n36
Anishinaabe nationalism, 24, 174–179. *See also* The Invasion
Anishinaabe religious/social practice, 134, 146
Anishinaabe songs, 106, 108–109. *See also* nagamonan (songs)
Anishinabe Adisokan (Beaulieu), 129
Anishinabe Nagamon (Vizenor, 1970), 132, 133, 134
antiestablishment sensibility, 63
apolitical commiseration, 74
Appleton Crescent (weekly), 28
approach, instrumental, 20
appropriation: of Anishinaabe narrative material by Longfellow, 181–182; as of both myths and very immediate things, 101; as cultural insensitivity, 122; as a form of colonizing, 205–206n93; of lands, 140; process The Invasion seeks to critique and avoid, 79; as reappropriation by Liz Howard in "Of Hereafter Song," 182; and simultaneous erasure of indigenous

culture, 9; as spending measures, 162; used by Anishinaabeg as strategy of resistance, 183
Aristotle, 167
Armstrong, Louis Olivier, 2, 6
"artist," 109–110
"The Aspen's Song" (Winters), 115
assaults on Natives by U.S., 143–145, 146–147, 156–157, 177–178
assimilation programs, 43–44, 90–91, 102, 118–119, 174. *See also* boarding schools
assumptions: about Hemingway's familiarity with Anishinaabe culture, 71, 72; about writing's role in Native life, 7, 13; of capitalism about fungibility of land and life, 143; of collective responsibility that drives the welfare state, 146; of critical approaches that limit understanding of texts, 17, 18; of Euro-American cultural and colonialist politics, 19, 24, 79, 86, 102–103; of exclusive national sovereignty as goal of Native nationalism, 175, 191n61; governing self-determination policies, 140, 147, 170; of internationalism guiding the book, 185; that cultural development moves from barbarism to civilization, 106; that overlook the coercive legacy of colonial violence, 128–129; of white supremacy and economic privilege, 150, 154
Astrov, Margot, 117
Ata, Te (Chickasaw actress), 114
Auginaush, Joe, 52
Austin, Mary, 98, 108–109
authenticity, cultural. *See* cultural authenticity
authenticity assessment, 136
authority, ethnographic text, 136–137f

authority, institutional, 141
authority, settler-colonial, 18
autonomy, 169

Baagone-giizhig (Hole-in-the-Day), 34
Baawitig (Anishinaabeg home), xviii, 1–2
backwardness, 38–40, 43–44
Bakhtin, Mikhail, 9, 19, 53–54
bands, Anishinaabe: and affidavits from six original at the Sault, 96–98; claims of exclusive usufructory rights, 85; as deeply heterogeneous community, 44, 47; dissolved with Treaty of 1855 and Ojibway nation ceased, 91, 201n64; a few joined British in War of 1812, xix; gather for celebrations and religious observances in summer, xviii; from Grand Portage to Mille Lacs, 34–35; would not leave their established territories for White Earth, 42, 62. *See also* Spry, Adam
barbarian, 110
Battle of Batoche, 37
Battle of the Plains of Abraham (1759), 82–84
Bauerkemper, Joseph, 21
Bay Mills Indian Community (1936), 97
Beaulieu, Augustus (Gus), 28, 35, 104
Beaulieu, Clement, Jr. (reverend), 28, 29–30, 34, 104
Beaulieu, Theodore (1850–1923): "the Demosthenes of White Earth," 63; efforts to remake self-governing homeland unsuccessful, 62–63; evinced ritualized sense of aadizookaanag, 193n30; family history, 28–29; "our paint is . . . writing fluid," 27; printed

Beaulieu, Theodore *(continued)*
    translations in the Progress, 23–24, 193n35; rooting stories in landscape of home-focused land claim, 194n62; translations represent time non-novelistically, 194n61; "Wah-Boose" (pseudonym), 39–40; work as self-conscious emulation of vision of nationhood, 194n57. *See also* Vizenor, Gerald
Beaulieu's radical reshaping of oral tradition: as anticolonial resistance, 55–61, 64; and comparison of translations to oral tradition, 48–54; and interiority of characters, 49; as "new tribal hermeneutics," 63–64; as replicable strategy for interpretation of oral material in writing, 129–130, 134; and vision of Anishinaabeg future, 24, 25, 39–44, 72
Bellin, Joshua, 8, 200n58
Bevis, William, 123
Bieder, Robert, 200n55
"Big Two-Hearted River" (Hemingway), 71
The Bingo Palace (Erdrich), 140, 141, 210n54
Blackbird, Andrew (1817–1908), xix, 72
Blaeser, Kimberly, 131, 135
"The Blue Duck" (Sarett), 113–114
boarding schools, 11, 109, 139, 143, 210n55. *See also* assimilation programs
Bodeen, Paul, 27
Bolton, Rich and Prudence, 68–69
border issues. *See* boundaries
Boston Transcript, 113
boundaries: challenging of as basis of indigenous sovereignty, 18, 178–179; between First Nations and Anglo-Canadians, 37; methodology of reading across contested, 4, 15–16; Ogimaag fixed these between hunting territories and settled disputes, 84–86; permeability of Anishinaabe and Euro-American, 87–89; reading across settler-states and indigenous nations, xx, 18; reduction of to insider and outsider dichotomies, 184; between "savage" Indian and "civilized" American, 16; between tribal nations and nation-states, 22
The Box of God (Sarett, 1922), 112, 115
Boyden, Joseph, 190n56
Brando, Marlon, 65
Bruyneel, Kevin, 15–16, 176, 205n86
"To the Buffalo" (Densmore), 111
"Buffalo Dance" (Henderson), 110
Bungi, xviii
bureaucracy, 139–140, 143, 210n55
Bureau of American Ethnology (BAE), 103, 107, 108
Bureau of Indian Affairs (BIA): cutting tribal services, 156–157; and dramatic policy reversal of 1936, 96–98; Erdrich's parents employed by, 141; raid by, 27–28, 31–32; takeover of, 143; tricksterlike failures of, 47
Bursum Bill opponents, 98
Burt Lake Burnout, 197n25, 201n64

Cadotte, Michel, 104
Canadian land claims, 36–38
Canadian Pacific Railway (CPR), 2, 3, 6
canon-formation, 20
capitalism, global: "acculturated" via free market, 127; as commodification, 169; cultural pressures of, 137f; as means of Native dispossession, 150, 177; vs. mino bimaadiziwin, 182;

natural world as resources to be exploited, 178; vs. redistributive obligations, 89–92; self-sufficiency as heroic virtue in, 146; unchecked expansion of, 185. *See also* labor
Carcieri v. Salazar, 136
Castro, Michael, 203n42
categorization refusal, 15
Cathay (Pound, 1913), 202n28
Cato Institute, 156–157
Ceremony (Silko, 1977), 121, 144, 210n54
chapbooks, 111, 120
Chautauqua circuit, 112–114
Cherokee Phoenix (newspaper), 28
Cheyfitz, Eric, 23
"Chief Petoskey" (Petosegay), 72–73
Child, Brenda, 87
child welfare officers, 169
Chippewa Music, 105, 107, 108, 119, 128
Chippewa tribe (Minnesota), xviii, 106, 109–110, 175, 190–191n60
Christianity, 127
Chrystos, 122
civilization, Euro-American, 40–42
clan (doodem), 88–89
Clapp amendment, 62–63
Claybaugh, Amanda, 142, 144
Cleland, Charles, 196n3
Clements, William, 123
climate change, 178
coalitions, 22
Coburn, Tom (senator), 162
cohabitation, 39
Collier, John (BIA chief), 96, 98, 117
colonial archive, authority of, 129
colonial control, 33
"colonial dynamic," 23
colonial history, 82–83f, 128
colonization, 42–44, 74
comedy vs. tragedy, 175–176
commiseration, apolitical, 74

communal identity, 141
communal life, 107
community vs. autonomy, 145
complexity vs. primitivity, 133
contesting boundaries, 15–16
continuity, 99
contraction policies, 155–157
Cook-Lynn, Elizabeth, 175, 211n62
Cooper, James Fenimore, 16, 80, 199n44
Copway, George (Gaagigegaabaw, 1818–1869), xix, 3, 9
cosmopolitanism vs. separatism, 175–179
Coulthard, Glen, 185
couvade, 70–71
Cox, James, 75
Crane, Gregg, 81
creative misunderstandings, 87–89
critical approaches: assumptions of, 17, 18; to contemporary politics, 64; to Erdrich's fiction, 174–179; nationalist vs. settler-colonialist, 17–18; Native to non-Native, 122–123; to settler-colonial ideology, 183; to status quo, 74; of U.S. Indian policy, 32–33
Cronyn, George, 108, 109, 115
cultural accommodation, 87–89
cultural authenticity: as adjudicated by non-Native courts, 136–137f; vs. alternate reasons for shaping cultural representations, 190n55; burden of asserting vs. "acculturated" Indian, 127–128; as double bind of settler-colonial dominance, 91; literature's ambivalent role in shaping perceptions of, 185; of novel as mode of address for the Anishinaabeg, 61; as to original meaning in poetry, 102–103, 124–125; and resistance to the rhetoric of, 164–166, 182; same misguided

cultural authenticity (*continued*)
  sense by which U.S. ended
  tribal nations, 24; undermining
  translation as, 129–130; use
  of written Anishinaabemowin
  to impart sense of, 6; whether
  traditional Anishinaabe culture
  is "truer," 14, 20, 49, 51. See also
  tribal hermeneutics
cultural change, 136–138
cultural commodification, 5
cultural compromise, 4–5
cultural development, 40–42. See also
  Anishinaabe songs
cultural difference, 127–128
cultural expression, 130–131
cultural heritage, 43–44
cultural identity, 4, 5, 14, 182–183
cultural loss, 120–121, 138
cultural politics, xiv, 2, 4, 5
cultural revitalization, 118–119
cultural separatism. See separatism
culture, xix, 1, 4–5, 20, 102–103, 190n55
cutover land, 65–67

Dakota Uprising (1862), 34, 103
Dawes General Allotment Act (1886), 23, 42–44, 117
Day-Dodge (centenarian), 46
Death Comes for the Archbishop (Cather), 78
"Death in the Afternoon" (Hemingway), 71
deforestation, 139–140
Delgamuukw v. British Columbia (1997), 136
Deloria, Philip, 21
Deloria, Vine, 116, 143, 184, 203n50, 207n12
Demon of the Continent (Bellin), 16–17
Densmore, Frances (1867–1957):
  background of, 102–107;
  confirms no tradition of ritual
  suicide, 70–71; Japanese style
  of translations, 131–133; notes
  on pictograph, 126; poetic
  translations by, 110–112, 115,
  119–125; published translations of
  Anishinaabe nagamonan, 24–25;
  role of ethnographic texts in
  politics of recognition, 128
depression. See economic depression
deracination, 145
Desbarats (Ontario), 2, 3, 5, 95
The Dial (Untermeyer), 109
"dialogic" processes, 19–20
dibaajimowinan (didactic stories), 25, 49, 192–193n29
dibaajimowin narratives (informative), 44, 46
dibaajimowin of the apichi (robin), 171–172
difference, 87–89
diplomacy, xix
dispossession, indigenous: brutal
  episode of, 197n25; by the colonial
  settler-state, 137f; down to present
  in continuity with past, 78; of
  intellectual resources as well as
  land, 90–91; of Odawa villages in
  Michigan, 73; our participation
  in and rationalization of, 74–75;
  role Euro-American writing played
  in project of, 67–68; as settler-
  colonial project, 128; and tribal
  right to undo damage of, 96–97;
  for which settlers in The Invasion
  acknowledge complicity, 79; of
  White Earth as Anishinaabe
  homeland, 62–63
"domestic dependent sovereignty," 174
domestic frontier romances, 81, 82
doodem (clan), 88–89, 167, 200n54
Dorris, Michael, 211n62
dreams, 134

dubitative mood, 52–53
Dumont, Gabriel, 36–38

ecological contamination, 25
economic depression, 119
Edwards, Chris, 156–157
Eliot, T.S., xx, 109–110, 112
Elliot, Michael, 175
emotional tourism, 74
English, Mary Warren (sister of WWW), 4, 104
English language, 127
"entitlement" programs, 142
epic vs. novel, 49, 51, 53–56
epistemology, indigenous, 116–117
equality vs. inferiority/superiority, 88, 90–92, 106, 151, 177–178
Erdrich, Angela (IHS physician), 163
Erdrich, Louise (b. 1954): award-winning Love Medicine (1983), 121; background of, 141; and Cook-Lynn's apparent animus against, 211n62; garnered widespread critical praise, xx; on "Ojibwe from the verb Ozhibii'ige, which is 'to write'", xvii; renders Native life intelligible to wide audience, 190n56; Tracks (1988), work of Anishinaabe nationalism, 98; widely cited passage from Tracks (1988), 139; writes paradigmatic fiction of the self-determination era, 25
Erdrich, Louise, fiction of: and indigenous nationalism in, 174–179; political work defends U.S. trust from neoliberalism, 157; on principles by which state operates, 139–145, 146–147
Erdrich, Rita and Ralph, 141
ethnographic standard, 127–128, 136–138
ethnography, biases of, 90–91
ethnomusicology, 107

"ethnopoetics," 121
eudaemonia, 167, 168
Euro-American colonization, 78–82
Euro-American dominance, 16
Euro-American land grabs, 98
European settlers, xviii
"At evening" (Winters), 115
exploitation, 89–92, 150, 157, 178, 185
expropriation, 90

factionalism, inter- and intraband, 47
federal Indian policies: from 1886 to present day, 23; and agents responsible for dispossession, 90; as antitribal, 117–119; and connection with the aadizookaanag, 47–48; with IRA passage, agent oversight ended, 96; and new era of nation-states, 144–145, 174–179; and recognitive logic remnants, 136; Termination Era as shift in philosophical basis of, 127; as threatening treaty-mandated subsidies, 156–157
federal termination policy. See termination policies (1950s)
feeling, structures of, 146, 150
Feinstein, Dianne, 136
field composition, 121–122
Fillmore, John, 103
first amendment court case (1886), 31–32
Fletcher, Alice, 103
forestland, government-managed, 67
forfeitures, 73
formal techniques, avant-garde, 121–122
Four Souls (Erdrich), 141
fraud, acts of, 73–74, 95, 96, 122
freedom of speech court case, 31–32
free market capitalism. See capitalism, global
Friends of the Indian movement, 103

frontier: as imperial core expanding out into unknown, 81; The Invasion as dark satire of domestic romances, 82; romance of violent conflicts with Natives birthed American identity," 81; transformation of wilderness into familiar homeland, 84–86; well-established theme of American life, made "new" by Hemingway, 69
fungibility, 143
fur trade economy, 89
fur trade era (1750–1819), 86–92

Ga'gandac', 102, 120
Gage'bīnes, 106, 107
Garden River (Canada community), 2, 3, 5, 77
Gellner, Ernest, 58–59
genres, 130, 183–184
geography, 59–60
gii'igoshimowin (ceremonial fast), 171
Gitche Gumee, 3
The Golden Bough (Frazer, 1890), 71
Gourneau, Patrick, 141
Government Accountability Office (GAO), 159–160
Grand Traverse Band of Chippewa and Ottawa Indians (1980), 97
Great Lakes region, xix, 2, 3
Great Spirit, 164, 168
Green, Simon, 68–69

haiku, 120–121
half-breeds, 36
Hall, Stuart, 179
Hallowell, Alfred Irving, 1, 70–71
"Harbor Springs" (Michigan resort), 73
Harvard Peabody Museum. *See* Peabody Museum (Harvard)
Haseltine, Patricia, 133

Hawthorne, Nathaniel, 80
"Healing Song," 108
Hemingway, Ernest (1899–1961): background of, 67–68; Burt Lake Burnout, 197n25, 201n64; family home on dispossessed land, 197n26; Nick Adams fiction and Lewis' The Invasion compared, 24; tragic story about Anishinaabe logging camp by, xx, 4; troubling fiction of, 98. *See also* "Indian Camp"
Henderson, Alice Corbin, 110, 115, 121, 202n28
"Of Hereafter Song" (Howard), 25, 181
"heritage," 109–110
hermeneutics. *See* tribal hermeneutics
Hiawatha, or Nanabozho (Kabaosa stage play): continuity between Howard's poetry and translational work in, 212n1; critical responses to, 4–5; differences among four scripts, 11; hyphenated Anishinaabemowin is for nonspeakers, 189n36; intertextuality of, 4; performance of, 1–3, 5; production at Desbarats, 95; production at White Earth between 1903 and 1917, 104; reimagination of, 5; reinterpretation by, 10–15; script held in libraries across U.S. and Canada, 188n8; translation is author's own, 189n35; young Hemingway attending, 69
historians, 97. *See also* Warren, William Whipple
historical grounding, 74, 77
historical narratives, 97
history, creative reinterpretation of, 97
History of English Literature (Taine), 40–42, 49–50

History of the Ojibway People (Warren), xvii, 98, 187n3
Hobomok (Child), 81
Hobson, Geary, 122
Hole-in-the-Day (Baagone-giizhig), 34
Hope Leslie (Sedgwick), 81
hospitals, 210n54
House concurrent resolution 108 (HR-108), 118
House Made of Dawn (Momaday, 1968), 121, 144
Howard, Liz (Anishinaabe poet), 181, 185, 212n1
Howard, Liz ("Of Hereafter Song"), 25
Howe, LeAnne, 190n56
HR-108 (House concurrent resolution 108), 118
humor, 32–33
Hynes, Dell, 121

"iceberg" theory of fiction (Hemingway), 71
idealized historical "narratives," 80–81
identification, psychological, 113
identity, 25
identity, American, 81
identity, Anishinaabe, 33, 84–87, 130–131, 163–164
identity, political, 15
imagination, tribal, xx
Imagists, 108–109, 111, 117, 130
imperialism, U.S., 33
inaabandjigan nagamowin ("dream singing"), 101–102
"Indian Camp" (Hemingway, 1924), 69–75. See also Hemingway, Ernest
Indian Child Welfare Act (1978), 158, 210n55
Indian Child Welfare officers, 169, 210n55
Indian Country, 117, 142–145, 155–157, 174–179

Indian dance, 112, 113–114
Indian Health Care Improvement Act (IHCIA), 162
Indian Health Service (IHS), 141, 158–163, 207–208n31, 208n34
Indian Killer (Alexie, 1996), 160
"Indian minstrelsy," 4–5
Indianness: embraced by Euro-Americans as mythic patrimony, 92; Euro-Americans' expectations of, 77; literary representations of, 5, 8, 9–10, 16–17; and "mysticism," 116–117; primitive imagery of, 16–17; rejection of imposed discourses of, 63; reworking ethnographic versions as resistance to, 129; romanticized descriptions of in Vizenor, 124; as "too much" interpretation, 115. See also savagery, Indian; Vizenor, Gerald
Indian past vs. American present, 54
Indian Reorganization Act (IRA, 1934), 23, 96, 97, 117
Indian reservations vs. illegal white settlements, 33
Indians, literary theme of, 69
The Indians in the Woods (Lewis, 1922), 76
Indian sovereignty vs. autonomy, 156–157
Indian statue proposal, 95
Indian Trade and Intercourse Act, 31
Indian Wars, 39
indigeneity, 5
indigenization, 15, 19–20, 183
indigenous agency, 5, 182. See also political agency
indigenous core enclosed, 81
indigenous cultural difference, 185
indigenous cultural practices, 127–128
indigenous dispossession. See dispossession, indigenous

indigenous in settler nations, 97
indigenous land claims, 136
indigenous literary nationalism, 183
indigenous nationalism, 22–23, 25, 99, 146–147, 182
indigenous nationhood, 18
indigenous peoples, 16, 185
indigenous poetry, 108–110, 115
indigenous political/legal rights, 127–128, 136–138
indigenous religion. *See* tribal religions
indigenous resistance, xx, 183, 184
indigenous sovereignty. *See* sovereignty, indigenous
"indigenous transnationalism," 22
indigenous-U.S. relationship, 33
individualism, 141, 163–164, 166, 167, 169, 209n48
industrialism, 185
industrial pollution, 178
inferiority, 33
inferiority/superiority vs. equality, 88, 90–92
"Initiation Song" (Vizenor, 1993), 134, 137f
injunctions, seasonal or ritual, 46
integrationist multiculturalism, 175
intellects, racial comparison of, 39–40
interconnectedness of natural world, 185
interdependency, 60, 166–168, 170, 173, 178–179
intermarriages, 87–89
internationalism, indigenous, 25, 185
interpretation, 102–103. *See also* tribal hermeneutics
interracial unions, 87–89
interventions (written reworkings), 110–111. *See also* tribal hermeneutics
The Invasion (Lewis, 1932): background history of, 75–82; critiques the novel's misrepresentation of Indianness, 79; as formally unsettled work, 82; juxtaposes Song of Hiawatha with Treaty of 1855 in furthering dispossession, 91–92; little-known historical novel compared with Hemingway fiction, 24; marriages in, 87–92; as nationalist literature, 98–99; publication history of, 98; recognition of coherent Anishinaabe historical perspective by, 97; rejection of settler-colonial ideology in, 78–82; revisions frontier as sovereign Anishinaabe nation, 84–87; scene as nucleus around which novel formed, 201n59; twists genre to imagine Anishinaabe women in domestic spaces, 81; unsettling pall cast over moment of colonial triumph, 82–83f. *See also* Johnstone, William Meddaugh

Jameson, Anna, 199n53
Japanese poetry, 117
Jarmusch, Jim, 101
Jeanotte, Alexandre, 36
Johnston, Basil, 70–71
Johnston, George, 78
Johnston, Jane. *See* Schoolcraft, Jane Johnston
Johnston, John (father of Jane and George), 77, 86–87
Johnstone, Howard (brother of Molly), 76, 77, 78
Johnstone, John Macdougall (father of Molly and Howard), 78
Johnstone, Molly (Anna Maria), 75–76, 77
Johnstone, William Meddaugh (brother of Molly), 78, 95–96, 97, 98. *See also* The Invasion
Johnstone family (kept oral tradition), 77

Johnstone family participation, 98
Johnston family, 8–9
Jones, Stephen Graham, 190n56
juxtaposition, 137f–138

Kabaosa, George, 2, 6–7, 55
Kabotie, Fred, 117
Kállay, Katalin, 71, 74
Keel, Jefferson, 162
Ki'tcimak'wa (Midewewin), 124–125
Kit Tatro (character), 165–166
Kohl, Johann, 70–71
Konkle, Maureen, 200n58
Krueger, William Kent, xx
Krupat, Arnold, 175, 204n64
Kugel, Rebecca, 21

labor: as diminishing market, 196n3; exile from, 55; as exploitation, 89, 150, 157, 178, 185; manual only available, 73; migrant, 66; recounting experiences of, 93; as traditional to Anishinaabe women, 165. *See also* capitalism, global
La Farge, Oliver, 98
Lakota tribe (South Dakota), 33–34
land, reservation, 73
land, traditional conceptions of, 59–60
land allotment. *See* allotment policy
land bases, reestablishment of, 97
land cessions, 143
land claims, 36–38, 144
"the land disease," 178
land dispossession. *See* dispossession, indigenous
land use, 84–86
land wars, 39
language play, 63
languages, Native, 73–74
The Last of the Mohicans (Cooper), 16, 81
law, national, 88
Lawrence, Jane, 208n34

legal censure, 135
legal rights of Indian nations, 96–97
legal status, 73–74
le Jeune, Father Superior Paul, xviii, 187n4
Lenoir, Louis, 36
Levinson Prize (poetry), 112
Lewis, Edwin (father of Janet), 76
Lewis, Janet (1899–1998): background of, 67–68, 76–77; claims The Invasion neither novel nor history but family "narrative," 80; and historical narratives on which The Invasion is based, 24; resources, activism of, 98, 117; unsettling implications of work by, 75; William Johnstone's letters on disappointing BIA meeting, 96
Lewis Institute (Chicago), 76
Library of Congress recordings, 107
literary forms, 15
literary genres, 130, 183–184
literary modernism, 67
literary nationalism, Native American, 98–99
literary or cultural tradition, 185
literature, 4, 15–16, 19, 184
literature, American, xx, 1, 175
literature, Anishinaabe, 13, 15–16
literature, English, 40–42
literature, Euro-American, 15–16, 75, 184–185
literature, Native: adaptation of the novel by, 61–62; and comparative work with settler literature, 184; "cultural separatism" of, 17–18; non-Indian audience for, 190n56; and state institutions, relationship to, 141–142, 144, 146–147; in "total translation," 121
Littlefeather, Sacheen, 65
Little Traverse Bay Band of Odawa (1994), 72, 97
Lomax, John and Alan, 107

Longfellow, Henry Wadsworth, 3
"Long time ago good. Now heap shit," 74
loss. *See* cultural loss
Love Medicine (Erdrich, 1983), 121, 140, 141
love of living for its own sake, 185
Luhan, Mabel Dodge, 98
Lyons, Scott Richard, 17, 22–23, 58–59, 167, 174, 184
lyrics, 101–102, 106, 111, 115

Mabo v. Queensland (1992), 136
"magical realism," 25, 141–142
The Magpie's Shadow (Winters, 1922), 115–116
Mallarmé, 117
Ma-mongazid (Ojibway chieftain), 82
"manabozho song" (Vizenor, 1970), 205n90
manidoog (legendary spirits): agentive existence whose aid can be called on, 167; considered to still be present and alive on the earth, 53; e.g., the cruel north-wind manidoo communicates not as in Longfellow's poem, 182; literally summoning or drawing their attention via rules, 46–47; medicine bags as material symbol of dependency on, 168; as nonhuman persons related to via a complex process, 166; other-than-human spirits that populate the Anishinaabe world, 44; who connect via ties of affiliation and affection, 59–60; with whom one solicits aid in achieving a good life, 171. *See also* nagamonan (songs)
manifest destiny, 33
Manitoba territory, 2, 37
Manitoulin (Anishinaabeg community), 77

man with hat, xvii
Many, Many Moons (Sarett, 1920), 112, 114
"Maple Sugar Song," 109–110
Matchi Manitou series, 145, 176
"May" (Winters), 115
McKenney, Thomas, 199n53
McNally, Michael, 5, 166
McNiel, Elizabeth, 47–48, 49
meaning, 19, 134, 135–136
medicine bags, 168
Melville, Herman, 75
methodology, 15–16
Métis of Canada, 36–38
Métis rebellion, 2, 36–38
metonymy, 91, 94
Meyer, Stephenie, 75
Meyers, Jeffrey, 69–71, 74
Meyers, Melissa, 192n17
Michigan Anishinaabeg, 65–66
Mide initiation song, 137f
"Mide Initiation Song" (Summer in the Spring, 1965), 124–125
Mide pictograph in "No. 64 'Initiation Song,'" 126f–128
Mide song practitioners, 128
Mide songs, 122
Midewewin healing society, 124–125
Midewewin songs, 106
Midewiwin healing power, 134, 135
Midwest, xix
"miigwech" (thank you), xiii, xiv, xv
Minnesota Anishinaabeg, 42–44
Minnesota Historical Society, 63
mino bimaadizi, 167–168
mino bimaadiziwin (Anishinaabe ideal): being open to spiritual and material aid is foundational, 170; as a coherent modus vivendi that structures social and cultural life, 209–210n51; as commensurate with state welfare institutions, 146; e.g., climate change is a threat to this principle, 178–179; as a

philosophical ideal, the good way of life, 25; shares with welfare state a sense of collective responsibility, 177; translated as "he or she lives well" or, better, "well-being," 166–168
missionary surveillance, 135
mixed-bloods, 31–32, 104. See also half-breeds
modern Anishinaabeg homeland, 43–44
modernism, literary, 4, 67
modernity: alienation by, 210n54; around which the U.S. state created an irresolvable paradox, 127–128; and Beaulieu's novelistic translations, 59; as closure of traditional life, 42–44; as "condition" of choice, 22; as cultural value of Anishinaabe nation, xix; and Dawes General Allotment Act, 34–35; Euro-American vs. "Indian primitivity," 16; "Indian consciousness" untouched by corrupting influences of, 9–10; rejecting trappings of, 164; and self-governing nation-state, 33; "to symbolically enter the culture of" via Hiawatha, or Nanabozho, 4–5; as transnational culture Anishinaabeg engaged in, 131, 135–136; whose forces form coalitions across boundaries of nations, 22. See also time, popular conception of
Momaday, N. Scott, 101, 117, 121
"monological narratives" of Indianness, 15–16, 18–19
Monroe, Harriet, 112
Montcalm (French general), 82–83f
Mort du Montcalm (Moret/Desfontaines), 83f
Mukwasibing (Bear Creek) community, 72–73

multicultural settler-states, 185
music, indigenous. See nagamonan (songs); tribal music
"muskrat," 1
Muting White Noise (Cox), 16–17

nagamonan (songs): and assumption as "primitive" form of poetry, 102; and haiku similarity with, 119–120, 131–134; impact of Anishinaabemowin syntax on, 184; Japanese haiku compared with, 131–134; as poetic potential, 111; reinterpretations of that rely on misguided sense of cultural authenticity, 24–25; spiritual vs. aesthetic view of, 115–116; traditional stories translated as critiques of contemporary politics, 64; translations of oral material into poetry that raise cultural questions, 101–107. See also Densmore, Frances
nagamon lyrics (The Sopranos), 120
Nanabozho mythos, 4. See also Hiawatha, or Nanabozho (Kabaosa stage play)
Nanapush (character), 139–140, 145, 176
narrative, Anishinaabe. See aadizookaan narratives; dibaajimowin narratives
narratives: alternative, in face of colonization, 17; cultural loss, 120–121, 138; dominant, 19; "erotic patronage," 147–151; historical, 36; of Indian disappearance, 13; questioning conventions of, 15; rationalization via, 92–93; romanticized, 80; solidity and power of via writing, 86–87; well-worn vs. adaptive, 182–183; writing as adaptive tool, 13

National Congress of the American Indian, 119, 155, 162
National Indian Youth Council, 119
nationalism, 17–20, 57–59, 98–99
nationhood, Anishinaabe: continuity of, 99; decentering of, 21–22; historical sovereignty of as realized in The Invasion, 78–79, 84–87; as multiplicity vs. cultural separatism, 15; rights to exist as independent, 96–97; as transhistorically stable concept, 17. *See also* transnationalism
"Native American Consciousness," 203n42
Native American Renaissance, 120–121
Native continuity, 99
Native critiques of settler-colonialism, 184
Native diversity, 184
Native literary criticism, 185
Native nationhood, 58–59, 61–62, 175–179
Native poetic tradition, 120–121
Natives, 31–32, 33, 74–75
natural world, 59–60, 119–120
Nawadaha (H. R. Schoolcraft), 9
Neebish Island, 75–76
negative behavior (sin), 168
Nelson, Judge R. R., 31–32
Nelson, Rep. Knute, 34, 62
Nelson Act, 34–35, 42–44, 62–63
neoliberalism, 142, 146–147, 156–157, 177
networks of affiliation, 191n62
New Ulm Review (1914), 63
Nick of the Woods (Bird), 81
Nixon, Richard (president), 144–145
"No. 64 'Initiation Song,'" Chippewa Music, 105, 124–125
Nokomis, 76
nonlinguistic elements, 121–122
Norman Conquest (1066), 40–42

North-West Territory, xix, 36–38
North Woods, 75–76
novel, Indian adaptation of, 61–62
novel vs. epic, 49, 51, 53–56

Obabaamwewe-giizhigokwe (Jane Johnston Schoolcraft), xix, 8–9
occupation, 143–144
O'Connor, Cork (fictional Chippewa detective), xx
Odawa, 66, 72–73, 96–97
ogimaa, 171
"ogimaa" (chief), xvii, 187n1, 187n2
"The Ojibwas, Their Customs and Traditions" (1887), 44, 45f, 46
Ojibwe/Ojibway (language), 1, 4, 13, 91, 125
Oka crisis (Canada), 143
"older woman" narratives, 147–149
Olson, Charles, 204n65
O-Non-E-Gwud, 75–76, 95
oral narratives, 193n35
oral performance, 121
oral tradition, 123, 135
original meaning, 102–103
Osborn, Chase, 78, 200n58
"oshkianishinaabeg" (new people), 138
Otchiptway, xviii
Other Destinies (Owen), 17
Our Fire Survives the Storm (Justice), 17
In Our Time (Hemingway, 1925), 69. *See also* "Indian Camp"
Our War Paint is Writers' Ink (Spry), xx, 4, 23–25
Outchibouec, xviii
Owens, Louis, 61
Ozah-guscoday-wayquay (mother of Jane and George Johnston), 77, 87–89
"ozhibii'ige," xvii

The Painted Drum (Erdrich, 2005), 146, 157–163, 209n48, 210n54

pan-tribal identities, 119
Parker, Robert Dale, 200n58, 205–206n93
paternalism, U.S., 145, 146
The Path on the Rainbow (Cronyn), 108–109, 112, 115, 117
pays d'en haut, 84–85, 87–88
Peabody Museum (Harvard), 103
Pearce, Roy Harvey, 10, 16
performances, artistic vs. ritual, 113, 127–128
personal responsibility, 163–164
Perspectives USA, 117
Petosegay ("Chief Petoskey"), 72–73
phonograph, wax cylinder, 104
Piatote, Beth, 150
pictograph, Mide, 137f–138. See also Mide pictograph in "No. 64 'Initiation Song'"
"Pictures from Brueghel" (1962), 117
picture-writing canto, 7–8, 10, 13
Pigs in Heaven (Kingsolver, 1993), 210n55
Pinkerton-Uri, Constance Redbird, 159, 208n34
Pitonoquod (The Invasion character), 93–94
pity, 106, 167, 169, 171
The Plague of Doves (Erdrich, 2008): Anishinaabe cultural values challenge white privilege, 153–154; Coutts' upward mobility in class and identity, 147–151; fiction balances ambiguity of state institutions, 154–155; imagines Anishinaabeg relationship to state, 146; and Judge Coutts's judicial activism, 141; parallels between Coutts and Louis Riel, 151–152; works to rehabilitate reservation bureaucracies, 25
Pocahontas (Disney), 16
Poems from Sioux and Chippewa Songs (Densmore), 111

poetics. See Anishinaabe songs
poetry. See Japanese poetry
Poetry (Henderson), 110
Poetry (Monroe), 112
policies. See federal Indian policies
political agency, 140–141
political authenticity. See authenticity, cultural
political bodies, 96, 99
political control, Native, 72–73
political elite (defined), 2
political power, indigenous, 41–42, 84–86
political resurgence, 50
political rights. See indigenous political/legal rights
political status, tribal, 96–97, 136–138
political time, secular, 58
politics, 17–18, 19, 51, 117, 185
polities, 21–22
post-treaty-making era, 23
Pound, Ezra, 196n1, 202n28
Povinelli, Elizabeth, 127–128, 185
power: Anishinaabe conception of, 171–172; drawn from sound of the vocables, 135; Euro-American literature's complicity in structures of, 17; as indigenous political, not martial, 84–86; never located in one identity alone, 146; often given animate nouns, 47; shifting differentials but reciprocal, 21; Wenabozho's, as trees bestow their gifts onto him, 57–60
Power (Hogan), 210n54
precontact indigenous culture, 74
prejudices, Euro-American, 33
"prejudicial sentimentality," 38–40
present as corruption of past, 74
primitive poetry, 109–110
primitivity vs. complexity, 116–117, 133
private property, 96. See also allotment policy

"The Problem of Speaking for Others" (Alcoff), 65
productivity, extractive, 178
profit motive, 89–92
Progress (1886–1889 newspaper), 23–24, 28, 32–33, 45f, 62–64
prohibition of alcohol, 164
propaganda wars, 39
property, rules governing, 84–86
Public Law 280, 118
Pueblo (of New Mexico), 98, 114–115
Pulitano, Elvira, 61

race conflicts vs. law, 88
"race distinction" (Canadians), 38
racism, Euro-American: as having to suffer anti-Indian racism, 73–74; illustrated in early twentieth century Michigan, 77; nationalism protects from devastating effects of, 185; rise of Judge Coutts from deracinated lay-about, 146–147; via conviction of cultural superiority, 177–178; via desire for Native land and resources, 150; which fails to compare educated rather than average Indians, 38–40; which hardens mistrust and fear into unconscious habit, 149
raid on Progress, 27–28, 31–32
rapids (at Baawitig), xviii, 1–2
Rasmussen, Birgit, 9
rationality, 85, 106, 111, 116–117, 167
rationalizing, 74, 79, 86, 88, 92–93, 174
reading, xx, 74, 75, 113–114
realism, 74
reciprocal-communalist system, 89, 174
recognition, 127–128, 205n86
redistributive vs. capitalist obligations, 89–92
Red River settlement (Manitoba), 37–38
reification, 17, 18, 102–103, 129

reinterpretation. *See* translation, theory of
relationships: between Anishinaabeg and Euro-Americans, 86–87; between Anishinaabeg and U.S., 146–147, 150, 182; in The Invasion, 87–92; between Native and non-Native readerships, 195n64; between Native and white, 87–92; between original and reexpressed forms arbitrary, 130–131; as web of relations, 179. *See also* mino bimaadiziwin
renewal, 138
research, archival, 24
reservation communities, 117–119
reservation land, 43–44. *See also* White Earth Reservation (Minnesota)
reservations, 143
reservations, break up of, 34
reservations, transformation of, 145
resistance, indigenous, 73
resistance to state vs. involvement of state, 174–179
responsibility, 169, 170, 173
responsibility, collective, 177
reversal of perspective, 94
reversal of policies, 97
revision of historical narratives, 97
Rexroth, Kenneth, 117
rhetoric, xix
Riding the Earth Boy 40 (Welch, 1971), 121
Riel, Louis (Métis leader), 2, 36–38, 151–152
Rifkin, Mark, 75, 93
right to free expression case, 31–32
ritual injunctions, 46
ritualized violence, 69
Robbins, Bruce, 146, 147, 149, 150, 173
Robin Hood encodes Anglo-Saxon politics, 49–50
robin story, 211n57

Rose, Wendy, 122
Rothenberg, Jerome, 24–25, 102, 121–123, 124–129, 135, 204n65
The Round House (Erdrich), 140
rules. *See* injunctions, seasonal or ritual
Ruppert, James, 195n64

Sandburg, Carl, 108
Sarett, Lew: as cultural insider, 112; Native consciousness in need of translation, 116; politics of, 114–115; quasi-shamanistic quality of, 113, 135; Rothenberg's "Red English" exoticism compared to, 125; "translation" in modernist tradition, 121
Saulteaux, xviii
Sault Ste. Marie (Baawitig/Ontario), xviii, 2
Sault Ste. Marie (Michigan), 75–76, 77, 78, 95–98
Sault Ste. Marie Tribe of Chippewa Indians (1972), 97
Sauteurs, xviii
savagery, Indian: as cultural prejudice, 38–40, 43–44; eliminating this drove the missionization of federal policy, 109–110; predictable narratives are the sine qua non of Euro-American literature, 75; vs. rationalism, 116–117; white ancestors as, 40; wild tales from older settlers that Densmore likely grew up with, 103
Say-coss-e-gay (centenarian), 46
Schoolcraft, Henry Rowe, 8–9, 78, 86–87, 108
Schoolcraft, Jane Johnston (1800–42), xix, xx, 3, 78, 89–92, 172
Scott, David, 22
Scott, Frank (Congressman), 96
seasonal injunctions, 46
Sebelius, Kathleen, 159
self-determination policies, 147. *See also* tribal self-determination

self-governing nation-state, 43–44, 72
self-governing political bodies, 96–97
self-reliance, theme of, 69
self-sufficiency, 146, 164, 169, 210n54
Senate Committee on Indian Affairs hearing, 31–32
separatism, 15, 17–18, 25
separatism vs. cosmopolitanism, 175–179
services, state, 141–144
Seton, Ernest, 109–110
settlement, 5
settler-colonial hegemony, 79
settler-colonialism: comparative criticism of conflict as a local phenomenon, 183; complicating our understanding of, 184; and contradictory drives of dominance, 90–91; as critique of "monological identities" for Native people, 16–17; and Euro-American writing, 67–68, 74–75; as ideology, 99; as indigenous in settler nations, 97; The Invasion as intimate critique of, 86; The Invasion casts unsettling pall upon victorious battle, 82–83f; as not inevitable outcome of Native-white contact, 89; and ongoing dynamic of indigenous resistance, xx; and productive troubling of the boundaries in, 18; as renegotiation of settler-indigenous relationship, 92; settlers as immigrants, 66; U.S. claims exclusive rights to define, 16, 90–91
Settler Common Sense (Rifkin), 16–17
sexual unions (Native-white), 87–89
Shaawano (character), 211n59
Shaking the Pumpkin: Traditional Poetry of the North Americas (Rothenberg, 1972), 121–123
shamanism, 113

Sharpest Sight (Owen), 210n54
Shawnee prophet, 164, 168. See also Tenskwatawa
Sheehan, Timothy (government agent), 30–32
Silko, Leslie Marmon, 121, 122, 174–175
simultaneity, 56–58
sin, as negative behavior, 168
Skeleton Man (Bruchac, 2001), 210n55
Smithsonian Bureau of American Ethnology (BAE), 108
Snyder, Gary, 121
social organization, Anishinaabe, 88
social responsibility, 146
Sommer, Doris, 80–81
"Song for the Cure of the Sick," 108
The Song of Hiawatha (Longfellow): assumptions of, 13; Beaulieu critique of as "corruption" of aadizookaanag, 54–56; concurrence of with Treaty of 1855's dispossession, 91–92; critical reappropriation by Anishinaabe poet Liz Howard in "Of Hereafter Song," 181–182; effacement of Anishinaabe literary sources for, xx, 8–10, 78; monological structure of, 9–10, 12, 14; "Picture-Writing" canto, 7–8, 10; rewriting of, 25; and staged adaptation titled Hiawatha, or Nanabozho by all-Anishinaabeg cast, 1–7
"The Song of Manabozho" (Vizenor, 1965), 205n90
"The Song of the Crows" (Vizenor), 132, 133–134
"Song of the Game of Silence," 108
songs. See nagamonan (songs)
song translations, 128
"Soo" (Sault Ste. Marie rapids), xviii
The Sopranos, nagamon lyrics in, 101–102

soul (the daimon), 167
sovereign authority, Native, 84–86
"sovereign peoplehood," 4–5
sovereignty, Anishinaabe, 84–86, 182
sovereignty, cultural and national, 17
sovereignty, indigenous, 18, 20–21, 23, 136, 175–179. See also The Invasion; "unsettled literature"
to "speak when absent," 8
"spirit-of-a-people," 122–123
spirits, attitude of, 106
spiritual power, 59–60
Spry, Adam (author), 159, 189n35, 190n55, 191n62, 209–210n51
stadialism, defined, 106
Stark, Heidi Kiiwetinepinesiik, 21
state, resistance to, 174–179
state institutions, 25, 139–145, 146–147, 163, 174–179, 211n69
state welfare institutions, 142, 146, 147–150, 163–164, 170, 177
state welfare institutions hurt by austerity measures, 155–157
sterilization cases of Native women, 159–160, 208n34
Stewart, Fenn Elan, 212n1
"stick shakers" (Jesuit missionaries), xviii
stories as cultural resource, 44, 45f
storytelling, Anishinaabe, xix, 44
St. Paul Globe, 63
strategies of resistance, 183
Strickland, Rennard, 176
"structures of feeling," 17, 20, 23, 61–62, 97, 189n45
A Study of Omaha Indian Music (Fletcher, 1893), 103
subjectivity, representation of, 133, 182
subsidies, treaty-mandated, 144
subsistence practices, 164–165
suffering, appropriation of, 74
suicide, ritual, 70–71, 73–74. See also "Indian Camp"

Summer in the Spring: Anishinaabe Lyric Poems and Stories (Vizenor), 24–25, 120–121, 124, 129–131, 133–136, 137f
Sunmount (Santa Fe sanitarium), 76, 114–115
superstition, 60
"surplus land," 34, 42, 73
The Surrounded, 144
survival, 137f, 164
"survivance," xiv, 5, 23, 63

Tabeshaw, Billy, 68–69
Taine, Hippolyte, 40–42
Tanner, James, 9
Tanner, John (Zhaazhaawanibiisens), 3, 9, 70–71, 168
Tatro, Kit (character), 165–166, 209n48
Tawil, Ezra, 81
taxation of Indian lands, 35, 73
Technicians of the Sacred (Rothenberg, 1968), 121
Tecumseh (political leader), 164
Tedlock, Dennis, 121
temporal boundaries, 15, 17
temporality, 51–55, 56–60, 102–103
Tenskwatawa (1775–1836), 164, 165, 168, 172
termination policies (1950s): as concentrated effort to end treaty-mandated subsidies, 144–145; driven by misguided sense of cultural authenticity, 24–25; fictional Nanapush leads resistance to U.S. efforts to terminate the tribe, 141; huge shift basing tribal sovereignty on recognition of cultural difference, 127; by official end in 1973, 109 tribal nations dissolved, 118–119; one of four major shifts in federal Indian policy, 23; relied on acceptance of narrative of cultural loss, 138; remnants of recognitive logic remain federal policy, 136; as tumultuous period resisted by Native peoples, 102
texts, 19
That the People Might Live (Weaver), 17
This Quarter (Walsh), 114–115
Three Day Road (Boyd), 210n54
thunderbirds (animikiig), 102
timber industry, 65–66, 139–140
timbermen, Anishinaabe, 66
time, popular conception of, 56–58
"total translation," 121, 123, 126, 128
Trachtenberg, Alan, 4–5
Tracks (Erdrich, 1988), 98, 139–140
tradition (Wenabozho), 46–47
traditional Anishinaabeg life, 5, 164–165, 166–168. See also indigenous cultural practices
tragedy vs. comedy, 175–176
tragic masculinity, theme of, 69
Trahant, Mark (Shoshone-Bannock), 155, 162, 207–208n31
Transatlantic Review, 68–69
transformation from oral to written: arc of reexpressed nagamonan via four Summer editions, 129–131; controversies arising from, 122–123; by ethnopoetic practitioners, 121–122; as poems, like the Anishinaabe, transform over time, 136–138; as "transvaluation of the heard to the seen," 123–124
translation, theory of, 23, 102–103, 113, 121–124, 129–135. See also English, Mary Warren
"transmotion," 23, 136–138
transnational corporations, 25
transnationalism, 20–23, 191n61. See also nationhood, Anishinaabe
treaty, White Earth (1867), 35, 42–44

treaty era (1820–1855), 90–91
treaty obligations, 84–86, 143–145
Treaty of 1836, 72
Treaty of 1854, 114
Treaty of 1855, 66, 91–92, 96–97, 201n64
Treaty of 1867, 63
Treaty of 1889, 114
Treaty of Paris (1783), xix
Treuer, David, 1, 52, 190n55
tribal "acculturation," 127
tribal communities, 33, 184
tribal cultures, 109–110
tribal governance, 141–142, 144–145, 146–147, 156–157
tribal hermeneutics, 63–64, 129–130. See also cultural authenticity
tribal identities, 118–119, 140–141, 165–166
tribal institutions, 142–143
tribal music, 101–107
tribal nations, 117–119, 174–179
tribal political rights, 155–157
tribal religions, 116–117, 122–123, 203n50
tribal rights, 96–97
Tribal Secrets (Warrior), 17
tribal self-determination, 23, 117, 155–157, 177. See also self-determination policies
tribal sovereignty, 127
tribe (doodemag), 167
"tribe of pressed trees," 140
trickster aadizookaanag, 47–48
trust relationship, 143–145, 156–157, 177
truth, narrative, 20
Tsireh, Awa, 117
Turner, Dale, 153
Turtle Mountain Reservation (North Dakota), 35–36, 141

United States (U.S.), 65–68

universality, 179
"unsettled literature," 67–68, 72, 75, 94–95. See also sovereignty, indigenous
Untermeyer, Louis, 109, 112
Upper Michigan, 75–76, 77–78, 79
upward mobility, 145–146, 173. See also The Plague of Doves
U.S. Circuit Court (St. Paul), 31–32
U.S. citizenship, 72
U.S. colonial policy, 15–16
U.S. government, 139–140, 142–144, 146–147, 155–157. See also state institutions; tribal governance
usufructory rights, 85, 95, 143

Valaskakis, Gail Guthrie, 128
Velie, Alan, 49, 51, 175, 193n41
Ventura, Jesse, 205n86
Veracini, Lorenzo, 97
Vive ut Postea Vivas, 88
Vizenor, Gerald (b. 1934): articulating tribal history of high culture not colonizing work, 205–206n93; authenticity of textual expression in, 124–126; background of, 119–120; chronotopic alignment of aadizookaan in "mythic time," 52; as essentialist thinking critic, 204n76; and guiding vision of survivance, xiv, 23, 63; as heir to White Earth literary resistance and experimentation, 63–64; as inspired by Theo Beaulieu's adaptations, 4, 63; Medewewin religious practice fragmented in poems, 135; poetic "reexpressions" of Densmore's translated nagamonan, 24–25, 120, 123–126, 129–130, 135–136; reexpressions embrace haiku-like form, 131–134; targeting Native audiences of marginal

marketability, 190n56; transmotion political theory reflected in poetics, 23, 136–138. *See also* Beaulieu, Theodore; Progress; tribal hermeneutics
vocables, 134–135

"Wah-Boose" (possible Theo Beaulieu pseudonym), 39–40
Walsh, Ernest, 114
Walzer, Michael, 142
Warren, William Whipple (1825–1853), xvii, xix, 98, 104, 209–210n51
The Wasteland (Eliot), 112
Waubojiig (ogimaag), 77
Way to Rainy Mountain (Momaday, 1969), 121
Weaver, Jace, 17, 61
Weekwitonsing (Little Bay Place) community, 72–73
Welch, James, 121
welfare state. *See* state welfare institutions
"wemitigoozhi" (Jesuit missionaries), xviii
Wenabozho stories: aadizookaanag told by White Earth elder Joe Auginaush, 52–53; Beaulieu's translations center around Wenabozho's home, 194n62; as culturally unifying resource, 47–48; mythic images of, 76; "Song for the Cure of the Sick" and "Healing Song," 108; temporal simultaneity in, 56–60; trickster and shapeshifter, 46; which only appear during wintry time, 193n30; written as continuous narrative, 51–57
"What Do We Want?" (Minnesota Anishinaabeg), 42–44
Wheeler-Howard Act, 96

White, Richard, 87
White Earth Reservation (Minnesota): aadizookaanag that appeared in Progress, 23–24; on ancestors of modern Anglo-Saxons, 39–44; for in-depth history of allotment at White Earth, 192n17; desirability of land in communal trust, 34; dispossession of, 62–63; home of literary resistance via Progress, 64; land dispossession of, 62–63, 95; Mary English performance of Hiawatha, or Nanabozho, 3, 4; and production of Kabaosa's Hiawatha, 104; radical plan to remake, 33; special recognition, xiv; Theo Beaulieu starts Progress in 1886, 29. *See also* Progress
White Earth treaty (1867), 42–44
White Lightning (E. Lewis), 78
white people, 164
white shamanism, 122
Wik Peoples v. Queensland (1992), 136
Williams, Angeline, 70–71
Williams, Raymond, 17, 189n45
Williams, William Carlos, 117
Wind River Reservation, 74
Winter in the Blood (Welch, 1974), 121
Winters, Yvor (husband of Janet Lewis), xx, 76–77, 98, 114–117, 121
Wolfe, Patrick, 78
Womack, Craig, 17
Wounded Knee protests, 121, 143
writing: ambivalence toward, 14; as compromised mode, 123–124; as cultural exchange, 4; pictographs as kind of (nonphonetic), 126; reflection of indigenous institutions in, 184; as tool of adaptation and survival, 13; "to write," xvii
writing, Anishinaabe, 33

writing, Euro-American, 67–68, 79
writing, perspectival, 86–87
written record, xvii–xviii, 49–54, 128–129

The Yemassee (Simms), 81

Zhaazhaawanibiisens. *See* Tanner, John

www.ingramcontent.com/pod-product-compliance
Lightning Source LLC
Chambersburg PA
CBHW030538230426
43665CB00010B/944